THE DAY IT FINALLY HAPPENS

ALIEN CONTACT, DINOSAUR PARKS, IMMORTAL HUMANS— AND OTHER POSSIBLE PHENOMENA

MIKE PEARL

SCRIBNER

NEW YORK   LONDON   TORONTO   SYDNEY   NEW DELHI

Scribner

An Imprint of Simon & Schuster, Inc.

1230 Avenue of the Americas

New York, NY 10020

First Scribner hardcover edition September 2019

SCRIBNER and design are registered trademarks of The Gale Group, Inc.,
used under license by Simon & Schuster, Inc., the publisher of this work.

For information about special discounts for bulk purchases,
please contact Simon & Schuster Special Sales at 1-866-506-1949
or business@simonandschuster.com.

The Simon & Schuster Speakers Bureau can bring authors to your live event.
For more information or to book an event, contact the Simon & Schuster Speakers
Bureau at 1-866-248-3049 or visit our website at www.simonspeakers.com.

Interior design by Kyle Kabel

Manufactured in the United States of America

1   3   5   7   9   10   8   6   4   2

Library of Congress Cataloging-in-Publication Data

Names: Pearl, Mike, 1984– author.
Title: The day it finally happens / Mike Pearl.
Description: New York : Scribner, [2019]
Identifiers: LCCN 2019012778 (print) | LCCN 2019014692 (ebook) | ISBN
9781501194153 (eBook) | ISBN 9781501194139 (hardcover) | ISBN
9781501194146 (pbk.)
Subjects: LCSH: Forecasting. | Technology—Social aspects—Forecasting. |
Social change—Forecasting. | Twenty-first century—Forecasts.
Classification: LCC CB161 (ebook) | LCC CB161 .P336 2019 (print) | DDC
303.49—dc23
LC record available at https://lccn.loc.gov/2019012778

Photo Credits: Pages 40–41, 61, 70–71, 107, 137, 196–199, and 211:
Quasicoherent Labs, Copyright © Mike Pearl 2019

ISBN 978-1-5011-9413-9
ISBN 978-1-5011-9415-3 (ebook)

For Paige,
my girlfriend while I wrote this book,
my fiancée around the time I finished it,
and my wife the week of its publication

CONTENTS

Introduction   ix

The Day the UK Finally Abolishes Its Monarchy   1

The Day a Tech Billionaire Takes Over the World   17

The Day Doping Is Allowed at the Olympics   25

The Day Humans Become Immortal   39

The Day Anyone Can Imitate Anyone Else Perfectly   49

The Day the Last Human-Driven Car Rolls Off the Lot   59

The Day Saudi Arabia Pumps Its Last Barrel of Oil   67

The Day a Real Jurassic Park Opens   79

The Day Antibiotics Don't Work Anymore   87

The Day the Last Fish in the Ocean Dies   103

The Day the US Completely Bans Guns   115

The Day Nuclear Bombs Kill Us All   131

The Day a Baby Is Born on the Moon   151

The Day the Entire Internet Goes Down   159

The Day the Last Slaughterhouse Closes   177

The Day Humans Get a Confirmed Signal
    from Intelligent Extraterrestrials   195

The Day the Next Supervolcano Erupts 207

The Day the Last Slave Goes Free 219

The Day the Last Cemetery Runs Out of Space 227

Epilogue 239

Acknowledgments 247

Notes 251

INTRODUCTION

If you consider yourself an informed reader who cares about the future in our supposedly post-truth world, you've probably learned the dark truth about expert forecasters. They supposedly don't know anything.

There's data to back up this cynicism. For the book *Superforecasting: The Art and Science of Prediction*, which psychologist Philip E. Tetlock wrote with journalist Dan Gardner, Tetlock gathered mountains of data about predictions, only to conclude that statistically speaking, "the average expert [is] roughly as accurate as a dart-throwing chimpanzee." But still, people who predict things aren't all idiots. Tetlock and Gardner discovered that some people have a knack for prediction, and they profiled them in their book. Here's what the two authors found:

Apparently, if you want to make a prediction about the future, you should base it on hard data, and that data should be completely divorced from any hunches or biases. You should deal in probabilities—never certainties—and offer an unambiguous time frame.

For instance, if you're like legendary physicist Enrico Fermi, you can make seemingly psychic deductions about information you don't have by determining what data you can easily access, and then extrapolating. In his famous "How many piano tuners are there in Chicago?" thought experiment, Fermi asked his students to guess the number of tuners (people, not forks) to a reasonable degree of certainty with simple number crunching. We know the population of Chicago, and we know how piano tuning works. We can also calculate with some accuracy how many pianos Chicago has. So if we crunch the data, and show our work, we can come up with an estimate with a better chance of being accurate, rather than a guesstimate. It's a cool trick, but it only works when the thing you're studying is already pretty well studied.

I'm not a statistician or a physicist. In fact, I'm terrible at math, but I do like to predict the future, and I've made a job of it. I just approach it a little differently because my main qualification is a paralyzing fear of things that are going to happen.

My fear comes from an anxiety disorder—a very common mental illness. It's a mixed blessing for someone who works as an explanatory journalist: it fills my head with ideas, but I hate the ideas. This might sound like a fun personality quirk, but if you've ever experienced a week-long string of panic attacks, or been afraid of closing your eyes because sleep brings extreme, graphic nightmares, you know anxiety can be a whole lot more serious than just stand-up comedian–esque neurosis. I'm hypervigilant. I'm very easy to startle (that cat-in-the-window gag is in seemingly every horror film, but it gets me every time). I'm fidgety. I constantly scan my surroundings for exits.

As part of what I guess you could call a "coping strategy," I started writing my *Vice* column "How Scared Should I Be?" in which I tried to assess the rationality of my own fears. Writing about what scared me—things like terrorism, pit bulls, choking, and getting punched in the face—was a revelation. That experience led to my series of climate change predictions called "Year 2050," and my hypothetical war series, "Hours and Minutes." These articles weren't just therapy; through them, I learned that millions of people share my fears. And for a time, I felt a twinge of guilt: *Is it okay to exploit people's fear for clicks?* I wondered. But then my girlfriend (my most loyal reader) pointed out that understanding the details of a terrifying topic is weirdly empowering, even comforting.

Of course, occasionally, after a thorough excavation of the facts, I've been forced to break the news—to myself and the readers of *Vice*—that we're not scared enough. For example: I assigned my highest fear rating ever to "never retiring" because, after researching the topic, I decided that my peers should be much more afraid of it than they already are. So yes: by definition, I'm fearmongering.

But I see that as a net positive, too. After all, we evolved to experience fear because it saves us from harm. Evolution may not have taught us inhabitants of the modern world to allocate our fears judiciously, but with a little research, we can make some necessary adjustments. I find it reassuring to know that some of the stuff that's *ostensibly* scary is also *actually* scary. It makes me feel sane.

But let me be clear: this isn't a self-help book, and I'm not going to make any claims about how *I can rescue you, too, from anxiety if you follow my step-by-step plan.* I still believe, however, that envisioning future possibilities in a sensible, fact-based way is a helpful habit that leads to clearer thinking. Since writing about speculative scenarios became my job, I've trained myself, whenever my knee-jerk response to something is fear, to stop and look at likely outcomes and real-world implications rather than imagine the apocalypse. Or, if I have to concede the possibility of the apocalypse, I ask myself, would it really be so bad?

The most therapeutic article I've ever written wasn't about the future at all. It was called "How Scared Should I Be of Pit Bulls?" I've dealt with a fear of dogs for most of my adult life, ever since 2006, when a dog I swear was the size of a lion lunged at me on a sidewalk in Budapest. It wasn't a life-threatening incident (the owner pulled the dog off me a second later, and the bite didn't even require a Band-Aid), but the shock has stayed with me. One moment that dog was someone's well-groomed pet—a good boy or girl, if you will—and the next it wanted me dead.

Even so, I brought an open mind to my investigation, and it turned out that, yes, dogs described as "pit bulls" are involved in far more fatal attacks than any other type of dog, but science can't really nail down what a "pit bull" is, which complicates the whole matter of the breed's inherent scariness. But I also learned that dogs—pit bull or otherwise—simply aren't dangerous enough to be a threat to most humans, There are only about twenty-six dog-related fatalities a year in the US, which is less than the number of fatalities from falling tree limbs. And the vast majority of human victims have either been babies or the very elderly. What's more, that's 26 out of the approximately 4.5 million annual dog bites—including nips on the hand.

Uncovering these facts has been good therapy; I now pet pit bulls all the time—but only if they seem receptive.

So with that in mind let's turn our attention to the next few decades, shall we?

Reports on what the future may hold for humanity aren't exactly full of optimism. For instance, a multidisciplinary panel of Australians at the University of Adelaide authored a report in 1999 called *The Bankruptcy of Economics: Ecology, Economics and the Sustainability of the Earth* that seems to spell certain doom. The Adelaide experts note that the demands of our expansionist economic models are putting too much strain on natural resources, and they predict "massive environmental damage, social chaos and megadeath."

To make matters worse, society's collapse might be irreversible, at least according to Fred Hoyle, the British mathematician and astronomer who coined the term "big bang theory." According to Hoyle's classic book *Of Men and Galaxies*, with "oil gone, high-grade metallic ores gone, no species, however competent, can make the long climb from primitive conditions to high-level technology. This is a one-shot affair. If we fail, this planetary system fails, so far as intelligence is concerned."

Then again, there are academics out there, like Harvard cognitive psychologist and linguist Steven Pinker, who would have us believe that humans' pursuit of knowledge will ensure our pulling together, dodging the apocalypse, and making the best of it. As Pinker wrote in his 2018 bestseller, *Enlightenment Now: The Case for Reason, Science, Humanism, and Progress*, "Despite a half-century of panic, humanity is not on an irrevocable path to ecological suicide. The fear of resource shortages is misconceived. So is the misanthropic environmentalism that sees modern humans as vile despoilers of a pristine planet."

Starting in 2011, with the release of Pinker's *The Better Angels of Our Nature: Why Violence Has Declined*, I began to really like Pinker-ism, because I found it enormously comforting to read passages like that one about humans not being "despoilers"—not just because they assure me humanity isn't on a path toward oblivion, but because they make me feel less guilty for being human. Still, when I read the news, my gut tells me that, yes, we're "despoilers," at least unwitting ones.

With *Better Angels*, Pinker brought to the surface a very important fact: human-on-human violence isn't on the rise; it's been dropping off precipitously over the last few millennia. But with an eye toward the future, his books contain a few too many hedges to quiet my anxieties.

They're punctuated with passages like "No form of progress is inevitable," and "Progress can be reversed by bad ideas."

Journalist Gregg Easterbrook is an optimist in the Pinker mold. In his book *It's Better Than It Looks: Reasons for Optimism in an Age of Fear*, he writes about watching a formerly endangered bald eagle soar through a smogless sky, a moment that "did not make me feel complacent regarding the natural world, [but] rather, made me feel that greenhouse gases can be brought to heel, just as other environmental problems have been." But Easterbrook also hedges, noting that just because "past predictions of widespread human-caused species loss did not come true does not mean the peril to other living things has concluded."

When it comes to prophesying the future it really *is* hard to bathe everything in sunlight when there are so many uncomfortable facts casting shadows.

One of the most famous predictive documents in my lifetime, the "World Scientists' Warning to Humanity," written in 1992 by the Union of Concerned Scientists, was pretty solid. It contained dire warnings about the atmosphere, water resources, oceans, soil, forests, and living species. When in 2017, for the organization's twenty-fifth anniversary, fifteen thousand signatories thoroughly evaluated that earlier report's predictions, they found that it had been partially wrong about the atmosphere—happily, the ozone layer has been stabilized, thanks to increased global awareness of the issue—but as for the rest, the Union noted, "humanity has failed to make sufficient progress in generally solving these foreseen environmental challenges, and alarmingly, most of them are getting far worse."

I'm sure you know the broad strokes of humanity's Big Problems before I even go into detail. Thanks to the greenhouse gases we can't seem to stop emitting, we've heated our planet around 0.8 degrees Celsius since the Industrial Revolution, and after a brief pause, we have—as of 2018—begun increasing our emissions once again. Never mind the famous 1.5-degree-high watermark; according to some estimates, we're on track to warm the planet by an average of 4 degrees Celsius by 2084 or earlier. That will, in turn, lead to longer and more severe droughts, subsequent famines, and a watery future for major coastal cities like Miami, Shanghai, Rio de Janeiro, Osaka, Alexandria, and Dhaka.

And in the midst of the crises engendered by climate change, we could lose the ability to treat bacterial diseases, as germs become more and more resistant to antibiotics. Adding to the gloominess, humanity's richest 1 percent pocketed 27 percent of all income from 1980 to 2016, while the entire lower 50 percent pulled in just about 12 percent.

And then, of course, there's the messiness of technology. I was born in 1984, placing me in the small cohort of people who experienced "an analog childhood and a digital teenhood." I created my identity in the Internet Age, but I can remember life before the internet, and like many people, I sense something bizarre is going on. Over 40 percent of Americans get their news from Facebook, and only 5 percent have "a lot" of trust in said news. Everything is being automated—and I mean *everything*—and while 33 percent of my countrymen are enthusiastic about that, 72 percent are worried. Those last figures are from Pew Research, which found that people are ambivalent about *many* aspects of technology. For example, 70 percent of us are excited about robots easing the burden of caring for our elders, but 64 percent think mechanized caregivers will probably make Grandpa and Grandma feel lonely, so, um, why are we excited again?

Summing it all up, it seems to me that if you're not both excited by *and* terrified of the future, you don't have a pulse.

But something's missing from all these conversations: *specificity*. A global mass extinction sounds grave, but shouting about a mass extinction just makes you sound like a scold or a street preacher. On the other hand, if I get specific and tell you we're going to lose Arabica coffee and the adorable aquatic mammal known as the vaquita (google it), you'll more likely feel the reality of a dawning ecological disaster at the gut level. Similarly, "political instability" sounds hazardous in a vague sort of way, but people tend to be more interested in where the civil wars are going to be and who will die. If the robots really take all of our jobs, doesn't that mean there'll be famous robots doing better, more exciting work than the others? They sound pretty cool to me. What will they be up to?

Maybe some of these things won't happen the way we think they will. But why waste time predicting when we can imagine? When I spoke to Dan Gardner, the *Superforecasting* author, he concurred. "The range of possible futures is absolutely immense and people don't appreciate that fact," he said, which echoed my own feelings on the matter, and made me feel better about not being a mathematician or a physicist.

So with apologies to Wall Street speculators and Vegas bookmakers, I'm afraid this isn't going to be the kind of book about the future that you can use to make a clever stock trade or start a business. Predicting outcomes is, in some cases, an exact science—but mostly for boring bean counters and engineers. "When you build an airplane, you're building a *new* airplane, but they've got some kind of a checklist, which is immensely long," mathematician and physicist James A. Yorke, coiner of the term "chaos theory," told me. If the checklist looks good, the plane will fly. On the other hand, he pointed out, "You don't have a checklist on items which are completely new."

Even though we're about to talk in this book about the real-world implications of some pretty outlandish things, I should warn you: there won't be anything here about time travel, dragons, or everyone on Earth jumping up and down at the same time. Myths, fantasies, and goofball what-ifs have their place, but I'm trying to bring you information you can actually *use*. So, yes, that means there won't be a chapter on zombies.

My specific brand of future-vision was pioneered, as far as I can tell, by a guy you may or may not have heard of—Matthew Ridgway, who served as chief of staff for the US Army. Before Ridgway was a high-ranking general, his military career got on track in the days just before US involvement in World War II when he cooked up a crazy hypothetical: *What if the whole American fleet in the Pacific got wiped out?* Ridgway says top brass considered his fictional scenario "fantastic and improbable," so, to work through the implications, they only agreed to schedule a single "command post exercise"—a "what-if" run-through carried out over the communications lines at headquarters rather than on simulated battlefields.

Then along came the attack on Pearl Harbor, which eerily echoed Ridgway's command post exercise. His fictional version of a Pacific fleet wipeout turned out to be somewhat inaccurate—for example, at Pearl

Harbor the whole fleet wasn't completely destroyed, and the US aircraft carriers survived, which sped up the navy's recovery. But the real event at least vindicated Ridgway *conceptually*, and his superiors took notice. He'd been promoted by then, but he was quickly shuffled further up the ranks, and became the US general best known for taking over command of the Korean War after Harry Truman fired Douglas MacArthur.

According to Gardner, the *Superforecasting* author, the lesson we can learn from Ridgway isn't that people who speculate about future events are geniuses with ideas that are consistently amazing. Rather, the lesson is that "it doesn't matter how probable or improbable you think [an] outcome is, let's start from that point and work it through, because in the working through there is value."

To that end, let's jump ahead in this book to some earth-shattering, horrifying, ridiculous, and wonderful days in the future. The scenarios I'll be describing won't all be Pearl Harbor–level nightmares. In fact, some will be downright pleasant. But all will be of the type that we don't usually contemplate in much detail, because on some level they're unsettling. As you'll see, most are the logical extensions of social, technological, or natural trends.

The hope is that, by indulging in what some might dismiss as crystal ball–gazing, we can actually avoid being caught flat-footed by events that are either outlandish or dangerously momentous. Also, that by looking ahead we'll develop a better understanding of the present.

There's comfort in that. Trust me.

THE DAY THE UK FINALLY ABOLISHES ITS MONARCHY

Likely in this century? > *Maybe*

Plausibility Rating > *5/5*

Scary? > *Only if you work in British tourism*

Worth changing habits? > *No*

It's election night, and bustling business districts are quiet across the UK. The voting results are earth-shattering, but no one is celebrating. Instead, the citizenry silently tunes in to see live footage of the consequences of the vote. Mexit has just passed, and now this thing is really happening. So the king has to . . . make a concession speech, right?

But this is the mother of all concessions—an admission that he's lost the election, and his extended family's multi-century reign.

The last time this many British subjects watched a live broadcast of their monarch giving a speech was when Queen Elizabeth II broke with her strict reading of royal decorum and comforted a grieving Britain as it mourned the death of Princess Diana. This king was born too late to remember that ordeal, but he's been reminded of it often, particularly as this day crept closer and closer.

The king speaks from the balcony of Buckingham Palace, facing inside, with London behind him—the illuminated Winged Victory statue jutting up from the memorial to Queen Victoria out on the Mall over his right shoulder. He's dressed in a dark gray suit, with none of his jewel-encrusted royal decorations or medals. He looks a little tired and morose, pale from the shock, but as his upbringing and royal genes might have predicted, he's unfailingly regal to the end. He begins with the same gentle abruptness he always uses at the start of a speech.

"Though it pains me personally, I'd like to extend my sincere congratulations to the 'Yes' campaigners for their success in today's election," he says.

"My father taught me that England's history is a special one," the king says, using his usual speech tactic of launching into a personal anecdote. "Elsewhere, the past can sometimes feel inert, or sealed in amber as they say. But Britain's story lives with us every day in all its grand scope. When we look around, we feel ourselves living in our history, and see ourselves as every bit a part of the story of this land as our ancestors. Momentous days have come and gone, and I've always viewed them with an eye to history—small in the grand scheme of things, like my role in them, and inevitably swept away by time. So I never saw myself as a featured character in the great play of history."

His speech becomes labored; the hard bit must be coming:

"But 'momentous' is too feeble a word for today, which ends an epoch. And so it seems that the spotlight of his-

tory has found me. I would be remiss in not honestly expressing, in this moment, what I'm feeling most of all: sadness. I also feel remorseful whenever I think today's result stems from some misdeed or character flaw of mine.

"But here's another phrase my father was fond of: 'When you can't change something, see the best in it.' If I'm to take his words to heart, I must believe, as we now know the majority believes, that this result will be an important step forward—for Britain, for democracy, and for civilization. I'm as confident as ever that Britain's future is bright, and what's more, I know I shall always remember today as a historic milestone—as, I suspect, will you. I hope you'll join me in praying for guidance as our great nation begins its new journey."

Then the picture cuts to a shot of Buckingham Palace. With that, there no longer is a United Kingdom, but a new country called the "Union of Great Britain and Northern Ireland"—though everyone will still reflexively say "the UK" for decades to come.

Then the video feed cuts to something even more difficult to imagine than the ex-king's speech: the speech by the acting president—a *British president*? What a strange combination of words.

The president, who only holds the position on an interim basis until a new one is elected, held the title "first secretary of state" until today. This man is a former MP representing Sedgefield who campaigned on affordable housing, and who made that one embarrassing speech on the floor of the House of Commons that everyone remembers, and *he* is the replacement for the King of England? Yes, he campaigned for this, and yes, he's just won. Must he give a speech, though?

All at once, Britain feels a twinge of regret—not enough to call for the night's result to be reversed, but enough to cause a queasy feeling in the nation's collective stomach. Britain collectively switches off the president's speech. It won't be the last time.

———————————— ◆ ————————————

If you're a new country, calling yourself a "republic" is, to use a right-wing neologism, a form of "virtue signaling." It can be a way of saying to the world that you're not an autocracy—that people in your country are ostensibly in control of their own destinies. Look at the "Democratic People's Republic of Korea." This is a bizarre, Orwellian name that makes it sound like a republic—to paper over the fact that it's actually a dictatorship. Regardless of what republicanism actually accomplishes for a society's well-being, establishing a republic on paper seems to be good public relations.

So it strikes me as stubborn and sort of rebellious that, as the third millennium approaches its third decade, the British don't live in a republic, and they're extremely unabashed about it. They regularly vote in what are widely considered fair and democratic elections, but they don't get to pick their head of state. Instead, the ruler of their country is born into the job, with only a few ancient customs and clarifying rules to keep everything tidy. The King or Queen of England is a person referred to as things like "royal highness" and "majesty," who sleeps in castles, wears a crown, holds a scepter, and taps people on the shoulders with a sword to confer accolades. He or she is a performer of rituals, essentially, even though most of the king or queen's time is spent in a modern city regarded as a global capital of culture and commerce.

And at the moment of this writing, that doesn't look like it's about to change. As it stands, the queen is Elizabeth II: adorable great-grandmother, lover of small dogs and pastel hats, and paragon of popularity. But when the inevitable happens, and Elizabeth gets replaced as sovereign by her much less popular, scandal-prone son, Charles, with his pink face frozen in that trademarked queasy grimace, will republicanism take hold *then*? What about when King Charles maneuvers to have his even less popular second wife—who is very much *not* the extremely popular mother of his children—styled "Queen Consort," to much public nausea, as he has signaled he plans to do? At that point, will the British public be so exhausted by the tawdry tabloid headlines that they'll want to toss the whole monarchy in the proverbial bin?

Probably not, but it's conceivable, according to Adrian Bingham, a history professor at the University of Sheffield focused on media and popular culture, if (A) there's a major scandal, and (B) the newspapers latch on to it. "If the scandal was sufficiently grave, I could see papers like the *Daily Mail* speaking in tones of outrage, 'Something must happen!' 'Somebody must go!' And with one thing leading to another, you can see a set of events where eventually this institution is now discredited," Bingham told me.

So here's a different question: Will the UK *ever* take the republican plunge? Definitely, according to Nicholas Barber, professor of constitutional law and theory at Trinity College, Oxford. "We're most certain to become a republic eventually," he told me. "It's bound to happen sooner or later, but it might well happen very much later," he said.

So in the spring of 2018, I went around England asking people "What would happen if the UK became a republic?" and very few had much of an opinion. Almost all said, "That's a good question," and wanted to leave it there. If I pressed, most would say, "Tourism will suffer." So let's start there:

Tourism revenue was the only concrete reason for preserving the monarchy that most staunch royalists cited, probably because of the river of journalistic ink that gets spilled whenever Brand Finance, a firm that estimates the values of brands, publishes one of its reports on how staggeringly profitable the monarchy is for the country. Their 2017 report declared that monarchy-related tourism accounted for £550 million in annual economic uplift—revenue related to tourists visiting royal homes and buying royalty-related souvenirs. But according to the Australian academic fact-checking site The Conversation, there's really no rigorous, transparent, academic research proving that assertion.

It's hard to feel confident, then, about specific totals.

But the idea that the royals attract tourism beyond what you might otherwise expect for a country of England's stature rings true. After all, there I was in England, having entered the country *entirely* because of the monarchy.

When I went to Windsor Castle to get a look at the queen on Easter morning, I got a further taste of this phenomenon. I ran into two American women from Florida who'd flown in for no other reason than that they wanted to glimpse Prince Harry and his fiancée, Meghan Markle, at a discount, by showing up at a royal appearance well before the big royal wedding in May—itself a clear boon for tourism. So they were there for the same reason as I, and they *weren't even planning to write about it*. (Alas, their dream didn't come true. The queen went to church that Easter morning, as did Kate and William, but Harry and Meghan couldn't make it.)

But according to Graham Smith, the CEO of Republic, a British pressure group demanding the monarchy's abolition and replacement with an elected head of state, we're all overstating the potential for a drop-off in tourism. After all, what are we imagining will happen if there's a republic? Will Buckingham Palace be paved over, or turned into public housing? Of course not. "These places have historic significance," Smith told me. If there were no longer a king or queen, places associated with the *past* king or queen would still be popular "revenue raisers" as tourist destinations, he said. In fact he thinks they'd be even better in a republic, because right now, "obviously, you can't go into them most of the time, so I think they would succeed quite well as museums and galleries."

That sends us back to Brand's reports. If they're going to be held up as a comprehensive defense of monarchy (which, to be fair, I don't think Brand ever said they were), a distinction should be made between tourism revenue that comes from the monarchy's *continuing to exist*—picture the vast crowd at a royal wedding—and the revenue from Britain's *having had a monarchy at some point*—consider the lure of all those castles, palaces, and museums full of shiny royal stuff. People still visit Versailles, after all.

And China is no longer a monarchy, but if you've ever been a tourist in Beijing, you probably went to the Forbidden City and Summer Palace, to see where the emperor hung out.

And as long as Brand is refining its data-gathering at my request, they might want to add some control groups to their tabulations of souvenir profits. Brand's 2017 report references a televised study demonstrating that 70 percent of Chinese shoppers in England prefer souvenirs featuring the Royal Warrant—that symbol you see sometimes with the lion and the unicorn that means "monarch-approved." The warrant is akin to a royal Nike Swoosh, powerful in its symbolic value, and ostensibly a mark of quality, even if it may not make the thing it's stamped on materially better. But should we conclude that Chinese souvenir buyers' desire for fine chocolates and soaps stamped with the Royal Warrant would, in the absence of an active monarchy, diminish? What about *non-Chinese* souvenir buyers?

While there are probably shoppers in England who insist on, say, monarchy-approved fidget spinners only, and *would absolutely reject* a red London phone booth fidget spinner, or a "Keep Calm and Carry On" fidget spinner, it's doubtful the number of these finicky shoppers is large enough to do much damage to the British economy.

Still, maybe that £550 million figure is accurate, and the British economy stands to lose all that. While that amount isn't chump change, it struck me as I conducted my research that people were defending an entire system of government over an amount of money about the same as the profit margin of a hit Marvel movie (as of this writing, the most recent, *Avengers: Endgame*, has made about £513 million in profit). And anyway, "Think of the lost tourism revenue!" isn't a very emotional appeal. I wanted to hear an emotional appeal. So I set out to find the non-royal who would be most upset on Republic Day.

My search brought me to Margaret Tyler, who was referred to in 2015 by the *Wall Street Journal* as "Britain's Loyalest Royalist." (She told me she likes the label.) Tyler's home in the northwest London neighborhood of Wembley is the Fort Knox of royal souvenirs. Her collection lines every shelf in the house and includes thousands of mugs, plates, dolls, books, flags, blankets, and cardboard cutouts. There's also a Princess Diana room, featuring custom stained glass windows. Tyler's collection

appears all the time on TV news programs and in the *Daily Mail*—
if it's a slow news day for the tabloids.

Over a cup of tea in Tyler's living room, I asked the seventy-four-
year-old royals enthusiast—who wore a Union Jack blazer with a giant
ribbon on it in celebration of the queen's ninetieth birthday—why she's
so dedicated to the royal family.

She compared the United Kingdom to a home, watched over by
a benevolent parental figure. She pointed to the 1992 fire at Windsor Castle and compared the queen's handling of that to her visits to
Northern Ireland at tense moments in 1995 and 2011. "Wherever she
sees something that's not quite right, she picks up on it," Tyler told me.
For victims of tragedies like the 2017 Manchester terror attack, a visit
from the queen "means that she cares. She knows. She understands. I
do think that means a lot to people. She's the mother of the country.
She holds it all together."

It doesn't bother Tyler at all that the head of state doesn't weigh in
on political matters. She returned to her household analogy: "When
you've got one child moaning about the other one, or whatever, you
don't get involved, but you listen to them, you know what I mean? And
probably she does the same."

England as a single, coherent "house," watched over by one parental
figure, is an idea that's "all based on this idea of family, and continuity
of family, and blood and soil," said Graeme Orr, professor of electoral
law at the University of Queensland in Brisbane, Australia—one of
the realms of the British monarch. "I think the monarchy has survived
because it has got aesthetic appeal," he added.

Aesthetics aside, the "blood and soil" aspect of the royal family more
or less started in the ninth century with the current royal family's distant ancestor (in spirit, though probably not blood), a feudal nobleman
named Alfred. Alfred was the grandson of Egbert, King of Wessex, a
warlord who terrorized much of England and established Wessex as
England's Anglo-Saxon base of power. Alfred's four brothers were all
regional kings before him, but they all successively died, so Alfred became
King of Wessex, but not before his family had more or less perfected its
defense infrastructure. As king, Alfred oversaw the defeat of the Great
Heathen Army—the quintessential "Viking horde"—in a series of gory

battles, and once they were on the run, he controlled all the non-Viking territories of England, which is what gave him the audacity to proclaim himself King of the Anglo-Saxons. Egbert probably had enough power to make a similar claim, but he didn't as far as anyone knows, and that's why Alfred is called "Alfred the Great" now.

The territory controlled by Alfred the Great's descendants slowly expanded. After some setbacks at the hands of the Vikings and others, the British royal family (which, again, is connected to Alfred by tradition, not actual DNA) eventually controlled the entire island of Great Britain, and, when seafaring technology improved, half the world. Later, their dominion shrank some when they lost important realms, such as India in 1947. And that pretty much brings us up to the present, geographically speaking.

In contrast to those earlier centuries when they were known for their scepter wielding and tribute collection, the royal family is pretty much regarded these days as a collection of smiling celebrities. "All I want of my head of state is someone who can smile, shake hands, be pleasant to people, that's it. And you'd think election would be better than birth at picking out that kind of person," Barber, the Trinity professor, told me. (He was quick to add, though, that the US system for picking heads of state is notorious for selecting people who are awful at shaking hands and being pleasant.)

British monarchs are legitimately quite good at shaking hands and being pleasant to dignitaries, even if their political function is just to give blanket assent to laws, and, generally, to approve whatever parliament does. That pointlessness is more or less the whole point, Orr, the Brisbane academic, pointed out, "The constitutional monarchists by and large are just talking about the institutional value of not having a politicized head of state."

Those wonderful smiles and waves, however, don't make the royal family harmless, according to Smith of the pressure group Republic. "The monarchy as an institution is part of our constitution, and certainly gets in the way of Britain being a full-blooded democracy." He feels that monarchs "push their own interests" and their own agenda. "They can do all sorts of things without recourse to parliament, and they can honestly control parliament as well, as a result of crown powers, so it creates a very strong motivation to resist any democratic reform."

When Smith gets his way and the monarchy waves good-bye, that will place the British in the company of, well, most people. Wherever you're sitting, there's a good chance that it was the realm of a monarch at some point, British or otherwise, and if you examine history, you'll see that most of these monarchies ended rather rudely. China's last emperor was forced to abdicate, and was eventually imprisoned. Russia's royal family was executed, mutilated, and dumped in a swamp. The last official king and queen of France (barring some brief flirtations with returning to monarchy on the way to the establishment of a Republic) famously got the guillotine. The Shah of Iran only avoided the wrath of revolutionaries by fleeing the country. The last king of Laos was forced into Communist captivity. In short, the prospect of facing pitchforks and torches has long been baked into being a monarch.

But Smith doesn't sound like he's pushing for revolutionaries to storm Buckingham Palace and drag the royals out into the streets for a summary execution. Instead, he thinks the idea of a better way to run things will simply take root and democracy will prevail. "Say that 55 percent or 60 percent of the population say *Yeah, we should get rid of the monarchy*, and parliament is willing to do it. Parliament can either pass a law to get rid of the monarchy, or it can go to a referendum first, *then* pass a law," he said.

Past monarchies have been abolished by popular vote, but for whatever reason, this almost never happens without the proceedings being marred by a whiff of corruption. In 1946, the child king of Bulgaria was voted out in favor of the ascendant Soviets, but, based on the final tally, the integrity of that election was suspect (close to 100 percent sided with the Soviets). In Greece, a right-wing military junta held a questionable monarchy referendum in 1973, which was invalidated the following year by elected leaders, who then held another referendum in the hope that it would earn more legitimacy. Wishful thinking on their part. They barred the deposed king from campaigning in Greece, and, predictably, he lost again. It is *possible* for a monarchy to be abolished democratically, though. In 1968 the Maldives—an island nation with a population of less than half a million—ended its 853-year-old monarchy via popular referendum. It's worth noting that prior to that referendum (which was far from their first) the king had clung to power for years after the population had made it clear that they wanted him out, but so far, it looks like the throne of the Maldives has been permanently retired.

While we're on the subject, many monarchies have turned into republics not so much by voting out *their* king or queen, but by getting out from under the thumb of a foreign monarch. The Icelandic constitutional referendum of 1944, for instance, was a polite, highly democratic affair in the midst of World War II that arranged for the King of Denmark not to be Iceland's head of state anymore. But that move had no bearing on whether Denmark would continue being a monarchy, and, indeed, it still is one. Similarly, over the years, the governments of Ghana, South Africa, Nigeria, Kenya, Malawi, Uganda, Guyana, Gambia, Malta, Sri Lanka, Trinidad and Tobago, Fiji, and Mauritius have all shown *their* queens the door, too. And each time, her name was Elizabeth II.

That brings me to a very important, and awkward, wrinkle in the process of abolishing the British monarchy: Britain can vote to make its monarch stop being the *British* head of state, but that doesn't change the fact that fifteen other countries still consider said monarch *their* head of state. In case you need a refresher, those are Canada, Australia, New Zealand, Jamaica, Barbados, the Bahamas, Grenada, Papua New Guinea, the Solomon Islands, Tuvalu, Saint Lucia, Saint Vincent, Belize, Antigua, and Saint Kitts and Nevis.

Mexit would *not* change the monarch's status in these places, according to Bob Morris, a scholar of monarchy and the law, and an honorary research fellow in the constitution unit at University College London. "The UK would be unable to legislate for what the independent realms would use for the monarchies abroad [and] could not independently legislate to abolish monarchy in their case," he told me.

But if the UK tossed out the monarchy, it looks like there might be an automatic shut-off valve for the monarchy in some of the realms, a stipulation built into their individual constitutions. If we look at what happened when the UK parliament changed the rules of royal succession in 2013, six realms passed equivalent local succession laws to maintain continuity: Canada, New Zealand, Australia, Saint Kitts and Nevis, Saint Vincent, and Barbados. Those, presumably, would need to make their own legislative decision about whether or not to keep the monarchy. In the other nine realms, however, the UK succession law jumped realms and took effect without the local government doing anything. Those nine were Antigua, the Bahamas, Belize, Grenada, Jamaica, Papua New Guinea, Saint Lucia, the Solomon Islands, and Tuvalu. So in the event of Mexit, it seems the monarchy would indeed vanish automatically in those places, unless local officials intervened.

Once Britain is officially a republic, the next chore will be figuring out what to do about the Crown Estate, the giant pile of investments and property valued somewhere north of £12 billion that pays for the royal family to exist. These assets include Buckingham Palace, Windsor Castle, Clarence House, Kensington Palace, and Saint James's Palace, along with self-perpetuating investment capital.

As I implied earlier, the ex-royals probably won't get to just keep all £12 billion—would you get to keep your work laptop if *you* got fired?

But the Crown Estate is also not *public* property, per se. It's a corporation designed to fund the day-to-day work of being a royal, and funnel the rest of the money into the treasury. To help you understand how the Crown Estate puts money in the monarch's pocket, let me give you a hypothetical: Suppose the Crown Estate owns 50 percent of an outdoor mall in Oxford called Westgate, which it does. And let's say I'm typing this sentence while wearing blue jeans I bought at the Primark in that mall, which I am. Some of my money from that transaction filters up to the owners as profit—two pounds, let's say (unlikely since Primark clothes are very cheap, but it's just a hypothetical), and one of those pounds goes to the Crown Estate, because it owns half the mall. Since each year the monarch receives a 15 percent "sovereign grant" from the Crown Estate's profits, the queen would actually receive 15 pence from that pound contribution of mine, and the rest would stay in the treasury. This routing of the bulk of the revenue to the government is why staunch monarchists maintain that "the queen pays 85 percent tax." But that's a bit misleading when you consider that the queen doesn't actually *own* the Crown Estate.

If you're a British monarch, and the monarchy ends, the good news is that the divorce won't be complicated, according to Smith, who, you'll recall, is an advocate for Britain's transition to a republic. "It should be a relatively straightforward process," he told me. "There are certain things which you [as a royal] do own personally such as Sandringham [a house in Norfolk] and Balmoral [a castle in Scotland]. And there are other things which you clearly don't own such as Buckingham Palace, and the Duchy of Cornwall, or the Crown Estate. So when [the royals] are thrown out we simply say, 'What's yours is yours, what's ours is ours,' and part company." It is simple. And depending how you feel about a family whose private wealth is estimated to be in the hundreds of millions of pounds, it's arguably fair. The British people get £12 billion, and the royal family (essentially, twenty-five individuals as of the weddings of 2018) keeps its personal £500 million or so (estimates vary wildly) as well as two huge residences with more than enough room to host the in-laws.

The only problem is, there's a hitch in that "you take your stuff, and we take ours" plan: royal assent. Lest we forget, the monarch has to put a stamp of approval on whatever monarchy-annihilating referendum or bill comes along. Would the monarch break with hundreds of years of tradition and kill the bill? Trinity professor Barber doesn't think so. "It sounds like it's going to be a huge crisis and a big problem, but I think in reality, once you got to that stage it would be settled and agreed," he told me. So assuming there's no civil war or guillotine-type situation, the king or queen would probably have a say in the divvying up of royal riches. To imagine that the royals will walk away with zero percent of the Crown Estate is, eh—let's just say it's unlikely. There's a radically different frame through which to view this, though.

According to Brand Finance, the Crown Estate's value is slight com-pared to the royal brand's share of the British economy—approximately £67.5 billion in 2017 (roughly the GDP of Egypt). How BF arrives at that immense figure is a little opaque, but that's their story and they're sticking to it. What happens when that powerful brand loses the mon-arch, its central figure? What would the tabloids cover if the royals were suddenly not technically royal? Would anyone watch royal-related TV shows or movies, or buy royal biographies? What about the branded chocolate and soap? In some ways, it would be a little like a doomed Hollywood franchise trying to keep going without its star—which can go well, like when the *Spider-Man* movies got rebooted without Tobey Maguire and carried right on, or it can go horribly wrong, like when Bruce Lee died and it plunged the entire martial arts movie genre into hell for years.

But Mexit wouldn't just destroy. It would also create. Specifically, a position for an elected head of state has to be created, which can mean making the prime minister the head of state, or creating a separate position like a *chancellor* who would be chosen by parliament after a government is formed. Or it could mean parliament would, like Switzerland, elect a *federal council*, a hard-to-describe executive branch of government which, depending whom you ask, features seven presidents, or only one, or none. Last but not least, there could be a regular old president, chosen by popular vote. But presidents come in many flavors. They could do what the British monarch currently does: not much. Alternatively, the president could set the country's political agenda, and tinker all he or she wants with the military and much of the bureaucracy, like the US president. Or, the president could wield godlike powers that allow him or her not only to unilaterally control the government, but to interfere in daily life in drastic and sometimes mysterious ways, like the Russian president.

But according to Smith, in addition to electing a head of state as part of monarchy's abolition, parliament itself has to change. In a republic, he said, you would have to "get rid of the House of Lords and replace it with another house."

The House of Lords is, let's face it, pretty odd. Once the monarchy is abolished, why should people get to be members of the government just because they hold titles of nobility? The House of Lords Act of 1999 aimed to make the House a little more equal, and that gave the British-American actor Christopher Guest (Nigel Tufnel from *This Is Spinal Tap*) the opportunity to give up the seat in the House of Lords that he had, bizarrely, inherited from his father. In 2004, Guest said of his stint as a parliament member: "There's no question that the old system was unfair. I mean, why should you be born to this? But now it's all just sheer cronyism. The prime minister can put in whoever he wants and bus them in to vote. The upper house should be an elected body, it's that simple."

So if Guest and Smith get their way, the House of Lords will be changed to something called, perhaps, "the Senate." They could change the name "House of Commons," too, but, if you want my opinion, that's a pretty cool name for a legislative body.

Finally, the Anglican Church has to figure out who runs it, because right now its supreme governor is the British monarch. "Just because we get rid of the monarch doesn't mean she stops being the head of the Church of England," Barber told me. It's not at all clear how the Church would thread this needle. There could be no "supreme governor," and the person in charge could be the Church's most senior bishop, the Archbishop of Canterbury. Or the church could ask the former monarch to stay on, a decision that would "look very silly indeed," Barber said.

Even though it would look "silly," having the king or queen retain status as head of the Church of England after Mexit could be a convenient back door that would allow the royals to preserve a modicum of their special status, and allow devout Anglicans to feel like they still have a king or queen, even if the government, well, fired the monarch.

Former royal families who now have no formal ties to the governments their family once controlled do sometimes cling to threads of royalness, which sets them apart from the rest of the old money at their yacht clubs. The Italian ex–royal family, for instance, hasn't been in power since 1946, but members still use their titles, and still occasionally go to court with one another to settle disputes about which member should hypothetically be king if Italy suddenly decides to be a monarchy again. In India, the royal family of Jaipur is one of many royal families that lost their crowns under the Dominion of India in 1949, but when I visited their former palace in 2018 the younger ex-royals still updated the walls with fresh family photos, and used the palace to advertise their charities.

It just might be that the British royals will want to hold on to some measure of power by availing themselves of the democratic tools at hand. "If there was a move towards republic, I could imagine someone like Charles saying, *fine*, stepping down, and then running for election as head of state. In many ways I think Charles would be much much happier being an elected head of state than a monarch," Barber suggested.

Bingham, though, sees the possibility of an entirely different career track for the highly opinionated Charles: punditry. "I'm sure he'd have TV show offers and all the rest of it. I can imagine a scenario where he would take that up, or pen acerbic columns, or write disgruntled letters to the *Times* and stuff like that. He wouldn't bow out easily."

Having gathered all that, I assured Margaret Tyler over tea that the royals won't disappear. They just won't be in charge. I asked what she thought of that, and it was frankly a little heartbreaking to watch her contemplate it.

"Wherever the royal family go there are crowds, aren't there? Imagine there weren't any crowds. Imagine they just turned up, opened something, and went home! It would be terrible, wouldn't it?" she said, growing forlorn. "Imagine if [the queen] went somewhere and wasn't carrying flowers! That would be awful. That shows we don't appreciate her. In fact, I think the word 'thank you' is not enough to say what she does. I would like to think of another word that means 'thank you so much, we really do appreciate you.'"

A few minutes spent imagining a world without a queen left Tyler wan and disheartened: "I just hope I'm not alive to see it."

THE DAY A TECH BILLIONAIRE TAKES OVER THE WORLD

Likely in this century? > *Probably not, but watch out*

Plausibility Rating > *2/5*

Scary? > *Extremely*

Worth changing habits? > *Yes*

The glasses were there one day, and the next day it was like they'd never existed. Lee can't be at fault. Lee is great. Everyone loves Lee.

Ever since they eclipsed smartphones, the market for augmented reality glasses has always been dominated by two Korean brands: Nex and Fantasee. Nex glasses, from Lee Cheong-Hoon's company, Nex Corporation, are ugly and clunky, but everyone has a pair. Fantasee glasses are elegant and they work better, but they never sold as well,

and Lee was always telling Fantasee president Kim Eun-hye that he wanted to buy her company. She always said no.

Kim always said she was friends with Lee. They were "rivals," not enemies. Everyone had a sneaking suspicion that was a lie—that they hated each other's guts—but no one would ever say that out loud.

For a decade, Nex Corporation had been the world's most valuable company, presided over by the world's richest man, Lee Cheong-Hoon. Nex was seemingly everywhere—its name advertised on restaurants, stores, news sites, clothing, and appliances—but it was also nowhere, because the company was governed, driven, and staffed by an advanced AI, which was a public relations masterstroke. Lee, ever the benevolent face of the company, could publicly scold the AI, his employee, for a particularly unseemly or underhanded hostile takeover, and people would continue to adore him.

You couldn't go anywhere in the world without seeing "tributes" to Lee. Nex Corporation had more cameras than anyone could count on many cars, planes, drones, and satellites, and a simple tribute like "I LOVE LEE" cut into a field of wheat, or spelled out in roofing tiles, or projected into the sky, could be singled out for a prize. A prize from Nex could be something small, like a gift card, or something life-changing, like a visit from Lee. Regardless of what you won, you were the person of the hour. The impact on your social media score made it all worth it.

And if some moron who didn't care about prizes spoke up and said something bad about Lee, or said they thought Kim was a better leader, the crowd knew what to do without prompting. Whenever Lee had a new enemy, winning the Nex leader's favor became like a contest. Get the person fired, ruin their marriage, or get their kids taken away, and a great prize was in store.

But still, Fantasee had always been right there next to Nex on store shelves. Nex glasses were cheaper, and much more customizable, and if they broke, you could repair them yourself instead of taking them to an authorized repair shop. You could access unauthorized custom realities with Fantasee glasses. For a lot of people—especially those who didn't care for Nex—these realities were their source of community. Winning prizes from Nex Corporation didn't appeal to everyone, but outside of Fantasee communities, it seemed like everything everyone did was an attempt to win a prize.

In fact, even though no one said it (who would dare, when there were Nex microphones in all of the company's products?), it was as if Nex had begun making all the rules. No matter what country you were in, the Nex terms of service document was the law. Lee was everyone's "best friend," or so they said. Since there was so much to gain from saying so, and since there was no telling what might happen if Lee heard you hated him, who would ever say otherwise?

But it was bewildering for everyone when Nex Corporation bought the last of the retailers that sold Fantasee glasses, and promised Fantasee would nonetheless stay in business. Almost everyone said the move was great news, and that Lee would definitely keep his word, but privately, people thought that couldn't be true. Still, there was no sense making a fuss about it. What could anyone do?

But in the "deep realities" you could access only with Fantasee glasses (and only after "jailbreaking" them), you could find a lot of people who didn't think this was going to be good. But by that time not a lot of people visited those places anymore. Everyone knew if you weren't using official Nex channels, you couldn't win a prize. And then all at once, they were gone. You couldn't buy Fantasee glasses in stores, and as an added layer of surprise, Nex bought up all those unauthorized realities in one fell swoop. They were gone. Fantasee glasses were worthless. One day, Kim appeared on TV looking happy with Lee, and she said she couldn't have been prouder of her friend Lee and his big success.

If anyone didn't believe her, they never said so.

◆

If I'm perfectly honest, I'd love to be the emperor of the entire world. Don't get me wrong, I'm not saying I live my life with the goal of ascending to some position of global power, and I don't think I actually deserve this kind of power—no one does. If you came up to me in a bar and asked me if I want to be the Lord of All That Exists, I would say, "No, absolutely not, don't be stupid," like a reasonable person. But things would be different if you shook me out of a sound sleep and said, "Quick! I have to get rid of the Crystal of Infinite Power!" I'm certain I would shout, "Give me the crystal!" before some nobler part of my superego had time to step in to tell me to cast it into a volcano instead of trying to possess it.

I suspect, however, that there are people who have the same wicked urges as I do, and would happily act on them given the chance. It's just that universal domination is kind of a vague concept.

That seems to be the whole joke in *Pinky and the Brain*, a cartoon in which a hyper-intelligent lab mouse wants, in no uncertain terms, "to take over the world." To do this, he usually wants to mix together some mind control drug with a silly secret ingredient, or he plans to distract the populace by some silly means, ostensibly so he can access the levers of power. But again, he never gets that far. Then there are the *Star Wars* movies. If you recall the evil emperor Sheev Palpatine in the *Star Wars* universe, he apparently rules over all known planets, even though his empire doesn't seem to govern with a heavy hand, which leaves large pockets of dissent all over the galaxy.

The clearest articulation I've seen of world domination in fiction was on *The Simpsons*. In the episode "Treehouse of Horror V," we briefly see a universe in which Ned Flanders is "unquestioned lord and master of the world." Flanders appears in the homes of his "slaverinos" via a dual-purpose surveillance and propaganda delivery screen à la the viewscreen in *1984*, and naturally, Big Brother Ned just wants everyone to be cheerful. When Homer expresses negativity, he's sent to a reeducation camp, given smile therapy, and, when that fails, he's placed in line for a lobotomy.

Silly as all this "taking over the world" stuff may sound, according to Hans Morgenthau's 1948 *Politics Among Nations: The Struggle for Power and Peace*, one of the foundational texts on foreign policy theory and power politics, it's a wonder it hasn't happened already. Morgenthau writes that theorists "have conceived the balance of power generally as a protective device of an alliance of nations, anxious for their independence, against another nation's designs for world domination, then called universal monarchy." The position of universal monarch has, thankfully, never been achieved, not even by Alexander the Great, who, according to legend, "wept for there were no more worlds to conquer." (Alexander actually stopped conquering worlds when he got to western India.)

But what if instead of killing your way to owning the world, you bought it instead?

Until Jeff Bezos came along—a guy whose fortune briefly topped the $150 billion mark in 2018 before a slight downturn—John D. Rockefeller was probably the richest person in history, assuming you adjust for inflation. His company, Standard Oil, had a monopoly in the US, and considerable control over the US economy—a grip that proved very difficult to loosen. But while Rockefeller may have possessed many Bond villain powers, he also confronted fierce global competitors who kept him in check, and Standard Oil itself was far from impervious to the intervention of the US government. The company's monopoly was eventually dissolved by order of the US Supreme Court in 1911.

*   *   *

Today's ultra-rich, on the other hand, create networks of power that can extend to any—and perhaps every—country in the world. Much of the control over the corporate world now appears to be in the hands of a single "super-entity," according to "The Network of Global Corporate Control," a 2011 study produced by three systems theory researchers at the Swiss Federal Institute of Technology. They analyzed the power structures of 43,060 transnational corporations, culled from the world's "30 million economic actors," and found that nearly 40 percent of the control over the global economy is held by a group of 147 transnational corporations that in turn form a single coherent entity with control over its own actions.

Taking things a step further, that study notes that about 75 percent of the businesses in that group are "financial intermediaries," or, in other words, banks and bank-like financial entities, such as pension funds. This means the reins of power are in the hands of the people who make those companies' investment decisions—though the study also points out that according to *some* theories of corporate control, "financial institutions do not invest in equity shares in order to exert control." But in any case, it looks like we've been headed down a path for some time toward the decline of states as the centers of global power, and toward a more corporate-dominated world.

According to sociologists like Gary Gereffi, emeritus professor at Duke University, the modern corporation isn't a citizen of any state, but a giant transnational blob having what he refers to as a "global value chain." There's a famous group of powerful individuals with notoriously expansive global value chains: the titans of Silicon Valley. Their business ethos is known as "disruption"—creating a piece of technology that violates norms and upsets the status quo. And some of them want to disrupt literally everything.

Balaji Srinivasan, a Silicon Valley big ideas guy and the chief technology officer of the cryptocurrency exchange Coinbase, believes that the momentum of tech companies is reaching an escape velocity that may soon propel them beyond being mere companies. Ultimately, that momentum will allow them to (A) do absolutely whatever they want, and (B) make governments obsolete. Consumer demand, he argues, is a force that simply won't be cowed by government regulators. "Uber,

Airbnb, Stripe, Square, and of course y'know, the big one, Bitcoin, are all things that threaten [Washington,] DC's power," Srinivasan told a start-up conference in 2013. "It is not necessarily clear that the US government can ban something that it wants to ban anymore."

Then Srinivasan transitioned into talking about "rule"—suggesting quite openly that Silicon Valley may soon be the center of power, at least for the US. He argued that Silicon Valley deserves to be in charge, despite the fact that, as he said, "the emerging meme is that rule by [Silicon Valley] is rule by terminators," so he offers a counterargument: "DC's rule is more like a ruined building in Detroit." And then he noted that trying to win a war against the US is probably unwise, saying, "They have aircraft carriers. We don't. We don't actually want to fight them." Nonetheless, "warfare is going to become software. Laws are going to become code. Management via robotics is going to become automation."

You probably already see where this is going, but I'll spell it out for you anyway: Srinivasan, with his antigovernment views and his clear megalomaniacal streak, would like to work for, of all things, the United States government. Specifically, he met with the US president in 2017 about possibly becoming head of the US Food and Drug Administration, an organization he allegedly thinks shouldn't exist.

Before I get carried away, please know that I am not about to take a hard right turn into conspiracy theories. Srinivasan hasn't expressed any interest in establishing a world government with himself as its figurehead, and I'm not saying that he could do so, even if he worked for the US government. But I *am* saying Srinivasan and his ilk clearly have the best shot at accomplishing this sort of thing. Srinivasan isn't nearly as rich as some of his disruptor friends like PayPal billionaire Peter Thiel (one of the venture capitalists who partly funded Coinbase and recommended Srinivasan to the president), but he's part of the tech establishment, a group that, for whatever reason, almost universally believes in the pursuit of limitless wealth and total autonomy as a kind of birthright.

But real-world domination probably requires a bigger fortune than Thiel's or Srinivasan's, and at the moment that means a good person to look closely at is Amazon founder Jeff Bezos, who cultivates a more affable image than his frenemy, the more openly villainous Thiel. Bezos nonetheless has well-publicized libertarian leanings. That's not a crime, but as of this writing, Bezos is (according to my own back-of-the-envelope number crunching) the proud owner of so much wealth that approximately 1/2000th of *all the money or assets in the world* belongs to him.

The sheer size of one tech titan's fortune is troubling when you consider that what Srinivasan said about regulations is actually very true. As Barry Lynn, executive director of the Open Markets Institute, a liberal think tank, told *New York Times* commentator Farhad Manjoo in 2017, "Individuals, lawmakers, we're all feeling a rapid loss of control and power around [tech] companies."

And as Manjoo pointed out, Bezos's massive wealth accumulation is coming at a time when tech companies are "creating machines that could one day approximate and surpass human intelligence—a technological achievement that may come with as many complications as the advent of nuclear weapons." Manjoo added that tech profits produce "vast riches to a relative few employees and investors in liberal West Coast enclaves, while passing over much of the rest of the world."

Philosopher Peter Asaro, spokesman for the Campaign to Stop Killer Robots, shares my fear (which I learned when I was investigating "the singularity" for *Vice*). The singularity risk that people worry about—the threat of computers becoming so powerful that they'll outsmart us and enslave us—doesn't make much sense on closer inspection, but Asaro pointed out to me that true artificial intelligence is nonetheless pretty scary if AIs start running companies with "no individual and no group of people [able to] really guide them anymore."

For a preview of what it would be like for everybody to be ruled by one unofficial but undeniable corporate dictator, one only need look at the soft power a large company is able to project when it flexes its muscles. The kind of reverence people once exhibited toward monarchs seems to be hardwired into their DNA, but today they seem to only show this kind of fealty toward corporations.

For instance, when Amazon announced plans to build a second headquarters outside of Seattle, city governments all over North America signaled their willingness to do absolutely anything to win the contest: New York City mayor Bill de Blasio turned every possible light in his city orange; Tucson, Arizona, offered up a giant saguaro cactus as a tribute; and the Ottawa Senators compelled a stadium full of hockey fans to cheer as loudly as possible for Amazon. Meanwhile, Tesla founder Elon Musk commands an army of social media followers who attack his critics, seemingly in their spare time, just because they admire Musk. In 2018, a Musk critic named Erin Biba was hounded on Twitter, on Instagram, in email, and elsewhere after the billionaire's followers saw him fire back at her. Messages she received included "Go shove your fake news up your grimy cunt."

In some ways, it's hard to imagine that an undisputed corporate overlord would have much of an interest in operating like a twentieth- or twenty-first-century despot. While Latin American dictators, for example, crack down on free speech, and kidnap and murder their critics, corporations, on the other hand, normally get what they want by offering people opportunities to advance or by simply giving them free stuff. Although it's worth noting that corporations like Chiquita are alleged to have been complicit in the activities of Colombian death squads in the late nineties and early 2000s. So maybe a corporate autocrat would be just as bloodthirsty as a regular autocrat.

Still, it's unlikely that Jeff Bezos or some other tech billionaire is on the verge of staging a global coup any time soon.

THE DAY DOPING IS ALLOWED AT THE OLYMPICS

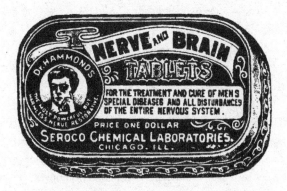

Likely in this century? > *I wouldn't rule it out*

Plausibility Rating > *3/5*

Scary? > *A little. Steroids can be nasty*

Worth changing habits? > *Not as long as drugs are banned, but when they're not, absolutely*

Transcript of live coverage of Olympic cycling from BBC One:

Desk Anchor: It's been an odd year. Great Britain's inchoate anti-doping policy has amounted to a mere *request* that athletes perform their events clean, but there are no tests any longer. Meanwhile, countries that have taken a hard anti-doping stance have paid dearly. The American, Russian, and Chinese competitors seem to have only increased their domination.

And doping is at center stage once again going into the keirin final.

If you're just tuning in to the keirin event, the sport can look a bit odd to newcomers. The cyclists line up in formation behind a motorbike, and that formation holds, keeping things tame until the bike leaves formation for the last two-and-a-half exhilarating laps.

This was a Japanese event introduced at the 2000 games in Sydney. In Japan, of course, keirin is a real moneymaker. Players are famously locked in hotels to prevent corruption in the events, and indeed to keep drugs out. We can see from the lack of Japanese competitors at these games that that hard-line policy may have extended to the Olympic team.

Is Great Britain a hair's breadth from a gold medal in cycling? Phil Evans is at the track, and he'll take it from here.

Evans: Team GB has nineteen medals at these games so far—*none* in cycling. That's quite a step down from past years. This keirin final could change that. It pits Geoffrey Jax and Gregory Price against a team of fierce competitors, in a year fraught with upsets, though Jax and Price are still the favorites.

Here we see Jax mounting up. He's had an easy go of it leading into the final, but as we've seen, anything can happen in these unusual circumstances—I should say this "new normal."

There's the shot, and we're off.

Starting the first lap here, all six cyclists are lining up behind the motorbike. Here's Alexei Ignatiev of Russia taking pole position. Asked if he was using GHB—as all cyclists were this year—he gave that now-infamous reply—*Absolutely. I'm not an idiot.* We'll see if it's paid off for him.

Ignatiev still up front, Price in second. Jax in third. The Chinese competitor, Ng, in fourth. Alba, the Spaniard, in fifth, and behind him the Frenchman, Anton. Anton, of course, a relatively obscure newcomer, was made famous at these games when he was photographed buying amphetamines.

Jax is comfortable in third. And don't rule out Anton in the back there. It's possible to get wind in your back in this open stadium. It's a breezy day out, so wind could be a factor, as well as chemicals.

Three laps to go, and we're seeing them start to strategize with less than a lap before those final two and a half, and that's where medals will be won.

And there goes the motorbike.

Look at Ignatiev pedaling in the hot seat at the front—that GHB certainly doing its work. He's looking over both shoulders to spot the competition, and they're coming in fast. That's Jax and Price past him. He tries to regain ground.

The Frenchman veers way into the outside, an odd strategy. Here comes Ng in the shoulder pushing into second past Price with one lap left.

And that's . . . That's Anton right there on his wheel. He took the long way round for the sprint and it's working.

Jax and Anton are in a dead heat, and trying to open a gap between them is Ng. Ng's wheel looks like it may scrape Jax there and . . .

And that's . . . a bad crash. Jax and Ng both taking a spill.

Anton is on his own planet out front now, certainly smelling gold in his future. And that's Ignatiev behind him as they cross the finish for first and second. Price crossing third. One medal, at least, for Team GB.

There we see Jax picking up his bicycle. The Chinese team hurrying out to help Ng.

A disappointing result, but not for France! Their man Anton, now famous for two very different acquisitions at these games, is sure to face some scrutiny from fellow cyclists over his amphetamine use in this race, though he'll get no such scrutiny from the officials. France, and amphetamine, now have a gold medal in cycling. Ignatiev and his GHB regimen have silver—though the other competitors have not shied away from GHB as we've seen, so we can't expect much pushback from the fans there.

And that's the news from the keirin final.

There's an argument raging, with staunch partisans on both sides, about whether doping should be allowed in sports. On one side are the moralizing traditionalists who see the honor and heroism of sports triumphs being threatened by the creeping menace of unfair chemicals. On the other side are contrarian eggheads who envision sporting events not as tests of honor and character, but as casino games, only sweatier, where drug use is tantamount to card-counting in blackjack, and shouldn't actually be considered cheating.

When the two sides meet, the result can be amusing. Here are two Giant Brains of the doping issue debating each other in 2016 for the science magazine *Nautilus*. Bioethicist Julian Savulescu argues in favor of doping and the philosopher Robert Sparrow argues against:

Sparrow: Julian has proposed [that doping be allowed]. It makes no sense. It's incoherent. It seems silly because why not put the long-distance runners on motorbikes? Why not have the people doing high-jump pulled up on strings? The sports would make no sense at all. If you're going to argue for an all-out Olympics, it's still got to be within a certain set of restraints.

Savulescu: You could allow a completely libertarian, laissez-faire form of sport where there are no rules. Take ultimate fighting. This is an example where you've got rid of the rules that protect people from injury.

Sparrow: But they can't bring knives.

Savulescu: No, that's right. You can set some rules. Obviously, to run the 100 meters, you can't come with a motorbike. You could say, "You're allowed to take any substance that enables your natural legs to run faster." If you want to take amphetamines, cocaine, alcohol, or steroids, you can take anything you want.

Sparrow: Let's be honest here. This is not a sport without rules. The moment you say you can't be on a motorbike, you've got rules.

Savulescu: Of course. You can't have a sport without rules because it's got to define the behavior that is meant to be the test of their physical excellence or skill. Sport requires rules. The question is what sort of rules. Could you allow any sort of performance-enhancing substance, no matter how dangerous? You could.

It's a preposterous debate, but it does get to the core of the issue. Red isn't blue, dogs aren't cats, and it would be wrong to ride a motorcycle in a footrace. If there's any actual substance to Sparrow's argument, it's that using a banned drug is a rule violation. Those who inspect urine and blood, sometimes years after a competition, are essentially high-tech referees.

But the rule breakers seem to be winning—both the debate and the Olympics. Each newly announced testing method results in dozens of disciplinary measures, and then the International Olympic Committee (IOC) allows dozens, if not hundreds, of known dopers to compete in the Games. Why? Well, it can't hurt that the Olympics' motto is "Faster, Higher, Stronger." Make no mistake: officials and athletes are equally invested in the business of breaking records, and only people with advantages break records. The Olympic Movement *claims* to be defined by "the fight against doping," and by "promoting sports ethics and fair play," but over time, perceived unfair advantages have become the norm. This is the inescapable contradiction at the heart of the Olympic Games, and it's hard not to see the people fighting this ever-evolving war against doping as anything other than lost souls, locked in a tragic Sisyphean struggle.

In various ways, the IOC and its associated organizations act as what you might call "fairness cops"—officials on the lookout for drug use, or anything perceived to be giving someone an advantage. Policing for fairness is a nice thing to do, but when viewed under a microscope, fairness in sports is an impossible goal, and when you get right down to it, it doesn't even make that much sense.

Let's start by weeding out the ridiculous parts of the Savulescu-Sparrow debate. Anti-doping rules—Olympic and otherwise—are much squishier than, say, anti-motorcycle rules in sprinting. Take, for example, tennis superstar Maria Sharapova. In 2016, the International Tennis Federation banned the Russian player for using a drug called meldonium after she failed a test less than a month after the substance was banned by the World Anti-Doping Agency (WADA). But Sharapova isn't some sinister cheater. She'd been taking a supplement that contained meldonium for ten years, and an arbitration panel later agreed that she wasn't at "significant" fault, having taken her supplement in good faith that it was "compliant with the relevant rules." But her suspension stood for over a year, all because she reportedly missed the email informing her about the rule change. Sharapova had broken a rule, and doesn't claim otherwise.

Olympic-level athletes like Sharapova frequently try supplements and remedies of all kinds that are meant to relieve pain, speed up healing, or generally promote good health, though they often have no measurable benefit. At the London Olympics in 2012, athletes showed up with their bodies covered in strange strips of colored fabric called Kinesio Tape, and judges allowed it because Kinesio Tape doesn't do anything different than an old-fashioned Ace bandage (except stay on in a swimming pool). But Ace bandages *do* make a difference for athletes with sore joints, as do other seemingly benign items available in any first aid kit. Why else would they be there?

But things start getting absurd when you consider that some commonplace performance-enhancing drugs are perfectly acceptable. If your first aid kit isn't designed for fully sanctioned and legal performance enhancement, you're doing it wrong. In 2009, the School of Sport and Health Sciences at the University of Exeter in the UK found that acetaminophen—also known as paracetamol in the UK and Tylenol in the US—provided cyclists with a 2 percent performance improvement. Most important, however, this effect was observed *whether or not* athletes reported pain. And acetaminophen is absolutely allowed at the Olympics. If you're an athlete, use it every time you compete. The stuff *makes you faster*!

But while banning something as benign as acetaminophen sounds silly, such bans do happen when authorities spot something being used by a large number of winning athletes and they fear a shift to full reliance on that enhancement. A visible example of this phenomenon is when in 2010 swimming authorities banned the drag-reducing full-body swimsuit made of a pricey fabric that American swimmer Michael Phelps had made famous at the 2008 Olympics. (In the year and a half following, he and other swimmers wore it while smashing records all over the world.) All that sudden success was proof enough that these ultra-aerodynamic unitards were doing something, so they had to go.

And that's good, right? We wouldn't want all swimmers to have to pay for those suits if they want to win. But then again, now that swimmers ostensibly can never wear those suits again, many of the records broken with their assistance are probably locked in for the foreseeable future, all of which is reminiscent of the notorious wave of records broken—famously in the West by East German, Czech, and Soviet athletes, but also by at least one American—in the 1980s and early 1990s when athletes were clearly doping (although there'll never be proof, because the proper controls weren't yet in place). In the name of fairness, human achievement in these areas has been given an artificial high-water mark, because the people who set those records weren't playing fair.

This brand of fairness policing seems especially rational when it's meant to help athletes burdened with an economic disadvantage. In 1971, American Olympic weightlifter Ken Patera said of his Russian rival Vasily Alekseyev, "Last year, the only difference between me and him was that I couldn't afford his drug bill. Now I can. When I hit Munich next year, I'll weigh in at about 340, maybe 350. Then we'll see which are better: his steroids or mine." Despite this admission, he apparently passed his drug tests, and competed in the Munich games the following year, but won no medals, which probably explains why he avoided further scrutiny. In his own brash way, Patera was making a reasonable, working-class appeal to his own inherent physical ability, and seemed to resent having to fork over money for his drugs—and why shouldn't he?

But it's important to note that the fairness cops once sought to do the exact opposite: make the Olympics a safe space for the wealthy only.

"In the 1920s and '30s, anyone who was on the track running 100 meters basically trained in the same way, if they trained at all, because prior to that, training was seen as cheating," said Mark Burnley, researcher of exercise physiology at the University of Kent. At the advent of what we now call the Olympics, "you turned up to a pedestrian race, and you basically just ran based on your innate talents. . . . You just went ahead and did it," he added. This idea carried on into the Olympic era, something you might notice in the 1981 movie *Chariots of Fire*—which depicts the 1924 Games—when John Gielgud, playing a persnickety old Cambridge sports guy, criticizes one of the protagonists for hiring a coach, which, the thinking went, was an ungentlemanly thing to do.

This was because, for the lavishly mustachioed nineteenth-century competitors whose athletic hobbies transmogrified into the modern Olympic Games in 1896, eligibility stemmed from being an especially athletic member of the luxury class. People who were more physically fit because their physically demanding, lower-class jobs made them that way were considered cheaters in any gentlemanly competition.

I'm not saying the fairness cops will ever return to the idea that training is cheating, but as bioethicist Thomas Murray once wrote, "natural talents are, of course, allotted in vastly uneven measure among us all." Fairness is in the eye of the beholder. If the Games only valued moral prowess—things like courage and dedication—and not the unfair advantage of, say, a genetic predisposition to huge muscles, then reconfiguring the Games to reward only those values could potentially be achieved via some kind of chemical handicapping process: growth drugs for the exceptionally weak, and atrophy drugs for the exceptionally strong. I don't think this is really what anyone wants, but the philosophical framework for "fairness" in sports has changed before, and it could change again.

So let's return to meldonium. It was seen as nothing but an over-the-counter circulation aid for cardiac patients that probably did nothing for athletes and had been added to Eastern European sports supplements decades before it was banned. The ban finally materialized in 2016 after sports labs noticed the unusually high prevalence of the drug in the blood of medalists at a European competition the year prior. This wasn't because there'd been some controlled, reputable scientific experiment proving that meldonium was effective, but rather just because it seemed to be a hot new trend. (As of this writing, the actual effects of meldonium on athletes were still "hazy," according to the *New York Times*.)

We know the fairness cops are capricious. Go ahead and show up to your Olympic event with something unusual on your body or in your blood. The assumption will most likely be that you're just superstitious, and the judges will give it the all clear if it's not explicitly forbidden. But if it looks like your unusual totem or tonic isn't just a lucky charm or a pre-event ritual and is actually helping you win—which, by the way, is why you brought it in the first place—there's a good chance the fairness cops will reverse themselves and ban it, and they won't even wait for cut-and-dried scientific proof.

In the next few decades, the IOC will have to solve new ethical puzzles as scientific and social advances arise and further complicate the quixotic search for Olympic fairness: genetically altered athletes and advanced prosthetic limbs and synthetic organs, as well as calls to end the bizarre machinations involved in testing female athletes for their biological sex. So let's say the IOC decides this whole doping fight is small potatoes and waves the white flag (the *solid* white flag I mean, not the flag they always wave, which is white but with five rings on it). What would happen then?

The IOC could start this process anytime, probably by creating a commission tasked with investigating WADA's value, in the vein of the disciplinary commission headed by Samuel Schmid, a former Swiss Federal Council member, which issued the report about Russian doping. An outside authority figure like Schmid would probably head the WADA commission. If that council came to the conclusion that rules against drugs were no longer worthwhile, they'd then write a report calling for WADA to be downsized, or for its mission to be changed.

Many, if not all, competitors in certain events would suddenly feel obligated to dose themselves with anabolic agents like steroids, and perhaps hormones like HGH, which are widely believed to work in chorus with steroids, along with erythropoietin (EPO)—also known as "the blood doping drug" because when injected it tells the body to produce more red blood cells, increasing the amount of oxygen available to exercising muscles and improving endurance. Athletes could also try out sketchier drugs that seem to move the needle performancewise like beta blockers, and cannabinoids, along with amphetamines, which have less of a proven track record than you might think (more on this in a moment).

Then what? All hell will break loose, by which I mean the public will flip out. TV viewers are fascinated by sports doping, as Americans saw when Oprah Winfrey achieved blockbuster ratings for her 2013 interview with Lance Armstrong about his doping, or when baseball player Mark McGwire's 1998 home run streak was briefly all anyone in the US talked about—even though pretty much everyone knew at the time he was using *something* performance-enhancing (he admitted as much more than a decade later). If it's hot news when British super-swimmer Adam Peaty announces what he eats, imagine the clicks publications will get when he talks about how he dopes.

That will lead to an interesting predicament for drug manufacturers: How will they navigate the danger and murky legality of these highly profitable products as they gain wider prominence, particularly in light of the impact the widespread use of opiate painkillers had on Big Pharma?

Recall for a moment the events that led to what we now call the opioid epidemic. In the mid-1990s, Purdue Pharma—to name just one manufacturer—figured out how to market morphine derivatives as pain pills when it released Oxycontin, which, according to the *New York Times*, brought in revenues of about $2.8 billion from 1995 to 2001. But today, opiate use is generally regarded as a plague, leading to addiction, overdoses, and widespread drug-related death and despair. For Purdue, it led to a big fat lawsuit, with multiple US states suing it for its role in the crisis.

So it's very safe to say that while Big Pharma will clearly profit from Olympic doping, companies probably won't come out in the open and offer, say, tips on how athletes should obtain and use their products safely. On the other hand, that bit of ethical prestidigitation could have fatal consequences. Doping requires athletes to get their hands on drugs, and figure out how to safely portion and dose themselves. Steroids, for instance, are illegal without a prescription in most developed countries. Presently, if you want to know how to use them—but don't have access to a highly paid crooked sports physician—you can buy your drugs somewhere like Mexico and take a deep dive into the unseemly world of sketchy bodybuilding forums like UGBodybuilding to determine dosage levels and frequency.

Then, there'll be the Games themselves. When drug enthusiasts are finally liberated from the IOC's burdensome restrictions, will they finally ascend to the Valhalla of true, liberated human prowess like visionaries finally unleashed from the stupidity and small-mindedness of society at the end of an Ayn Rand novel? Will sprinters finally accelerate to Autobahn speeds? Will wrestlers snap each other in half like comic book villains? Will javelins glide into the air above the Olympic stadium and into low Earth orbit?

Sadly (or thankfully?), that libertarian super-Olympics is almost certainly a fantasy. Bill Mallon, an orthopedic surgeon and Olympic Games historian, hypothesized that these hypothetical Games would look like the 1988 and 1992 Olympics (and "not a heck of a lot different from [the Games] today," he added), when the East German and Soviet women dominated just about every strength-based event, like hammer throw, discus, and shot put, setting records that still stand. Mallon expects that those records could finally be beaten by a fresh crop of athletes using modern training techniques alongside anabolic steroids.

But most of that record-crushing, Mallon predicts, would be in women's competitions, because, as he put it, "anabolic steroids have an effect on men but not as much as on women."

Burnley, the University of Kent physiology researcher, had a similar assessment. "There'd be an initial flood of drugs into sports. Everyone will use them indiscriminately," he said. "A few people . . . [would] get pretty injured. Other people would excel," which would result in some broken records, as athletes figured out their dosages, regimens, and sensitivities, and then there'd very quickly be a plateau, after which everything would more or less feel normal again.

The first fully doped Olympics, in other words, won't look like some Hulked-out Circus Maximus, but, rather, like the Olympics we all know and love, with a few more broken records and a few more injuries.

According to Mallon, this is because much of what athletes ingest to get an edge is rooted in ritual and superstition, so a lot of the things on the WADA prohibition list might not actually be performance-enhancing. But this extends to actual drugs on the WADA ban list, including amphetamines.

According to the memoir *Rough Ride* by Paul Kimmage—Irish professional cyclist and sometime-doper—amphetamine use is prevalent among athletes in part because they can be habit-forming after someone tries them. "Once you experience the feeling of invincibility, it is so hard to race with just Vittel in your bottle—especially when you see other riders taking the stuff," Kimmage writes. Amphetamines do improve focus and wakefulness, and those effects might help you train, perhaps by reducing your tendency to just not feel like getting on your bike that day, and they're very addictive. But dosing yourself with speed in the Olympic Village before a competition probably serves little to no purpose. A 2014 lab test on rats showed what happens when you use amphetamines to stave off fatigue in real-world conditions. According to the report, amphetamine use makes rodents less tired in some cases, but "any benefit conferred by higher doses of [amphetamine] are quickly offset in a warm environment with the animal achieving critical temperatures faster." So elite athletes on speed might overheat in summer conditions, something athletes already have to worry about as the Earth gets hotter.

"I think a lot of it is a placebo effect," Mallon told me. He agreed with Burnley that once the ban is lifted, athletes will finally find out which drugs are truly effective, because they'll all finally be studied. But mostly, he said, all that research will allow them to better "optimize their steroid regimens."

The WADA list is long, and full of likely placebos, but there may be some wonderful drugs out there that still haven't been tried in a sports context. Time, and a lot of open-ended experimentation, will tell us which mystery drugs will turn into staples, and in which sports. Take LSD, for example. It doesn't instantly spring to mind as the go-to drug for athletic enhancement, but in 1970, Pittsburgh Pirates pitcher Dock Ellis pitched a no-hitter while allegedly on LSD. Maybe after a little bit of rigorous scientific research, we'll learn that all pitchers should be fried out of their minds on acid (or maybe not).

In the meantime, there are the two categories of banned drugs that almost certainly boost athletic performance, according to Mallon: anabolic steroids and blood doping drugs. With steroids it's an open-and-shut case. A 2004 review of studies focused on steroid use in men showed that across many diverse experiments, a ten-week steroid regimen was shown to boost lean body mass by two to five kilograms, and gave users a 5 to 20 percent strength increase. Other hormones, like HGH, are thought to work alongside steroids, but more research is still needed. With blood doping, the real world effects are much less clear. In fact, one 2013 study published in the *British Journal of Clinical Pharmacology* concluded that blood doping may not be effective for elite competitors.

Then again, "blood doping" will no longer be necessary after the ban is lifted. Rather than jumping through the hoops Lance Armstrong did to pass his drug screenings—taking drugs well before a competition to achieve the desired effects, extracting blood with boosted red cell counts, and then dosing himself later on with that blood—Olympic athletes will instead just be able to take drugs like EPO to boost the number of red blood cells in the bloodstream, and then hop right on their bikes.

According to Burnley, mixing steroids and EPO into a training and competition regimen will take time to optimize. Some athletes will respond well to drugs, and others won't, meaning some of today's ultra-elites might drop down a peg when it turns out their bodies are, for whatever reason, just not in the sweet spot for drug receptiveness. Conversely, it's possible that some relatively unknown fifth-place sprinter from today would, with the help of a little EPO, be a record-smashing leader of the pack. Burnley compared the possible outcomes to present-day surges in competitiveness that can be observed when athletes attain some training breakthrough.

What about all those injuries? Steroids aren't good for you, after all, but the effects are chronic. "They can cause liver damage and testicular atrophy, but it's not going to manifest itself in the Games," Mallon told me. Torn tendons, he said, would be the more common, immediate effect there. At the 1987 US Olympic Festival, he took care of a shot putter who'd torn both patellar tendons. "He was obviously taking steroids," Mallon said. "That's more common when you're on steroids than not."

But even though steroids mostly cause adverse health effects in the long term, there'll be a whole lot of new variables impacting the bodies of Olympic athletes. Injections will be widespread, meaning more open veins, and possibly more contaminated needles, which can lead to the spread of contagious diseases and bacterial infections. Moreover, each drug also comes with its own unique—and potentially life-threatening—hazards; for example, one of the side effects of EPO is blood thickened into a syrupy sludge, leading to potential heart attacks; and amphetamines' side effects range from overheating, to agitation, to psychosis.

If something is lost when the Olympics become a drugged-out free-for-all, it may be the notion that Olympians are our wellness role models (though the perceived physical perfection of the Olympians has always been a bit exaggerated).

Olympic athletes *do* have a documented history of living longer than the rest of us, but not decades longer. Perhaps you've read the *British Medical Journal* (BMJ) 2012 analysis of the life spans of former Olympic medalists, which found that Olympians have an average life span gain of 2.8 years over the slovenly masses. (Interestingly, even medalists from couch potato events like shooting or golf live longer than the rest of us, just like the sprinters do.)

That there's at least a marginal life span advantage to seeking Olympic glory is probably due to a constellation of effects—including the psychological boost that comes from success, and the systemic advantages that lead someone to feel they can start down the road toward an Olympic career in the first place. In previous years, might a would-be Olympian, having been forced to steer clear of certain drugs to stay within "the rules," have gained an advantage from that avoidance as well? I'm going to go out on a limb and say yes.

THE DAY HUMANS BECOME IMMORTAL

Likely in this century? > *Nope*

Plausibility Rating > *3/5*

Scary? > *It turns out yes, a bit*

Worth changing habits? > *Not right now, but someday longevity will be all about whether or not you change your habits*

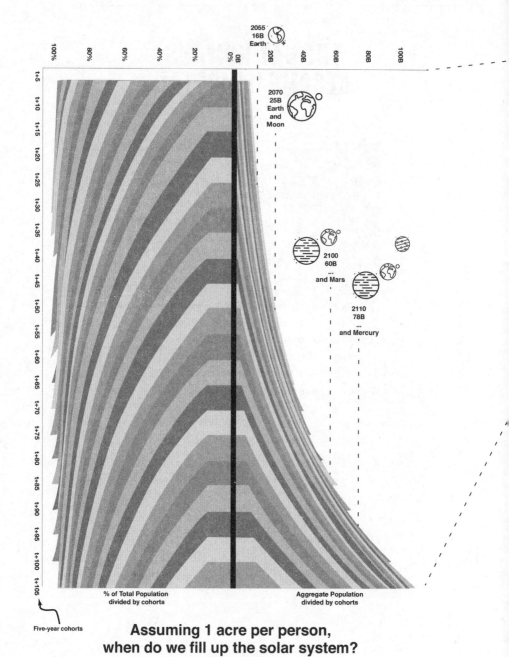

% of Total Population
divided by cohorts

Aggregate Population
divided by cohorts

Five-year cohorts

**Assuming 1 acre per person,
when do we fill up the solar system?**

(assuming a survival rate at the Makeham Baseline)

2055
16B
Earth

2070
25B
Earth
and
Moon

2100
60B
... and Mars

2110
78B
... and Mercury

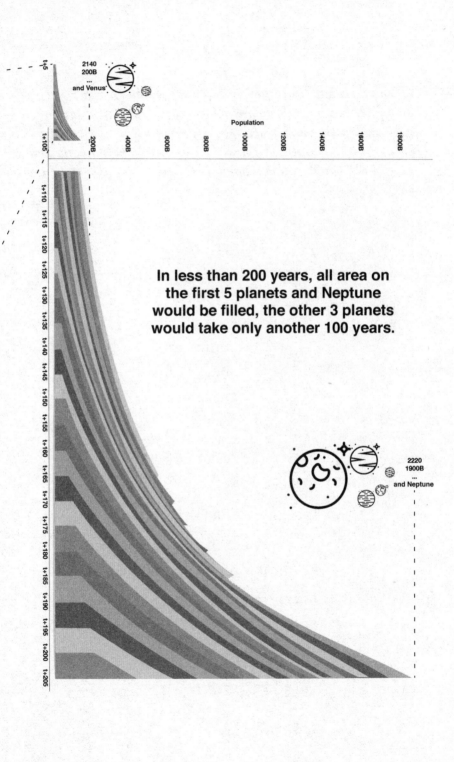

In less than 200 years, all area on the first 5 planets and Neptune would be filled, the other 3 planets would take only another 100 years.

Before I explain the graphic on the previous pages and go into detail about the bizarre day in which our ageless species fills up the last available living space in our solar system, and achieves true immortality by launching itself permanently into interstellar space, let's get something out of the way: it seems to me that it's okay to want immortality—or at least a much, much *longer life span.*

Statements like "technology that allows people to avoid dying from diseases would be good" are controversial. For no rational, evidence-based reason that I can see, many of my fellow humans have decided that death isn't just okay, but great! It's the secret sauce that makes life itself meaningful. "Immortality—how tempting, how appalling!" Roger Cohen wrote in a 2013 op-ed in the *New York Times*. "What a suffocating trick on the young! Death is feared, but it is death that makes time a living thing. Without it life becomes a featureless expanse."

There's a kind of superficial bravery in Cohen's attitude: accepting eventual oblivion because it supposedly enriches the present. But anti-aging activist and biologist Aubrey de Grey—whose long wizard beard and skeletal frame make him look, quite fittingly, like Father Time—considers this kind of talk cowardly. "People are shit scared of getting their hopes up," he said in his 2016 TED Talk. "Nobody wants to get their hopes up, so they like to make their peace with aging, and put it out of their minds, and get on with their miserably short lives, and make the best of it."

De Grey has a point. Before we all decide on behalf of our fellow humans that our life spans are great as is, that we should all only live to be about eighty, shouldn't we *try* living to be thousands of years old, and see if we still feel that way? My suspicion is that once we try living for eons, we won't collectively say, "Actually, this sucks. Life was more meaningful when we only had time to watch the Olympics eighteen or so times."

Just a hunch.

But let's move on from the "why" to the "how" of immortality. Can it really be done? Quite possibly. For starters, we just have to do what we've already been doing since we invented modern medicine: at the start of the twentieth century, the three leading causes of death were pneumonia, tuberculosis, and diarrhea-related conditions, and when you added diphtheria to those three, that murderer's row of torturous diseases accounted for one-third of all deaths globally. Being able to shift our attention to cancer and heart disease has been a triumph of modernity (although antibiotic resistance is a growing menace, which is why we'll be dedicating an entire chapter to it shortly).

But more important, we have to fight *aging itself*, which kills 90 percent of people in industrialized countries and two-thirds of all people, according to de Grey's research. This may be more possible than it sounds in the abstract, since we've recently learned how to pinpoint the biological causes of aging. According to a 2013 paper by Carlos López-Otín and his team at Spain's University of Oviedo, aging is the damage to our bodies that is caused by nine processes, such as DNA degradation, mitochondria gone wild, and having the wrong proteins in the wrong places.

All these inevitable—for now—forms of wear and tear in our bodies at the microscopic level are responsible for the conditions young people don't get, but old people do, including arthritis, cataracts, type 2 diabetes, atherosclerosis (the narrowing of arteries), and Alzheimer's disease. However, López-Otín and his team note that some of these factors, which they call "hallmarks," have upsides, and warn that the potential "cures" for each can negatively interact with one another, so they can't all just be halted at once.

For each of the nine causes of aging, López-Otín and company propose nine equally jargon-laden future therapies—in other words, they provide the recipe for immortality (spoiler: it's a bunch of drugs and therapies, most of which don't exist yet), which I will now break down for you:

- Clearance of "senescent" cells (cells programmed to die).
- Therapies to continue production of new stem cells.
- New anti-inflammatory drugs and "blood-borne rejuvenation factors."
- "Elimination of damaged cells."
- "Telomerase reactivation," which will stop the degradation of our DNA.
- "Epigenetic drugs," which stop us from literally mutating.
- Activation of "chaperones" for protein creation gone awry.
- Dietary restrictions.

- Drugs or therapies called "mitohormetics" and "mitophagy" (these keep the mitochondria in our cells from going haywire).

Throw those nine treatments in a pot; simmer; now you're basically immortal.

Of course, it's not going to be that easy. Since these can't all be knocked out with one drug, there won't be some big rollout of López-Otín's nine therapies—say, in the form of a miracle serum that each patient has to inject once a day. Instead, each of these processes will be perfected slowly, increasing life spans incrementally. If you're imagining some lucky test subject—a Silicon Valley billionaire who bankrolls the research effort, perhaps—getting to try the big immortality drug first, and becoming an ageless Count Dracula–type character in the process, surrounded by death but cursed with an endless life, that's not what will happen. Sorry, goths.

Instead, immortality will arrive piecemeal—knocking out López-Otín's nine hallmarks one by one. Perhaps we'll perfect "mitohormetics" first, to pick a random example. That will only extend life so far, without, say, "telomerase reactivation," the thing that keeps your DNA from breaking down.

As these age-fighting drugs and treatments get adopted—perhaps being prescribed when people are still quite young, to halt the aging process early—we should nonetheless expect negative drug interactions to slow down progress here and there. Perhaps your telomerase reactivation therapies will interact with your mitohormetics, and horrible side effects will ensue, making the whole endeavor not worth it. After all, who cares if you're not aging if your anti-aging drugs just caused your rib cage to cave in and crush your organs?

And about those dietary restrictions: remember, many of these will be medications that patients will take *forever*, sort of like anti-rejection drugs for transplant patients. That means the drug regimens will require lifestyle alterations, forcing patients to eliminate certain foods, or stop drinking coffee, or alcohol, or who knows what else. For instance, patients taking atorvastatin (aka Lipitor), a common drug used to treat high cholesterol, can't eat grapefruits without a risk of serious side effects, including death in extreme circumstances. So given the high number of drugs likely to be involved, we should expect the immortality lifestyle to be restrictive in as yet unpredictable ways. Is it worth it to live forever knowing you'll die if you eat, say, an everything bagel? Personally, I could live with that.

This will lead to a very interesting phenomenon: young people who haven't started certain immortality treatments yet will be able to eat and drink whatever they want, creating still more of a divide between the carefree hedonism of youth and the moderation of adulthood. Moreover, there'll be the nagging issue of self-control. Will it be harder to stay on your diet and faithfully take your meds as a healthy teenager when the long-term effects seem so abstract?

Another vexing question: Can this mix of therapies really be called "immortality"? These therapies won't make patients impervious to accidental death. There's no drug that could ever cure, say, having a wooden stake driven through your heart and then being beheaded— again, like Count Dracula.

But that's a bit of a red herring. When you get right down to it, immortality can't ever actually be achieved, since eternity isn't some endpoint at which you arrive. No one will ever look at their calendar and say, "I did it! I made it to eternity! I must be immortal," because, well, that makes no sense. So immortality is a moving goal that one must pursue literally forever (see the epilogue of this book for more about *the end of all existence*), but an end to aging is obviously the most important step in the direction of that goal. That makes defining the point at which immortality is achieved sort of a sticky business.

So I consulted someone who could help me define it.

Bryan Bischof is a mathematician and data scientist who founded a data consultancy firm in the Bay Area called Quasicoherent Labs (which also created the graphics for this book). He and his team crunched the hard numbers on immortality and told me that the best guess we have as to how long a person can live if they're "immortal" is probably around 1,132.925 years. As Bischof put it, "A thousand years is a long time to avoid accidents."

Bischof's statistical model for "immortality" makes us all eight years old. "The rate at which humans age is called the rate of senescence," he told me. "The minimum value of this senescence is called the Makeham Baseline, and it's generally around eight years old." In other words, according to demographers, fewer eight-year-olds die than any other group. They're safe from the sometimes fatal vicissitudes of infancy and early childhood, and they certainly don't die of old-age maladies like heart disease, but they do sometimes die by accident, or because of infections. So immortality would just give everyone the same odds of dying as an eight-year-old.

The computer program Bischof built created a "damping function," which assumes a thirty-year rollout as the immortality technology gets adopted more and more widely. During that time, the population will creep up. For this he computed the "Leslie matrix," a mathematical tool for seeing how many people in an age group are alive, dead, and having babies.

Which brings us to the graph that opened this chapter. The left half on page 38 shows the adoption of immortality as it becomes more popular. To see what happens once it's adopted, you might want to tilt your head to the right and look at the other half. What you see now is a skyrocketing human population. If we assume that each person requires one acre of land use—for living and for cultivating food—we'll fill up the Earth and the moon in about fifty years.

So I hate to break it to you, but this whole "live for a thousand years" plan plunges humanity into a kind of hell in a very short time. Assuming there's not a fertility crisis, we'll start to fill up our solar system as our population grows, meaning immortality will quickly create an existential crisis akin to today's climate change crisis and, paradoxically, jeopardize human life itself.

It's not at all clear how much usable living space there is in our solar system. For the purpose of this discussion, we're assuming one acre of livable space per acre of planetary surface. That makes for a somewhat crude calculation, but one that assumes there'll be space on moons and asteroids, and on man-made spacecraft. If that's the case, when the human population skyrockets to a mind-boggling 1.9 trillion people after less than three hundred years of immortality, the solar system will be full. (Okay, okay, we're *still* finding new planets, some with their own moons, way beyond Pluto, but close enough. You get the idea.)

So for my money, the day when humanity as a whole achieves immortality will also be the day we escape from the immortality crisis, by which I mean the day that there's a permanent human settlement outside our solar system.

This planting a flag among the stars will have the added benefit of giving humans a chance at surviving for the long haul, after our own solar system becomes uninhabitable. It's only once we're sophisticated enough to fly to another star, like Alpha Centauri, and extract the resources we need to live, rather than relying on the energy given off by a single star, that humans with life spans of more than a thousand years can possibly survive.

Otherwise we're in trouble. Achieving immortality may or may not damn our species to meaningless lives, like Roger Cohen thinks it will. But if we have to live out immense life spans on one tiny, resource-starved planet, then—to butcher the famous Thomas Hobbes quote—if our lives cease being short, we may have to become more nasty and brutish than ever.

THE DAY ANYONE CAN IMITATE ANYONE ELSE PERFECTLY

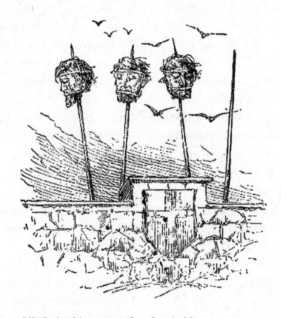

Likely in this century? > *Inevitable*

Plausibility Rating > *5/5*

Scary? > *Extremely*

Worth changing habits? > *Have you not been paying attention to the past twenty years of cybersecurity news? Of course it is!*

The call is coming from an unrecognized number. You answer, and the person on the other end of the line is sobbing, but it only takes a split second to recognize your sister's voice.

"He locked me out! We had a fight and he threw me out. I have nowhere to go!"

You've been wondering for months if someone in your family would ever get a call like this. After all, you never liked that guy she is dating, who breeds scorpions for a living.

"Whoa, slow down. Everything's going to be okay," you say. "Are you safe?"

There's a long pause, and then,

"I don't have any friends in Houston! Where am I gonna sleep?"

"Can you get a hotel?"

Another unsettling pause. "With what money?" she asks with a hint of bitterness.

"You don't have any money?"

"Can you wire me a thousand dollars? Just to get me through the next couple days?"

Wire? Can't she just use Venmo? And anyway, the last you heard, she was doing pretty well at work, and had just bought a car. Then again, Houston is on the other side of the country, and you haven't been checking in as regularly as you should have.

You tell her you're going to call your mom and then call her right back.

"Don't hang up!" she pleads. It's disturbing—bizarre even—how far she seems to have fallen in such a short time. You hang up.

Before your call to your mom can connect, she's calling again, on FaceTime now. You answer, bracing for the worst.

You see your sister's tear-streaked face as she hurries down an empty downtown sidewalk. "His friends know where I am," she says. "They know what happened, and I'm worried they're looking for me. I need that money. I'll be fine if I can get a motel room. I just need a thousand and I'll pay you right back."

"Go to the police!" you say.

"I don't get why you're making such a big deal about a thousand dollars! You've always been like this," she says,

passing through the front door of what looks like a high-tech Western Union. "Look, I'm at the place. I'll text you the info. Please, just wire me the thousand, and then I'll go straight to the motel and call you as soon as I'm safe. Okay?"

You're not rich, but you can afford to part with a thousand dollars if it means keeping your sister safe. "Okay," you say. "I'm sorry this is happening to you."

"Thanks," she says, and a warm feeling of relief washes over you as your sister's smile returns to her face. "I don't know what I'm gonna do tomorrow, but I'll figure it out," she says. "I love you. I'll call you right back."

"I love you, too."

The text arrives a few seconds later. "This place only converts Bitcoin into cash????" she writes. "But you know how that works, right?" You do, fortunately. You have a few thousand dollars in savings stashed in a Bitcoin wallet.

"Weird," you text back. "But no problem."

You transfer the one thousand dollars, and wait for her call.

After fifteen quiet minutes, you FaceTime your mom. When you tell her what happened, she's furious. "How could he just leave her stranded like that in Scottsdale? They don't know anyone there!"

"She's in Houston," you say.

"No. They're on vacation in Arizona until Friday," your mom says. "She just sent me a photo. They went hiking."

"Well, she FaceTimed with me, so I'm pretty positive she's in Houston," you say.

You can hear your father's voice in the background. "I just texted her. She says she's in Scottsdale," he says, before reading the texts aloud. "'I'm still on vacation. What money?' 'LOL. Is she okay?'"

Your face goes red. "I saw her, and she was definitely in Houston!" you shout. You know what you saw. It's not like you can't recognize your own sister's face.

You hang up and text your sister, or at least you text the number your sister was using.

"Hey is everything okay now? Are you at the motel?"

No reply.

"BTW why do Mom and Dad think you're in Scottsdale?"

No reply.

"What's going on? Did you get the money?"

Finally you get a reply. It's an image of that white, goateed mask you've seen online. It's a Guy Fawkes mask, that irritating "Anonymous" symbol.

Then comes a text. "Got it! LOL, thx sis!"

You have an incoming call. It's your sister, calling from her old number. Her real number, it turns out. In the "INCOMING CALL" notification, your phone displays a picture of her smiling face. Her real face.

You feel your lunch coming back up on you. *Not now*, you think, and reject it.

◆

The technology referenced in this unfortunate scenario isn't just some plausible future nightmare; it already exists. In fact, it's not only real, it's open source. One free version I've found is called FaceIt Live. It allows anyone to send a live video feed of their own face digitally "wearing" someone else's face like a mask. For now, the results aren't exactly convincing, but that won't be the case for long.

Granted, this technology could, say, save you time if you're a busy actor. On a 2016 episode of the Netflix animated series *BoJack Horseman*, the eponymous main character had his likeness secretly digitized, and that digital version was used to make an entire film—to much critical acclaim—even though BoJack performed no actual labor. But beyond facilitating fantastic feats of laziness, this technology could also allow you to make convincing videos of the dead, which may sound terrifying but, if used judiciously, might prove a valuable aid in grief counseling. It might also be an amazing—if, once again, somewhat ethically problematic—tool for reconstituting forgotten or suppressed memories.

That ethical stickiness is just the beginning, according to Peter Eckersley, who was chief computer scientist for the Electronic Frontier Foundation (EFF), a digital rights–focused nonprofit at the time I interviewed him, and who is now director of research at the computer industry consortium Partnership on AI. Eckersley's job at EFF was to be on the lookout for devices and software that might, unbeknownst to users, be violating their civil rights, and he and his team devised software solutions for those potential violations.

So prepare to wake up in a world in which almost anyone can create a truly uncanny fake version of anyone else, who can appear to do anything. Until the darkest imaginations of the general public get their hands on this technology, it's hard to know just what the applications will be.

The idea of creating convincing computerized imposters has been in the pop culture ether at least since the 1946 short story "Evidence" by Isaac Asimov, about a candidate for public office who's suspected of being a robot impersonator. The idea became unsettlingly—and realistically— possible when, in 2016, software designers from the Max Planck Institute for Informatics, the University of Erlangen-Nuremberg, and Stanford University created a video demonstration called "Face2Face: Real-Time Face Capture and Reenactment of RGB Videos." With the software, a user could, in real time, capture video footage of someone's actual face—Russian President Vladimir Putin, say—and then, by pointing a camera at their own face and changing expressions, also real-time, the user could make the target face move however they wanted, though not in a way that was fully convincing.

The demo resembled the Snapchat selfie filters that had been introduced the previous year. Though those were pretty trivial by comparison, they detected faces and could alter them by changing, for instance, the user's mouth in such a way that it would vomit rainbows. This technology alone was surprisingly sophisticated, but Face2Face was even more advanced. It made it possible for just about anyone to easily and instantly make someone appear to say anything. With this technology, anyone with enough sample images of the face they want to turn into the "mask," and the face that will wear the mask, can hand those photos over to an algorithm, which will then do all the work of swapping the faces. No Hollywood special effects skills required.

The lesson from this demo is that with enough hardware, you can already make anyone look like they're saying anything, as long as they're saying it rather stiffly, with nice TV studio lighting, and as long as the viewer doesn't watch for signs of humanity, like movement of the body. So what I'm saying is the demo worked amazingly well on politicians and not anyone else.

For the next several months similar technologies were refined, open source tools were applied to the concept, and several ideas converged to allow individuals like you and me (as opposed to researchers in high-tech labs) to produce ever more convincing face swaps. The process became more user-friendly, and digitally mapping any face onto a target face became something anyone with enough devious creativity and time could accomplish.

I suppose what followed was inevitable: in late 2017, a Reddit user with the moniker "deepfakes" superimposed the faces of mainstream celebrities onto the faces of porn performers, generating a series of fake, but unsettlingly realistic (and, importantly, nonconsensual) celebrity sex tapes. It had taken just over a year for the technology to find an application that was, if not overtly illegal, certainly abusive and scummy. Reddit banned the deepfakes community less than two months after journalists had discovered it.

But the term "deepfake" lives on as internet shorthand for videos in which faces are swapped out for other faces, and, as a corollary, face replacement technology has become a microcosm for the scary, "post-truth" future we're creating for ourselves. In 2018, filmmaker and comedian Jordan Peele appeared in a comedy PSA for BuzzFeed about fake news, in which former president Obama appeared to be saying things like "Stay woke, bitches," before being revealed as a deepfake, ostensibly perpetuated on the viewer by Peele.

I say "ostensibly" because Jordan Peele doesn't really sound like Barack Obama when he does his Obama impression, so no one was actually fooled (no offense, Jordan). This voice issue is the biggest obstacle in the way of creating fake videos of people seeming to do things they didn't really do: they can't talk. For now.

One day in 2018, I spent a couple hours reading hundreds of sentences into my laptop microphone, and feeding them into a piece of free online software called Lyrebird. Some of the sentences seemed to have been cooked up by a sadistic elocution teacher, like "Science has been arguing about the zoological classification of the species for decades," and some were rather ominous in the context in which I was being asked to read them, like "Besides encryption, it can also be used for authentication." Once two hundred or so examples of my unique vocal style were digitized, the software was able to create a text-to-speech engine that generated sentences and phrases that absolutely sounded like me—timbre, inflection, and all.

Well, they sounded exactly like me *if my words were being spoken through a desk fan and into a mobile phone*, but hearing it was still pretty frightening.

So let's say someone hacked into my Lyrebird account and used it to leave my girlfriend a voicemail telling her I was a hostage and needed $500,000 transferred into a Swiss bank account. How effective would that be? Well, my Lyrebird avatar is a terrible actor, because it can't make me sound agitated or scared, so the manufactured voice sounds like me—the real me—calmly reading the words "I'm being held hostage by terrorists, please help." And no con artist could have possibly fooled my girlfriend with such a recording, because right from the get-go, the voice bombs familiar greetings. "Hello" is too formal, and Lyrebird's "hey" is way off. And if you call your significant other by a special nickname, like I do, and the con artists aren't privy to that knowledge, the intended deceit is a non-starter. Even if the tricksters knew the nickname I use for my girlfriend, Lyrebird gets the delivery freakishly wrong.

Eckersley, the computer scientist formerly at EFF, told me that for now, these limitations affect not just Lyrebird, but the more sophisticated versions of this technology that currently only exist in computer labs. "The voices people use while giving public talks are a little different than the ones they use in personal conversation," which for now affords us some protection, he explained. "But that's thin protection, and it's protection that's going to crumble, potentially, to algorithmic techniques. There'll be a button that turns on and off the public speaking intonation." As it gets more robust, presumably, you'll just hit the emoji that matches the mood you need to hear in the computer voice's inflection.

You see where this is going: fake phone calls, then fake voicemails, and then fake video calls, not from obvious spammers, but, seemingly, from your loved ones. Maybe the deceivers will ask for your credit card information, but more likely, the ruse will be more clever. As it stands now, you wouldn't believe a text from a strange number, would you? It's a safe bet that in the next few years, you won't be able to believe a similarly strange phone call, or even a Skype call, without trying a little trick such as asking a question only the real person would know the answer to.

Imagining a future when this fakery technology gets in the hands of scammers, let's say your mom Skypes you while you're away at college, and says she saw your bank account is getting low, and she wants to transfer you some money, but she needs you to remind her what your account number and routing number are. Don't buy it—not unless you run your mom's face through some kind of authentication software, which will either confirm your mom's identity or unmask the imposter, like at the end of an episode of *Scooby-Doo*.

According to Eckersley, we need to work on strengthening phone number and email authentication protocols, since the only thing that lets you know to whom you're speaking is the caller ID, which scammers will easily be able to hack. But he's not entirely confident that those protection measures will be in place in time to prevent a lot of fraud, since the phone companies have really dragged their heels on computer security protocols.

The elderly have been targeted for decades by scams, but as younger baby boomers and Generation Xers hit retirement age in the next few decades, scams will have to become more sophisticated to dupe the tech-savvy elderly, who won't be so eager to believe that the IRS is calling and needs a cashier's check right away. But scammers have already found ways to target the next generation of seniors. For instance, they've begun using internet dating sites to target the elderly with catfishing scams, pretending to be fellow single seniors looking for love, and then convincing their smitten marks to write checks. Those kinds of scams will become easier, and more prevalent, when anyone can place a Skype call to a senior that *seems* to prove that the caller is a dreamy—but *plausible*—potential mate.

When imposter audio and video find a home on sites like YouTube, the implications are even more troubling. The danger then is that, in

Eckersley's words, "the epistemic, or sense-making, fabric that has to some degree held Western society together over at least the past fifty years, if not longer, [will start] to crumble and tear apart." That may sound overly hysterical, because even perfect fake videos can be proven false with thorough reporting. For example, if a video shows a candidate for office saying something damaging to the candidate's reputation, reporters will seek out the truth. Was the person really at that place at that time? Is there other footage corroborating this?

But I think we all know by now that journalistic rigor goes out the window when news is spreading online. As is the case with written fake news, concocting a totally wild, out-of-left-field fiction isn't the ideal way to spread a rumor. Instead, it stands to reason that videos containing a kernel of truth are likely to spread, perhaps videos depicting public figures saying plausible things that fit their public persona.

Imagine a large army of anonymous fake video creators, paid to generate hundreds of plausible-looking videos of a political candidate saying awful things. Yes, that candidate's enemies might spread the lies, and the public might believe them, but a potentially more unsettling outcome could follow. Assuming the public is aware that a high volume of fake videos exists, they'll doubt everything they see and hear, whether it's flattering or unflattering—or even worse, whether it's true or false. And this is just *one* political outcome that may or may not come to pass. There's no doubt that the technology will materialize and spread. When it does, Eckersley told me, "We're going to find ourselves in a super-weird topsy-turvy world."

But here's some good news: this technology will also be harnessed for non-evil.

Face and voice filters for video chat and vlogging, for instance, will allow people to change their faces, so they'll look and sound not so much like celebrities or innocent people whose identities they're trying to steal, but rather, just *someone else*. People who wish to conceal severe craniofacial anomalies, or anyone who might otherwise never feel comfortable on video, could, if they wanted, choose to use something like this to communicate openly and engage in public life.

These technological advances would also allow for the creation of seamless video footage of anonymous witnesses and information leakers in documentaries. Instead of being blurred, pixelated, or cloaked in shadow, these individuals could simply look and sound like a different person—provided the documentarian makes it clear that a disguise is being used.

But, in concluding this discussion, let's return to lazy actors and digitally resurrecting the dead. The biggest reason to be excited about this incredibly creepy technological frontier is that it will—mark my words—usher in a day when you can create your own custom movies and TV shows with a few keystrokes (or by then, maybe just some hand swipes or blinks).

Let's say your deepest, darkest fantasy is a slasher movie with Frank Sinatra as the killer, but since Frank is dead, you know you'll never get to see him wield a bloody chain saw. And now you can! There's no end to the possibilities for diversion if, you know, things like hiking in the woods, watching sunsets, or petting your dog just aren't enough.

THE DAY THE LAST HUMAN-DRIVEN CAR ROLLS OFF THE LOT

Likely in this century? > *Yes*

Plausibility Rating > *3/5*

Scary? > *Depends how much you enjoy driving*

Worth changing habits? > *Only if you hate driving*

TripAdvisor Reviews of Chandi Chowk Tuk-Tuk Tour Company, Delhi

★ ★ ★ ★ ½ Wonderful sightseeing trip!

Be sure to bring a camera, as you're going to be taking a wild ride through some of the most beautiful sites in the area formerly known as Shahjahanabad in a vehicle very much like an old-fashioned motorized rickshaw. I recommend going on a Sunday morning to see everything quickly. One small complaint: the speaker system is faulty and cuts out, plus the spoken audio script should probably be rewritten. It might be better to have a tour guide onboard, but since the driving is all automated, I understand why the owners made this choice.

★ ★ ★ Not so safe . . .

This tour was fun, but I can't recommend one of these "tuk-tuk" style vehicles. Since they're open on the sides, anyone can just reach in. There were automated warnings about this, but my wife had her scarf snatched by a monkey. The automated warnings didn't say anything about that. Also, I was in India a few years ago, and I seem to remember a lot of different colored rickshaws kind of like these. Those were very charming. Where did they go?

★ ★ ★ ★ ★ What a beautiful city

I took one of these tours several years ago, and India has transformed since then! Riding across town in one of these rickshaws meant getting stuck in a jam, or waiting for ages in a gridlocked roundabout. Now you never stop moving, so the tour goes pretty quick. Make sure and master the "stop" command, so you can buy delicious jalebi for a snack while you're in Jama Masjid, otherwise, the algorithm will just take you right past all the best booths.

★ If I could give zero stars I would

I grew up in Delhi and now I live in the UK, but I'm back on business. I wanted to see my former city today, so I paid the 350 rupees (5 USD) for one of these all-day tours. I cannot recommend this. First, this is not a "tuk-tuk." I used to drive a motorized rickshaw, or tuk-tuk, when I was a young man. I learned to navigate the city myself, decorated the cabin of my tuk-tuk, and I knew all the best alleys and shortcuts. This is a robotic golf cart, and it doesn't even point out many of the best historic sights. Second, it fails to take part in the community aspects of driving in Delhi. These carts move impressively among other cars, but they don't stop for children, and ours came uncomfortably close to a large bull that was in the road. Furthermore, a robot driver can't provide food recommendations. I'm an old man, but I'll walk next time I want to see Old Delhi properly. It seems I have no choice anyway.

◆

When the last car with a functioning steering wheel rolls off the lot—or indeed, when that car is eventually crushed into a cube, and the humans of the world achieve full reliance on autonomous wheeled, passenger-carrying robots—assuming that's something that makes the news, I'm confident that I'll feel hugely relieved. To me, the death of human-driven cars will be somewhat ugly, but fair, akin to when I hear about the trial and sentencing of some genocidal war criminal. *Good to know the trash has finally been taken out*, I'll think, narrowing my eyes for villainous effect.

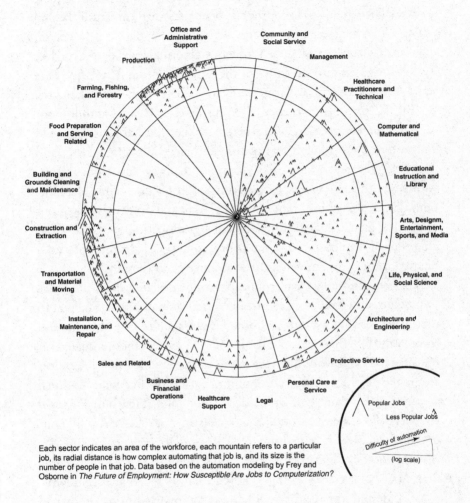

Each sector indicates an area of the workforce, each mountain refers to a particular job, its radial distance is how complex automating that job is, and its size is the number of people in that job. Data based on the automation modeling by Frey and Osborne in *The Future of Employment: How Susceptible Are Jobs to Computerization?*

Granted, the loss of driving-related professions will cause tidal shifts in the world economy. (It's worth pausing to note that most, or perhaps all, human jobs are at risk if the future of AI lives up to the wildest theories available.) How long it'll take for you to be replaced by an AI depends on how far you are from the center of the wheel in the above diagram (the farther from the center, the safer your job).

As you can see there in the lower left corner, transportation is one of the easier sectors to automate, and I think we all know it's got a very short time left. That's a whole lot of human beings who won't have jobs.

But it's hard to not welcome the end of driving when I'm actually behind the wheel. Driving scares me—particularly, when I'm traveling the hellish, dog-eat-dog freeway system of Southern California. It makes me feel like I've been drafted into the ranks of the War Boys from *Mad Max: Fury Road*. Autonomous cars will supposedly fix all that, which sounds fantastic.

This is more than a theory. Even in the early days of autonomous car development back in 2001, researchers like Shin Kato and Sadayuki Tsugawa of the National Institute of Advanced Industrial Science and Technology were working on reimagining roads as harmonious places with "algorithms for cooperative driving or flexible platooning of autonomous vehicles." Using empty robocars, Kato and Tsugawa worked out one of the first such algorithms, aimed at "compatibility of safety and efficiency of road traffic." In their paper about the algorithm, they even referred to the experimental vehicle as "smart and friendly."

Let's be absolutely clear: robocars haven't declared their allegiance to humans, and have, in fact, already tasted human blood. Since 2016 there have been at least four autonomous car fatalities, one in China and three in the US. But ever since the bloodshed started, the automated car industry has been working overtime to calm our anti-robot prejudices and make us process these autonomous car deaths like hyper-rational actuaries, rather than pearl-clutching technophobes. How humanity will wrap its collective head around this issue is anyone's guess. As Gill Pratt of the Toyota Research Institute told *Car and Driver* magazine in 2017, "Our hypothesis is that, because it's harder to empathize with a machine than a person, society is going to hold machines to a higher standard."

Still, despite the deaths—which mostly involved privately owned Teslas in self-driving mode—it looks like the case for self-driving cars holds up. As of this writing, Alphabet Inc.'s autonomous car division, Waymo, had racked up seven million miles of test driving on public roads—far more than any one human could ever drive in a lifetime—and Waymo's most serious accident was another driver's fault (footage of the crash shows that the driver swerved wildly into the robocar's lane while it was minding its own business).

So for our purposes here, we're going to buy the idea that robo-cars will be safer than human-driven cars. If it turns out they're death machines—or for that matter, that they destroy the global economy, steal all of our location data, or generally turn out to be a fiasco—you have my permission to turn one of those death machines on me. And it may be easier than you think to use a self-driving car as a murder weapon. According to a 2018 study published in *Nature*, you'll most likely just need to place me on the road next to something people intuitively value more than an adult man, such as a stroller, and the car will be programmed to swerve to avoid the stroller, and kill me instead.

But what will it be like when cars drive themselves? (Apart from the fact, of course, that—according to a 2018 paper by tourism researcher Scott Cohen—there'll be a rash of people having sex in them.)

Some very thorough speculative research and writing about this has already been done—particularly by the *New York Times Magazine* in November 2017 in an entire issue dedicated to the idea of robocars. One article, "Full Tilt: When 100% of Cars Are Autonomous," posited a number of plausible scenarios for the day we say good-bye to the last driver-driven car. Busy intersections won't involve the concept of "stopping" anymore, and will instead just look, from a distance, like two perpendicular schools of fish that momentarily converge, and seamlessly negotiate each other without colliding. Stoplights, and indeed all road signs, will be unsightly and unnecessary relics to be disposed of, creating a sign-free, utopian cityscape. The driverless city can include legions of mobile stores and warehouses, which will reduce delivery times and potentially disrupt the whole concept of retail stores. Driving algorithms will be more sensitive to the needs of the natural world than human drivers, easily dodging even the smallest of animals, and rerouting in real time to avoid animal-dense areas. At the same time, these algorithms will also be vulnerable to hacks, can be tricked out in ways that disregard safety, and will constitute a new frontier for petty crime.

This is admittedly a somewhat parochial view of a driverless future. Using the United States as the model for the soon-to-be-here driverless world may be unwise. Yes, the US is defined in some ways by its twentieth-century automobile mania, but the biggest car story right now is being written by the country that's about to be Earth's population leader if it's not already: India. Its love affair with cars started in the mid-2000s, and, as I write, it's just wrapping up a giant, multi-decade public works project to modernize its road system. So while the US and UK seem like places where robocars will take to the streets without much of a problem, India is the final frontier.

If you've spent time in India recently, you'll know that it's next to impossible to visualize roads full of robocars there. There are no "smart and friendly" vehicles to be found. Once you escape the polite, organized, and distinctly British-seeming road culture of the area around Mumbai Airport, the patterns of movement that most people in the developed world associate with driving become illusory. What you get on the Indian roads is a glorious and terrifying form of chaos that must be seen to be believed. The guiding philosophy that seems to rule every road in the country is "This is public space, to be used however anyone—be they driver, motorcyclist, pedestrian, vendor, cow, monkey, or elephant—sees fit." Since footpaths are practically nonexistent, walking two blocks in a city center feels like wading into a circus's center ring during the climax of the show. It's both liberating and frightening, requiring constant adaptation and improvisation. And it seems like the chaos would be utterly impossible to automate.

Which is not to deny that the whole system is in dire need of anything that can make the roads safer. The rate of road fatalities is appallingly high. According to injury data from the World Health Organization, India's road deaths per 100,000 vehicles are 130.1, compared to 12.9 in the US, 6.8 in Germany, and only 5.1 in the UK.

The surreality is ratcheted up on the open highways, which are also overflowing with scooters, animals, and even pedestrians, but which are made all the more dangerous by the fatal rate of speed. One night on a highway in rural Rajasthan, my girlfriend and I sat in the back of a taxi, clutching each other for dear life as our driver navigated the winding roads through the hill country. Our driver's time-saving strategy involved overtaking slower cars by entering the oncoming lane, *even on blind curves.*

Vivek Wadhwa is an Indian-born American technology entrepreneur, academic researcher, and tech pundit, and the coauthor of the 2017 book *The Driver in the Driverless Car.* Wadhwa is the consummate tech optimist. He has an expansive knowledge of the inner workings of present-day technology and, like me, loves to predict the future. Unlike me, he exudes hope, and has a tendency to make claims about technological paradigm shifts that will take place in the very near future, like when he predicted that 2012 would see the downfall of social media. (That didn't happen, but social media *did* transform from a lauded staple of the tech world to a reviled wasteland that we all vaguely tolerate.)

With that in mind, I called him to ask if and how an India dominated by driverless cars might come about, not *when* it would happen. (Though, if you must know, Wadhwa told me that it would happen within the next seven years, so by the year 2025. You don't have to ask him to make these predictions. He just does it. "Worst case: 2027," he added.)

"The irony is that I happen to be in a Model S Tesla in self-driving mode right now so my car is driving itself," Wadhwa said at the start of our phone conversation. "Someone got in the way and just stopped, and I just took over it because I didn't want to give that bastard, y'know, the right of way." Wadhwa had, whether accidentally or intentionally, given me a real-time example of what I perceive to be one of the biggest drawbacks of the "smart and friendly vehicle" ethos. What if you're willing to be smart behind the wheel, but not friendly?

Wadhwa acknowledged that revolutionizing the roads in India will be a huge project. But he expects the government will set aside roads for "self-driving only" in the next few years. He predicted that the highways would essentially be barricaded to exclude scooters and pedestrians, though he recognized that this would be a drastic change—one that will "require a state of emergency over there."

He predicts that since India is more than aware of its car fatality problem, as well as its crisis-level air pollution in cities like Delhi, the robocar-only highways will be just the beginning of the "state of emergency" project. More rules will be put in place to govern the city center. Wadhwa pictures citizens being told, "You can have your traditional automobiles on roads *outside* the city, but *within* the city it can only be this new generation of self-driving electric cars."

Government regulations requiring Indians to pay for a nationwide fleet of ultra-modern cars would be onerous. But this cost impediment might soon not be as formidable. The price of a converted self-driving car is currently in the hundreds of thousands of US dollars, but in 2017 the high-tech auto parts manufacturer Aptiv told Reuters that self-driving car hardware will only cost $5,000 by 2025. That same year, the Chinese software mega-conglomerate Baidu made its self-driving car software free.

With some generous government subsidies, the numbers really *could* make sense. All that is required is for the stars to line up and self-driving technology to be made practical in the most extreme driving environments.

THE DAY SAUDI ARABIA PUMPS ITS LAST BARREL OF OIL

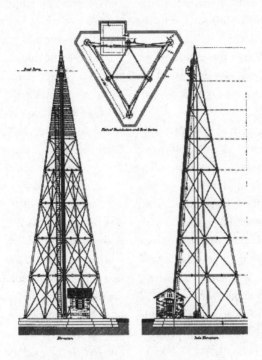

Likely in this century? > *Highly doubtful*

Plausibility Rating > *5/5*

Scary? > *In many ways, yes*

Worth changing habits? > *If you're a Saudi, or you do business in Saudi Arabia, it might be a good idea to speak out, but then again, that might also be a bad idea for you personally*

Port of Dhiba, Saudi Arabia. 6 p.m.

Women began working at the port decades ago. It was momentous when the first woman took a job sealing oil drums, but Norah pauses with her crimper in her hands as it dawns on her that she may be the last. Living the easy life in her home country was nice while it lasted, but she already has a plane ticket back to England, where she earned her engineering degree. She has enough saved up for a few months of job hunting.

The forklift returns empty, which is puzzling. Norah frowns at the driver, Faisal. "Are we done?"

"No." Faisal was never bright, but this evening he looks exceptionally confused. "They have a question about the barrels."

At times like this, Norah usually loves to explain the difference between a drum and a barrel. A metal drum, like the ones they load onto ships here in Dhiba, is fifty liters bigger than what the Americans call a "barrel." That's because a drum is a physical object, and a barrel is a liquid measurement, decided by the Americans. And where does this measurement come from? It comes from whiskey barrels! Every time they talk about "the cost of a barrel of oil," even here in Saudi Arabia, they're talking that which is *haram*—forbidden by their Prophet.

But she knows this would just confuse Faisal.

"Let's go talk to them," Norah says, hopping into the cramped passenger seat of the forklift.

When they get to the dock, four men in starched shirts with epaulets—the ship's crew—stand around an open shipping container. Once upon a time, tanker ships moved oil in such huge quantities that drums were unnecessary—the hull of the ship was one giant drum. But for years now, orders have been shrinking. Lately, buyers order a few dozen drums, if they order any oil at all.

Next to the shipping container there's a stack of red plastic drums marked "Hazardous Waste." The black oil drums in the shipping container are the same exact size and shape, but metal, and unmarked.

One of the men is Abdullrahman, Norah's supervisor, and he looks relieved to see her. "How do you open it?" he asks.

"A waste container?" she asks.

"An oil drum," says Abdullrahman.

She hoists one of the full drums onto one corner and rolls it out into the open. She pulls out her plug wrench, which, if you turn it backward, has an attachment that breaks the plastic seal. Then she unscrews the cap, and unscrews the second plug—allowing the contents to be poured out. She hands Abdullrahman the wrench. "Keep it. I have another one at my workstation."

"Thanks!" Abdullrahman says. "But actually, you can go early. You'll be paid through the end of the month."

She'd known this was coming, but she's shocked to be dismissed so abruptly.

"Wait. What are you doing?" Norah asks. The ship's crew has a funnel, and they're pouring the contents of the metal drums into the plastic ones. "That's perfectly good oil."

"Yeah, but they don't want the oil," Abdullrahman says. "They said they'd pay more for the drums if they're empty. Oil is worth less than nothing now, I guess."

"I get it. I see," Norah says.

She looks at Faisal. He could drive his forklift for a drug company, or a chemical company. They have a couple of those here in Saudi Arabia, but not many. It doesn't sound like they're hiring, though.

"You can go, too, Faisal," Abdullrahman says, gesturing not to the workers' dormitories at the port, where Faisal has been living, but at the highway to the nearby city of Duba, where just this week, nine men and six women—all unemployed—were killed in clashes between unemployed workers and police.

"Okay," says Faisal. Then he looks back at Abdullrahman, confused. "But what do I do when I get there?"

◆

The game is simple: you're the new reigning monarch of Saudi Arabia, and you can approach your kingdom's uncertain future one of two ways: (A) take the lower path to follow the UN's and international community's suggestions to the letter, or (B) follow the upper path to basically keep doing what you're doing. For the purposes of this game, there are only two paths, and they don't cross each other. You win the day you pump your last barrel of oil, no matter how ugly things have become in your country in the meantime.

Either path is fraught with setbacks, but as the decades roll on they'll both lead to the finish line. According to the game, the international community's approach will give you a diversified economy and greater regional peace, and the status quo will bring you economic devastation in the absence of the single resource that drives your economy, and if you're really unlucky, it will bring you war. Is the game correct? We're about to find out, because the game corresponds to Saudi Arabia's real predicament. Saudi leaders acknowledge that their economy is precarious, and they've made concessions that suggest they know their regime's human rights record is repugnant. But what's more, as we'll see, these two problems are intimately linked, and one can't be tackled without sorting out the other.

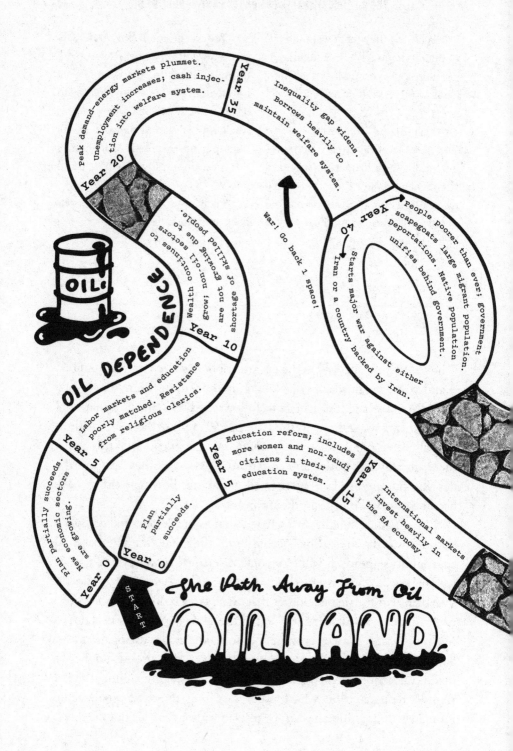

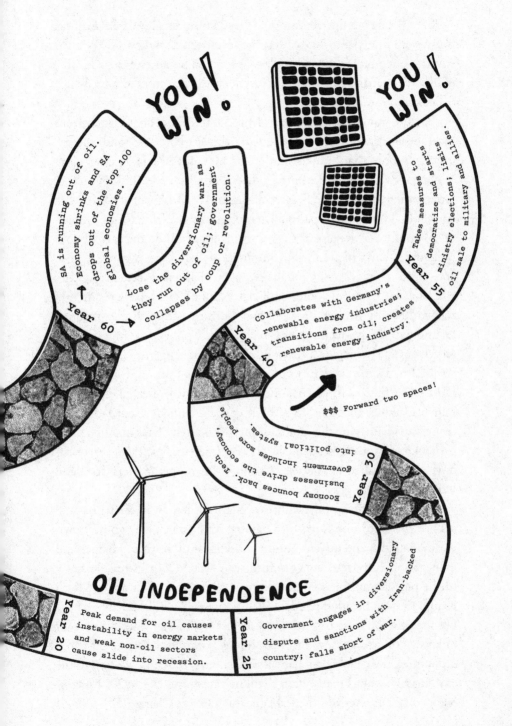

YOU WIN!

YOU WIN!

Year 60 → Economy shrinks and SA drops out of the top 100 global economies.

SA is running out of oil.

Lose the diversionary war as they run out of oil; government collapses by coup or revolution.

Year 55 Takes measures to democratize and starts limiting elections; limits oil sale to military and allies.

Year 40 Collaborates with Germany's renewable energy industries; transitions from oil; creates renewable energy industry.

$$$ Forward two spaces!

Year 30 Economy bounces back. Tech businesses drive the economy; Government includes more people into political system.

OIL INDEPENDENCE

Year 20 Peak demand for oil causes instability in energy markets and weak non-oil sectors cause slide into recession.

Year 25 Government engages in diversionary dispute and sanctions with Iran-backed country; falls short of war.

But looking out the window over Riyadh from the Royal Palace, things must seem fine. Saudi Arabia has the seventeenth highest GDP in the world—one notch below Canada—and it's all because of the country's oil reserves (and Saudi Arabia's idiosyncratic domestic economy, which I'll talk about more in a minute).

But the implications of the real-life Saudi Arabia board game aren't local, or even regional: they're global. The last barrel of Saudi oil will be much more than just the last barrel in Saudi Arabia. According to F. Gregory Gause, head of international affairs at the Bush School of Government and Public Service at Texas A&M University, "The last barrel of oil traded internationally is going to come from Saudi Arabia."

Mentally, set the global stage for this event in the manner of your preference—by which I mean your *political* preference: if you're a hardcore, Silicon Valley–style capitalist, imagine that renewable energies and efficient new batteries, along with clever carbon taxes, have resulted in the world being weaned off fossil fuel–burning energy sources through technological advancement and technocratic policy making; if you're an eco-socialist, imagine a vast consciousness-raising campaign that has resulted in a shift away from growth and consumption in the world's most powerful countries, meaning everyone now lives small-scale, sustainable, nature-focused lifestyles; if you're a climate science–denying conservative, imagine the "globalist puppet masters" have manufactured such an enormous inescapable lie about climate change that everyone is now a brainwashed lib, hopelessly under the puppet masters' spell and doing their bidding.

No matter which of these three scenarios is closest to the truth (and it's not the third one, sorry), the global oil business isn't going down without a fight, and oil isn't going to disappear on its own. Hedge fund managers in 2018 were "super bullish," and were still investing like crazy in the petroleum industry, according to Reuters market analyst John Kemp. But on the other hand, climate activists like Bill McKibben have been saying for years that we need to just walk away from 80 percent of known oil reserves, even though doing so would obliterate oil-based economies. If we don't do what McKibben says, the consequences of the ensuing runaway climate change will be catastrophic. The 2018 special report by the Intergovernmental Panel on Climate Change (IPCC) said carbon pollution—which comes mostly from fossil fuels—needs to be cut by 45 percent by the year 2030, and then go down to zero by 2050. Petroleum has to go down, one way or another.

It doesn't look like that will happen on the IPCC's time line—and the result of our collective indifference to climate degradation will be catastrophic—but that final barrel *will* be pumped and sold someday. In the majority of the world, that most likely means a rather choppy shifting of gears from the unbridled use of greenhouse gas–emitting energy sources and transportation methods to a more judicious approach to energy and transportation. Cars can probably become electric without drastically changing the way humans do business. Electric planes, on the other hand, don't seem like a realistic possibility anytime soon, so flights might simply have to become rarer and more expensive. Cargo ships, too, might have to go away entirely, which means a less globalized economy.

So there are economic shocks ahead in many, if not all, countries, but Saudi Arabia, the nation that's practically synonymous with "oil," is setting itself up, as far as I can tell, to dive into a horrific death spiral. The government has several decades to find an alternative way to feed its people, and, as we shall see, it's decidedly not availing itself of that opportunity.

Okay, it's a little misleading to imply that Saudi Arabia doesn't have a backup *at all*. Their ideas are just, let's say, less than practical. For instance, the Saudi Arabian government says it's building a city called Neom—one of several planned megacity projects—to be completed in the next few decades. The image of Neom that the kingdom is projecting to the world is that of a literal utopia, an idealized vision of Saudi Arabia's oil-free future. A fantastical commercial from 2017 showed a simulation of Neom, filled with placid, multicultural people performing high-tech jobs, walking barefoot down beaches with mostly white children, doing cartwheels, tending to fresh vegetables in futuristic greenhouses, sailing, scuba diving, skydiving, high-fiving, and just generally loving their lives. A narrator with a British accent promises nothing short of heaven. Neom, he says, will be "a land created to free people from stress. A place where pioneers and thinkers and doers can exchange ideas, and get things done. A start-up the size of a country that will change the way we live and work forever."

The city will include twenty-five thousand square kilometers of Saudi land (about the size of Vermont) along with small slivers of land from neighboring Jordan and Egypt. Neom will be an independent economic zone, with "neighborhoods that can feed and clean themselves." But more to the point, Neom will rely almost entirely on sustainable sources of energy, rather than Saudi Arabia's signature export. The project website for Neom boasts "perennial solar resources" of 20 mega-joules per square meter, and an "ideal wind speed" of 10.2 meters per second, so there's plenty of cheap sustainable energy to be harnessed by anyone who wants to install the turbines and solar cells.

Neom is supposed to reach its phase one landmark in 2025, but that estimate is pretty dubious. The British nonprofit group Middle East Monitor compared the prospect of Neom working out to that of another special city, King Abdullah Economic City. About the latter, it noted, "More than a decade since its launch, the project is only one-fourth developed or under development."

Saudi Arabia likes to offer at least the *appearance* of a shift away from its oil-centric economy, but then not follow with anything substantive—sort of a "hope for the best; don't prepare for the worst" strategy. But the country controls 18 percent of all proven petroleum reserves in the world, according to OPEC. That means asking Saudi Arabia to find a new way to sustain itself is like telling the Spanish pop group Los del Río to go on tour without performing "Macarena" if "Macarena" were on track to cause tens of millions of deaths. Sure, under all that pressure, Los del Río would diligently record a new record, but when they hit the stage, saw all those blank faces, and began worrying about ticket sales, we all know what they'd play.

And Saudi Arabia is playing the hell out of its "Macarena." According to the Observatory of Economic Complexity, crude petroleum, refined petroleum, petroleum gas, and ethylene polymers—a petroleum derivative—make up 82.3 percent of Saudi Arabia's exports, and that estimate of the country's reliance on oil is probably at the low end. While the "Saudi Vision 2030" plan promoted heavily by Crown Prince Mohammad bin Salman promises better things ahead—specifically, that non-oil exports will rise from 13 percent to 50 percent by 2030—don't count on it.

When asked about the 2030 time line, James Gelvin, a Middle East historian at the University of California, Los Angeles, said, "It ain't gonna happen."

Gause, of Texas A&M's Bush School of Government and Public Service, was similarly pessimistic in 2018, noting that Saudi Arabia hasn't been trying all that hard because the disastrously low prices of oil that were plaguing Saudi Arabia two years before had since improved. "Vision 2030 was conceptualized in an atmosphere of oil under forty dollars a barrel. Well, now it's up to seventy dollars," he told me. (It has since dipped somewhat, but not below forty dollars.)

You get what I'm saying by now: Saudi Arabia, like much of the world, has an oil addiction, and it keeps relapsing. Like any addict trying to get clean, the Saudis can't just quit cold turkey when their whole world revolves around using. The new, geopolitically correct economy the rest of the world longs to see in Saudi Arabia involves a kind of sociocultural sleight of hand that will swipe away the current entrenched status quo like a magician's tablecloth and—an even more difficult feat—slip another tablecloth underneath the dishes without spilling a drop.

To wit: Saudi Arabia is unlikely to slap its own oil industry with costly regulations, because the government itself owns Saudi Aramco, the monolithic oil company at the center of Saudi life, and this arrangement allows the government to provide eligible citizens with cushy jobs and large paychecks. And if you're looking for a culprit for the country's lack of enterprising creativity, it certainly can't help that all aspects of life revolve around a hegemonic form of religious conservatism through which the state maintains unequal status for women.

Gelvin thinks, "It's no coincidence that the neoliberal revolution took place at the exact same time as the human rights revolution globally, because the two are very dependent upon each other." The theory goes a little something like this: You want new sources of revenue so your country won't collapse? You need new ideas. Want to foster new ideas? Let people say things that might make you uncomfortable. Want people to be able to cope with change without becoming frightened and violent? Encourage pluralism. Freedom, this thinking goes, begets enterprise. (It's just one theory about how innovation works, and China might beg to differ.)

Instead of welcoming new ideas, though, Saudi Arabia often suppresses them. Critics of the regime face crackdowns, like blogger Raif Badawi, who was publicly flogged and imprisoned, or, most recently, *Washington Post* journalist Jamal Khashoggi, who vanished in 2018, with the CIA concluding that the crown prince had him murdered. The book *Daring to Drive: A Saudi Woman's Awakening* is a rare firsthand account by a social activist in Saudi Arabia who actually lived to tell the tale. Author Manal al-Sharif battled local traditions to be allowed to drive a car to and from work—instead of begging her coworkers for a ride day in and day out as women had been doing for decades. She writes that as her protest campaign rolled out, she had to remain patriotic at all times. "I kept saying respectful things, emphasizing that I am a Saudi, that I am proud to be Saudi, and that I love my country. I just want to change this custom," al-Sharif writes. She was imprisoned anyway.

Nonetheless, in 2018 women began to receive driver's licenses.

"I think women driving is going to be a huge change for the place socially and economically," Gause said. Not only does greater autonomy for women improve human rights, it's also a win for the neoliberal world order. To boot, organizations like Aramco will benefit from greater access to the huge brains of educated women like al-Sharif.

This points to a separate problem: the uneducated. Imagine a man with only a high school education. Maybe he's a driver at a ministry, but he has two wives, and kids. This is where Faisal, the driver from the fictional introduction, comes in. Without oil, Faisal will have to find work in a much more American- or European-style labor market—a "free" market where jobs for unskilled laborers are anything but guaranteed. And if Faisal manages to get one, it probably won't pay all that well, or come with any sort of job security.

Faisal will, in all likelihood, have to take a big step down in socioeconomic status. He'll have to become a janitor or some other kind of manual laborer. To keep their heads above water, one of his wives might have to become a domestic worker. Currently in Saudi Arabia, these kinds of jobs are reserved almost exclusively for migrant laborers. As unskilled Saudi workers crowd the domestic labor market, migrant workers, in turn, will suffer even more than they do now, seeing their rights disrespected and their voices ignored. "If there's a peep out of them, they'll be deported immediately. That's the way things go," Gelvin told me.

One factor that will turn this dawning economic crisis into a full-scale catastrophe is the country's extant unemployment problem. A 2016 report by Bank of America and Merrill Lynch projected that the youth unemployment rate in 2030 will be a shocking 42 percent. According to the *Financial Times*, "About forty-five percent of private sector jobs in the kingdom are in construction, a sector unattractive to Saudi men and largely off-limits to women who make up about eighty-five percent of job seekers in the kingdom."

Many people I spoke to offered the famous "frog in a pot of boiling water" as a metaphor for understanding this slowly intensifying crisis. The day the oil stops, Saudi Arabia will have been plagued by skyrocketing unemployment for years. There'll be a collection of crumbling, failed, multibillion-dollar planned city projects, and not a whole lot of goodwill from other countries.

"If the world doesn't need oil anymore," Gause said, "nobody will care." He *was* quick to point out, though, that since the holy cities of Mecca and Medina are in Saudi Arabia—literal must-see destinations for all the Muslims in the world—many people of that faith will care. But the vast majority of the world has no such obligation, and likely wouldn't notice.

You might think that the obligation all devout Muslims feel to visit the kingdom could be a revenue generator, and you'd be right: the country does at least *try* to make religious tourism into a cash cow. For example, it has opened the government-owned Abraj Al-Bait, a Las Vegas–esque complex of hotel towers in Mecca just a stone's throw from the Kaaba, Islam's holiest site. But according to *Time* magazine, Saudi Arabian tourism is a one-trick pony: you can only visit Mecca if you're a Muslim; if you're not, you can check out, what, an oil derrick? Or maybe leave the country altogether and grab some drinks next door in Bahrain.

Gentle sarcasm aside, there's nothing to do in Saudi Arabia anymore, and the government has made sure of it. Over the past few decades most relics and historical sites have been destroyed. This is, in part, because prevailing readings of Islam in Saudi Arabia frown on the visiting of such sites, considering such jaunts a slippery slope to idolatry. According to *Time*, even the birthplace of the Prophet Muhammad is facing demolition.

So what does Saudi Arabia get the day it pumps its last barrel of oil, apart from massive unemployment and a tanking economy? Unless something changes drastically, and soon, it gets unmitigated ecological disaster. According to a 2015 report published in *Nature Climate Change*, between the years 2071 and 2100, temperatures are expected to "exceed [the] threshold of human adaptability" at several points over those thirty years. That threshold is the "limit of survivability for a fit human under well-ventilated outdoor conditions," meaning the heat is so harsh that simply going outside puts you in mortal peril. And sometimes a person can't just stay inside. Aside from normal daily activities that require leaving the house, pilgrimages to Mecca are a "necessary outdoor Muslim ritual," and the report says the ritual is likely to become "hazardous to human health, especially for the many elderly pilgrims."

Perhaps even more depressing: Saudi Arabia doesn't have many friends. A 2016 survey of citizens in G8 countries ranked it number sixty-seven in terms of "reputability" on a list of seventy countries. Fifty-five percent of Americans have an unfavorable view of Saudi Arabia according to a 2018 Gallup poll. That means when the country tanks, destroying the livelihood of millions of innocent people, there may be no one for the government to turn to.

THE DAY A REAL JURASSIC PARK OPENS

Likely in this century? > *Surprisingly conceivable*

Plausibility Rating > *3/5*

Scary? > *In a fun way, yes*

Worth changing habits? > *No*

John Hammond: I don't think you're giving us our due credit. Our scientists have done things which nobody's ever done before.

Dr. Ian Malcolm: Yeah, yeah, but your scientists were so preoccupied with whether or not they could that they didn't stop to think if they should.

So goes one of the most famous exchanges in *Jurassic Park*, one of the cinematic juggernauts of the 1990s. The movie, which sparked a seemingly endless multibillion-dollar film franchise, is set on an island and is about zoo-kept cloned dinosaurs running amok and eating people. The above argument is between John Hammond, a theme park entrepreneur, and Ian Malcolm, a contrarian mathematician. Malcolm's words always annoyed me as a kid. *Of course they should*, I thought. *Who doesn't want to see real dinosaurs?*

It struck me in April 2017 that the world is full of real John Hammonds. That was when music festival fans were lured to an island in the Bahamas for something called the Fyre Festival. Rather than be greeted with plush accommodations, attendees found themselves stranded on a beach in tents built for disaster relief, where they had to fight extreme heat and were sometimes deprived of food or water. Worse, they were almost entirely deprived of the A-list musical acts they had been promised.

Fortunately, no one was eaten by a prehistoric animal, but the festival's organizer, an entrepreneur named Billy McFarland—later convicted of fraud and sentenced to six years in prison—was a charlatan with too much money and ambition, and not enough sense, just like Hammond. And just like the victims in *Jurassic Park*, the festival-goers probably should have had more sense than to take McFarland's bait. That doesn't mean they deserved what they got.

In literature, ambitious rich guys have been making big messes and causing other people to suffer ever since Macbeth, and probably earlier. But it was Mary Shelley's *Frankenstein* that put the tools of modernity in their hands, treating science like Promethean fire and giving us the timeless moral: *Those who play God are themselves damned. Jurassic Park* alludes to this old saw pretty directly when Ian Malcolm, played by Jeff Goldblum, quips, "God creates dinosaurs, God destroys dinosaurs, God creates man, man destroys God, man creates dinosaurs." And Malcolm is indeed the film's Cassandra character, who seems to know everything is about to go wrong before it does. But the reason he cites is mathematical, not religious: chaos.

Ultimately, just as Ian Malcolm predicts, a lot goes wrong in Jurassic Park, and a lot of people get eaten by dinosaurs, which is why people have paid billions of dollars to watch the movies.

At the time of the first film's release, science journalists took the movie's claims seriously, even if they dismissed them a moment later. Robert Lee Hotz wrote in the *Los Angeles Times* in 1993 that some promising prehistoric DNA recovery research "takes scientists no closer to the science fiction fantasy embodied by the book and film 'Jurassic Park,'" before lamenting that extinction "is still forever," according to the scientists in the article.

But with the benefit of hindsight, we now know that this level of certainty about extinction wasn't justified by the facts.

We'll have to get into the weeds for a moment, but that's as it should be. *Jurassic Park* was based on the rather in-the-weeds novel by Michael Crichton, a medical doctor who wrote jargon-heavy popular science fiction inspired by the very real breakthroughs emerging from the biotechnology revolution of the 1970s and '80s.

In the novel, Crichton imagined finding mosquitoes from dinosaur times preserved in amber (prehistoric tree resin), extracting dinosaur blood from those mosquitoes, piecing together complete DNA sequences from that blood, splicing that DNA onto live cells, cloning those cells, and producing living dinosaurs. This stuff sounded eerily plausible to the average popcorn-chomping moviegoer.

But how plausible was it, actually? Here's a quick plausibility breakdown of *Jurassic Park*'s crazy assumptions about science:

1. Yes, scientists can really get their hands on amber from the Jurassic period, although most of it is from the Cretaceous period or later. But that's okay, because most of the really scary dinosaurs are from the Cretaceous period anyway. And besides, Jurassic, Cretaceous, who cares? It's all dino-times.
2. Yes, some amber actually has mosquitoes preserved in it, and yes, we know mosquitoes almost certainly bit dinosaurs, because they bite birds.
3. It's conceivable that DNA could be harvested from very old blood. But eighty-million-year-old blood was already thought to be a bit of a stretch in 1993.

4. Cloning a big, multicellular organism from harvested DNA was an idea in the zeitgeist, even if it still wasn't quite ready for prime time. Breakthroughs in the '70s and '80s like the Cohen/Boyer patents allowed scientists to build proteins by splicing genes, and had laid the foundation for cloning, even if no vertebrate had actually been cloned yet.

5. Turning a cloned vertebrate cell into an embryo, bringing that embryo to term, birthing it, and producing a living, breathing animal? Still total science fiction.

Thanks to a 2012 study of fossilized prehistoric animals called moa—dinosaur-like birds that existed in Australia until the fourteenth century—we now know that intact DNA only has a half-life of about 521 years, but it can be readable as information (albeit information that's scattered like jigsaw puzzle pieces) for about one million years. That's a much longer life span for DNA viability than we previously assumed, but one million years only takes us about 2 percent of the distance into the past we need to go to gather dinosaur DNA.

So if that's the end of the story for fossilized DNA, it's a very discouraging sign. If the secrets in even the most perfectly preserved DNA dissolve after a couple million years, that closes the door on cloned dinosaurs forever. But at the same time, this finding opens the door to the cloning of extinct animals like the Pleistocene megafauna, a loose collection of giant extinct species that were around at the same time as some early—and unfortunately very hungry—humans. And even if Jurassic Park is still out of reach, the same can't be said for Pleistocene Park.

And someone will most certainly take a stab at cloning these preserved prehistoric monsters. This includes not just moa, but other bizarre animals from the past, like glyptodonts, which were armadillos the size of cars, or immense cats like the smilodon and the American lion, and, of course, the woolly mammoth.

Animals that went extinct more recently—like the Pyrenean ibex, a species of goat that went extinct in 2000—have been successfully cloned (although the cloned ibex born in Spain in 2009 died almost immediately from a lung defect), proof that some types of extinction *are* reversible.

But no cloned dinosaurs? Not ever?

Good news: it still might happen.

Prosanta Chakrabarty is an ichthyologist and evolutionary biologist based at Louisiana State University. He's also the creator of a viral TED Talk called "Four Billion Years of Evolution in Six Minutes," and has, for several years now, been the person I call whenever I'm fixating on a trivial—often puerile—biology question (he has seemingly infinite patience for my immature questions). He told me if we ever want to bring back dinosaurs, we may just have to combine bioengineering with phylogenetics—the study of evolutionary relationships between organisms.

"The cellular material is there, but not the DNA," Chakrabarty said. To get our hands on the DNA, then, "we can model what the DNA would have looked like." In other words, we would have to get creative. There are plenty of living archosaurs—the category that includes birds, crocodilians, and dinosaurs—and we can use them to figure out the shared DNA that conveys the traits that give us those types of animals at the genome level. According to Chakrabarty, that's about 95 percent of it.

The other 5 percent requires us to ask, "What are the protein coding genes that create things that actually make a dinosaur?" Once that's determined, Chakrabarty told me, "You stuff all the exons—the protein coding genes—into a chicken, and you see what makes a chicken have things that we think dinosaurs have."

It would be an imperfect, and somewhat disturbing, trial-and-error process. A whole lot of mutant chickens would be created, but eventually we could end up with animals that cut dinosaur-like profiles, insofar as we have any idea what dinosaurs are. We'd have animals that match the skeletal remains, and have scales and feathers, and lay eggs. Would those really be dinosaurs? Absolutely not. But put them in a zoo, and kids will love them.

But will it all go haywire, with humans being chased and eaten by horrible prehistoric monsters? And if not, will it be worth the price of admission?

I ran these questions by James A. Yorke, the mathematician and physicist who, in 1975, coined the term "chaos" as a scientific and mathematical precept, with coauthor Tien-Yien Li (coincidentally, Yorke also served as inspiration for Ian Malcolm). Yorke isn't too worried about the events of

Jurassic Park playing out in reality, he told me, because as an illustration of chaos theory, it has a glaring flaw: Dennis Nedry, the corporate spy who undermines security at the park to steal the underlying technology. "He destroys everything," Yorke told me. "What that's got to do with chaos I really don't know." Indeed, having someone turn off the electric fences that keep the giant predators in their cages is certainly a shortcut to cinematic terror. Still, if we take Nedry out of the equation, *Jurassic Park* offers some powerful lessons—the rules, basically, for creating a very hazardous dinosaur amusement park.

"It's not that it's a super-complicated process," Yorke told me. It's just that "there are too many new things being introduced in this project."

Dino-creating zillionaire John Hammond put too much faith in the genetic trickery he used to control the animals—his choice to create an all-female menagerie, and a genetic alteration that made all the animals dependent on supplementary nutrition.

"They didn't take into account that the base animal that they were using—what were they using, frogs?—could change sex. That's a chaos type of thing," Yorke explained.

Meanwhile, Malcolm spots a graph at one point, showing the heights of dinosaurs on the island, and when the bell curve is too tidy, he knows something has gone wrong: in a small sample, it shouldn't be so tidy—there should be more *chaos*. In science, this is a very real warning sign, Yorke said. "There are different ways of getting too smooth of a curve. Usually the way to get too smooth of a curve is, somebody's fudging the data."

In the novel, the island's monitoring system counts the total population at one point, producing the expected count of 238 animals. Then Malcolm queries the system for 239, and it finds 239—proof that the dinosaurs are breeding. When asked how many it can find total, it reports that there are 292. It's revealed that the computer had been programmed to save energy by searching only for the expected number of dinosaurs, and then stopping, which had prevented everyone from noticing that dino reproduction was going on. The computer had the information, but no chaos-minded mathematician had been there to ask the right question.

It all adds up to a lot of screaming and death, and the reason, according to Yorke, doesn't take a mathematician to comprehend: "Nothing works the first time, and it may fail for multiple reasons, but hopefully not too many." He added that "the most successful people are those who are good at plan B." He then told me to imagine myself getting to my goal by walking along a balance beam with a chasm on either side, and that if I were to fall into the chasm I would die. The problem with this plan is that there's no good plan B. So, word to the wise, he told me, "You don't choose that as plan A!"

And generally speaking, the creators of amusement parks *don't* choose that as plan A. When I was at Six Flags Magic Mountain recently, a roller coaster I was riding came around a corner, and I saw a bunch of rather eerie objects: a dozen or so giant plastic water jugs vaguely shaped like seated humans, and they looked well worn. I knew at once that these were the fake people used to test the very coaster I was riding. If something on the ride had been tweaked recently, I took comfort in the fact that the car had gone around the track a few times with a weighted jug full of liquid in my seat instead of me—a very different jug full of a very different liquid.

The basic rule is simple, Yorke said. In systems where you introduce new components, it's difficult to predict what's going to happen. So if you're being asked to help test out any new piece of technology, keep in mind that you're a guinea pig. If the technology involves things like claws and teeth, be cautious, but keep an open mind. Do the technologies that are protecting you from said claws and teeth seem comprehensible and trustworthy to you? Or do the security measures sound like the ones touted by John Hammond in *Jurassic Park*? Are they still in the testing phase? Are you supposed to take comfort in experimental genetic modifications and proprietary data-gathering software? That's troubling.

If you've ever gone bungee jumping you've seen this in action, assuming you hired someone reputable. I'm not talking about the obligatory safety-first ethos that permeates the experience, but the sheer systematization and mind-numbing repetition of the bungee technician's job. When I went bungee jumping, groups were sorted by weight, fitted with vests, checked and rechecked, and then run through a sort of assembly line process that resulted in about one person per minute safely jumping off a bridge. It made the experience feel a little less special, while also making my bungee technicians seem *a lot* more trustworthy. In a real

Jurassic Park, what could be more reassuring than the sight of thousands of satisfied customers filing out of the park in an orderly fashion—and, more important, in one piece? They've seen every dinosaur, and lived to tell the tale.

Physician John Rex gave me another way of looking at this. "If you ever need a surgical procedure done, what you want is a place that does twenty of them a day," he told me. This is the best way to avoid infections, he explained. A place working in high volume, he said, is "counting every one of their infections and they know their rates—they know their process and nobody is allowed to go out of step."

My takeaway is that at the grand opening of an extinct animal zoo, I'll be confident that I'm not going to be subject to any dino rampages. But use some common sense if a wealthy eccentric—perhaps a gray-haired Billy McFarland—flies you on an all-expenses-paid trip to his private island featuring a zoo full of once-extinct predators. I'm now convinced that when it comes to any complex, untested, high-tech tourist attraction where I don't understand and trust the process that was used to iron the kinks out before I got there, I have every reason to say no. Those kinks are called "chaos," and they can be deadly.

THE DAY ANTIBIOTICS DON'T WORK ANYMORE

Likely in this century? > *Yes*

Plausibility Rating > *5/5*

Scary? > *Extremely, but probably not the apocalypse*

Worth changing habits? > *Yes*

A-Day Minus 2

8:00 a.m. EST: In the midst of a fit of enthusiasm over a popular cartoon duck, children across the United States receive baby ducks as gifts. Following a series of depressing news reports about dead ducklings—casualties of neglect and cruelty—Jacqueline Meeks, director of quarantine control for Orlando, Florida–based Orange County Animal Services, issues a warning: "Don't touch any baby ducks found in public waste containers or bodies of water. Four Orlando ducks were just tested positive for Chlamydia psittaci, a type of bacteria that can spread to humans."

12:00 p.m.: A few emergency rooms in southern Georgia and northern Florida encounter patients showing flu-like symptoms, severe headaches, and in some cases even heart problems. Doctors suspect it's a severe flu, and send the patients home. The news about ducks hasn't yet spread to doctors, and the patients aren't asked whether they own or have come in contact with ducks.

2:00 p.m.: Two young children are kept for observation after showing signs of meningitis, and heart problems. Doctors are puzzled. Suspecting typhoid fever, they administer the antibiotic ciprofloxacin.

A-Day Minus 1

1:00 p.m. EST: Laura Boggs, a four-year-old girl in Waycross, Georgia, dies of a mystery illness. Her postmortem examination finds psittacosis—sometimes known as parrot fever—a bacterial disease that can spread from birds to humans. It's widely assumed that she received a baby duck for Easter, but this is never confirmed.

3:00 p.m.: News reports about parrot fever spread throughout Florida and Georgia. Parents read about parrot fever online, and pass information around on social media.

5:00 p.m.: Another child hospitalized in Orlando, Esteban Lozano, tests positive for parrot fever. Reports say Esteban is receiving intravenous antibiotics, and is expected to recover fully.

A-Day

2:45 a.m. EST: In a shocking and tragic turn of events, Esteban succumbs to his illness.

4:00 a.m.: The Centers for Disease Control and Prevention, based in Atlanta, Georgia, issues an emergency report about Esteban's treatment. Antibiotics, it turns out, had failed in Esteban's case very early on—specifically, doxycycline and tetracycline hydrochloride. When intravenous doxycycline hyclate proved useless, doctors moved him to quarantine, where he later died. Now bacterial cultures from both Esteban and Laura have been examined, and the bacteria are known to be "superbugs" and show resistance to all available antibiotics. The disease is effectively incurable.

6:30 a.m.: The Japanese creator of the cartoon duck character publicly apologizes for his part in causing this disease outbreak.

7:00 a.m.: As a precaution, many owners of parrots, parakeets, and canaries take their pets to be euthanized. Many of these are veterans with PTSD whose birds are therapeutic service animals.

After watching an instructional viral video about "mercifully" breaking the necks of ducks, nearly one hundred thousand confused, guilt-ridden parents wring the necks of their kids' ducks to prevent the proliferation of parrot fever.

7:15 a.m.: Tens of thousands of children are hospitalized with flu-like symptoms, and three more confirmed cases—two adults and one toddler—of parrot fever are reported in Florida.

A Louisiana veterinarian finds a case of parrot fever in a backyard chicken farm in Baton Rouge. The media rushes to pick up the story without asking follow-up questions about whether this is the drug-resistant form of the pathogen.

8:00 a.m.: Airlines have canceled flights to and from Georgia and Florida. Highways are clogged with residents fleeing their homes. Residents of South Carolina, Tennessee, and Alabama are demanding state borders be closed, but governors warn that this would be illegal.

9:30 a.m.: A Florida woman on vacation in the resort city of Puerto Vallarta, in western Mexico, dies of untreatable parrot fever. US airlines agree to ground flights from the US to Mexico.

The Florida woman is reported to have contracted parrot fever from her husband—now in a Florida hospital—rather than from direct contact with a bird. In a puzzling footnote to the news story, her husband mentions to a reporter that he'd met the family of Esteban Lozano while sightseeing in Georgia several weeks earlier.

1:00 p.m.: More than one-quarter of international flights to and from the US are grounded. An entire container ship is turned away in Japan when a harbormaster learns that a single container is carrying duck meat from a US farm in Indiana. Air- and seaports in more than one hundred countries post emergency

notices: no vessels shipping live birds or poultry can land or dock. When the news reaches the US, it triggers a commodities sell-off.

In response, US poultry farms rush to euthanize their animals. This includes chickens, turkeys, ducks, and geese, along with ostriches and emus being raised for meat and eggs. The number of birds set aside for euthanasia totals about one billion. Hospital waste incinerators rated for the disposal of hazardous biological waste experience a backlog of animal corpses to destroy. Farmers construct pyres, generating smoke clouds that darken the skies across the US.

2:00 p.m.: News reports come in from around the world: at least a dozen individuals in a dozen different countries have parrot fever. Once again, the reports don't mention whether the pathogen is drug-resistant.

2:30 p.m.: The president addresses the White House Press Corps: it's important to be cautious, but as there have only been a handful of drug-resistant cases, there's not yet cause to declare a state of emergency. The president's critics call the move cowardly, and very quickly the debate turns partisan and flies off the rails.

4:00 p.m.: At the closing bell, US stocks have plummeted an average of 220 points.

5:00 p.m.: An investigative reporter working for a popular youth-oriented news site finds that everyone who has contracted drug-resistant parrot fever so far camped out in Okefenokee Swamp Park, near Waycross, Georgia, the previous week.

6:00 p.m.: Video surfaces of a group of sightseers on a boat tour in Okefenokee Swamp, attempting to rescue an injured crane. Despite pleas from the captain to leave it alone, several people can be seen handling the bird. Among them are all the recent victims of drug-resistant parrot fever.

7:00 p.m.: The patient in the last confirmed human case of drug-resistant parrot fever, currently in a quarantine unit at the University of Nebraska Medical Center, is reported to be recovering nicely without antibiotics.

A-Day Plus 1

7:00 a.m. EST: Kentucky Fried Chicken issues a press release. All US locations will be closed indefinitely, but contrary to a rumor, this is due to supply issues, not a food safety problem at any of its locations.

8:00 a.m.: A duck farmer in Waycross, Georgia, confirms that he treated several cases of parrot fever with antibiotics, and that a recent case claimed all his birds. He disposed of them by burial.

9:00 a.m.: After a series of frantic calls, all EU countries reopen their air- and seaports to US vessels, but the President of the European Commission insists there was a real threat, and refutes the US president's characterization of the outbreak as a "false alarm."

◆

What you just read should come as no surprise. Americans are extremely talented at misapprehension, blame, and generally losing their minds. But that doesn't mean drug-resistant bacteria *shouldn't* scare Americans, and indeed the whole world.

As British economist Jim O'Neill noted in a report commissioned in 2014 by British Prime Minister David Cameron, by 2050, superbugs will kill an estimated ten million people per year, and put at risk "a cumulative 100 trillion USD of economic output." In 2017, Sally Davies, chief medical officer for England (the equivalent of the United

States surgeon general), claimed that superbugs could bring about "the end of modern medicine."

This problem didn't exactly sneak up on us. Alexander Fleming, the discoverer of penicillin, tried to sound the alarm about superbugs in his 1945 Nobel Prize acceptance speech. "It is not difficult to make microbes resistant to penicillin in the laboratory by exposing them to concentrations not sufficient to kill them, and the same thing has occasionally happened in the body," he warned the crowd assembled in Stockholm. "The time may come when penicillin can be bought by anyone in the shops. Then there is the danger that the ignorant man may easily underdose himself and by exposing his microbes to non-lethal quantities of the drug make them resistant."

World War II had been one giant coming-out party for penicillin, and Fleming was trying to tell the world to take it easy. No one listened, and it wasn't even a decade before antibiotics were everywhere, including in the hands of "the ignorant man," as Fleming called him (although he presumably meant simply "men"). In 1950, a team of scientists discovered farm chickens that had accidentally ingested antibiotics that had somehow gotten into a pile of manure. They were growing 50 percent faster, laying more eggs, and dying less, which was great for business. A few decades later, it was commonplace to pump farm animals of all sorts full of antibiotics—so commonplace, in fact, that in the United States, farm animals account for 80 percent of all antibiotics being used, period, according to a 2010 article by Ralph Loglisci, a food policy writer working for the Johns Hopkins School of Public Health. (In this article, he urged lawmakers to introduce legislation limiting the overuse and misuse of antibiotics. Seven years later, the US did finally put some controls in place; as of 2018, China was still slowly rolling out similar controls.)

Meanwhile, according to the US Centers for Disease Control, a third of prescriptions for antibiotics in humans are unnecessary—proactive courses of antibiotics given to hypochondriacs like me, and anyone with what they think is a particularly bad cold. A third of these conditions don't come from bacteria, and the prescriptions do nothing except inform a few more bacteria what our secret weapons are, and nudge those bacteria a tiny bit closer to resistance.

So in the roughly seven decades between Fleming's 1945 warning and our collective decision to act in the twenty-first century, we ignored all the warning signs. Right under our noses, the problem went from vague to dire. On the "vague" side, a report in 1985 found that the drug methicillin had lost some of its efficacy in cattle because the microbes had mutated, but that didn't spur a crackdown on agricultural antibiotics. On the "dire" side, there are now mountains of reports about the spread of the dreaded methicillin-resistant Staphylococcus aureus (MRSA), which was responsible for about a third of those alarming "flesh-eating bacteria" cases made famous in the US and UK by fear-mongering news stories in the 1990s. In that way, MRSA is kind of like the Michael Jordan of superbugs, if Mike had just gotten better with age instead of retiring.

Even in the early 1990s we were all told repeatedly that MRSA was thriving in places like convalescent homes. Then in 2003, NBA all-star Grant Hill contracted MRSA and developed "a high-grade fever and convulsions, before fully recovering six months later," according to Hill's page on a MRSA awareness organization website. In 2015, New York Giants tight end Daniel Fells developed a career-ending MRSA infection, and nearly lost his foot. And in an informal and unscientific survey of friends and family I performed, five out of ten respondents were personally acquainted with someone who had acquired a MRSA infection at some point.

But according to physician and drug developer John Rex, who currently works as an expert-in-residence at Wellcome Trust, a medical nonprofit based in the UK, the first major outbreak won't be a global pandemic. Primarily, this is because when there is an outbreak of something—like Zika or Ebola—people "work like crazy to control it, and most people aren't at risk." He then redirected, proposing a hypothetical that gets to the root of my question: "Could we have an outbreak where we don't have a tool?"

Could we indeed?

I'm not the first to game this question out. The Infectious Diseases Society of America, an association of doctors and other medical professionals that lobbies for public health policies aimed at combating infectious disease, explored this hypothetical in a 2004 document called "Bad Bugs, No Drugs," which is essentially a policy white paper with a very grim first page, starting with the heading: "The Next Epidemic Begins . . ." What follows is a brief but compelling piece of speculative fiction about an outbreak of untreatable salmonella found in a bad batch of milk. And you'll recognize the tone, because I mimicked it in the scenario at the start of this chapter:

> *Day 1: A 34-year-old New Hampshire expectant mother visits her doctor's office complaining of severe stomach pain, vomiting, diarrhea, fever, and chills. She is diagnosed with an intestinal infection, given intravenous fluids and a prescription for a fluoroquinolone—an antibiotic—and is sent home.*
>
> *By Day 5, 325 souls have perished. By Day 6, there are 1,730 deaths and 220,000 sickened in the United States alone. But the bug is spreading to other countries, threatening global stability.*

The authors were really just writing a scarier and deadlier version of a real story. In 1985, salmonella-tainted milk sickened about two hundred thousand people in northern Illinois, and caused somewhere between two and twelve deaths. Antibiotics in livestock had clearly made that outbreak stronger. Moreover, a report from two years later showed that those taking antibiotics at the time were at five times the risk of infection of those who weren't. This was most likely because the bacteria in the milk had less competition for resources inside the guts of people who were in the process of killing a bunch of their other gut bacteria with antibiotics. The antibiotics had in essence created vacancies in the victims' gastrointestinal hotels.

Salmonella can also be an efficient, if non-deadly, biological weapon, because it spreads quickly and easily when someone sneaks it into the food supply—something that actually happened in 1984 when members of the Rajneeshee religious commune in Oregon nonfatally poisoned 751 people. Forty-five were hospitalized, but the other 706 mostly recovered without even having to take antibiotics.

This is why the term "bacterial outbreak" typically conjures imagery of small groups or communities eating tainted food, and experiencing

cramps, diarrhea, and vomiting, but not much in the way of mortal danger. Historically, however, bacteria brought about the sort of huge-scale
epidemics we associate with fictional depictions of mutant flu viruses.
Just look, for instance, at *Yersinia pestis*, also known as the Black Plague,
a pesky little bacterium that did a naughty thing back in the Middle
Ages and killed perhaps half of all humans alive at the time. (While it's
well documented that the plague killed approximately half of Europe,
researchers are amassing evidence strongly suggesting that the plague
also swept through Africa and Asia, and was just as deadly there.)

Plague is relatively rare in the modern world, and it's also less deadly
than it used to be. In 1994 a plague outbreak in and around the Indian city
of Surat, which is just north of Mumbai, spread to five other Indian cities.
And to be clear, this was an outbreak of hyper-contagious "pneumonic"
plague, rather than bubonic plague, meaning it had two main forms of
transmission: fleas carried by rats, and person to person via coughing.
Incidentally, the density of rats in India's metropolises is mind-boggling.
Mumbai has about eighty-eight million rats in a city of about eighteen
million people, while New York City—a municipality in which a popular
myth says there are more rats than people—only has about two million
rats, despite having almost half as many people as Mumbai.

Still, as terrifying and widespread as the Surat outbreak was, it only
claimed fifty-six lives. Once upon a time, the plague was the king of all
diseases (it's *the* plague, after all), capable of annihilating half the known
world. Now, when its most contagious form shows up, it fails to kill the
equivalent of a full double-decker bus. I went to Surat to find out why.

First, Surat residents who were there at the time told me they consumed the antibiotic tetracycline like candy during the outbreak; if you
wanted, you could see that as a sign of just how reliant on antibiotics we
are in the event of an outbreak, and how powerless we'll be when there's
a superbug infection looming, but that would probably be overstating
the impact of antibiotics a bit. In preventing mass casualties, antibiotics
aren't the only bastion against bacterial outbreaks, "because we do have
some tools and we do have knowledge of how things get transmitted,"
John Rex told me.

Not to put too fine a point on it, but the Black Death was a global
pandemic in the fourteenth century partly because of two separate

epidemics occurring simultaneously: extreme widespread poverty and extreme widespread ignorance. According to Italian historian Carlo Cipolla's book *Before the Industrial Revolution: European Society and Economy, 1000–1700*, clothes cost a literal fortune so "during epidemics of plague, the town authorities had to struggle to confiscate the clothes of the dead and to burn them: people waited for others to die so as to take over their clothes—which generally had the effect of spreading the epidemic." The global market for cheap textiles may come with a lot of downsides (crappy merchandise and exploitative working conditions, to name just two), but at least you probably won't be tempted to steal clothes from any plague-ridden corpses—a huge win for public health.

Humans have come a long way in terms of overcoming ignorance as well, and that could help in quelling an outbreak before it becomes a global pandemic. Dr. Vikas Desai, a physician and teacher of public health who was working in Surat during the 1994 outbreak, told me that part of what saved India from disaster was public awareness. In the average Indian person's imagination, she explained, "there are stories related to plague, including maybe some English movies talking about plague. So we all were afraid of transmission." When I spoke to people all over India who were around during the plague, they recalled covering their faces with their shirts when they went outside, and since the contagion was in fact airborne, that precaution no doubt saved lives.

Still, Desai looks back at the plague outbreak now as something that could have, and should have, been prevented outright. "That efficiency was not there," she told me. Had Surat been better equipped, she said, the city "would have picked up cases earlier. A week or ten days earlier." Surveillance for deadly pathogens existed back then, but it wasn't very good. Public health officials had received reports of rats dying by the thousands, but it took about six more weeks, and no fewer than ten deaths, before a public alert was issued, which in turn triggered a mass exodus of hundreds of thousands of people from the city.

Mass die-offs of rats are a big clue, and obviously if you detected plague in rats before it could be transmitted to humans, and, preferably, controlled the number of fleas in a city, that would be a brilliant and lifesaving public health strategy—assuming a system for detection and bug control could be implemented in every densely populated urban area in the world. But am I living in fantasyland to think that could be implemented?

I requested a tour of the new plague surveillance unit created by the Surat Municipal Corporation in the wake of the outbreak. Shri J. P. Vagadia, Surat's insecticide officer, showed me his entire operation. Long story short: it was neither high-tech nor expensive, and it wasn't for the fainthearted.

The Municipal Corporation traps a handful of rats in cage traps, and then a small crew gathers the traps in the wee hours of the morning. In the morning, the rats are taken to a lab where a lab technician gives them a visual once-over for "buboes," which are signs of plague, then combs them with a plastic comb and counts the fleas on each rat. When the flea count exceeds a certain threshold, the team dusts known rat holes with malathion powder, a cheap industrial insecticide.

And that's the entire process by which India's eighth largest city spots one form of bacterial outbreak before it spreads. Feel free to replicate it if you believe your community needs a plague surveillance program.

And of course in 1994, the people of Surat also took all that preventative tetracycline I mentioned, which undoubtedly saved lives—but that won't be available when there's a superbug outbreak happening. For decades, it's been very easy to buy antibiotics over the counter in India. In fact, it's way too easy, according to Dr. Philip Mathew, a public health researcher. "Reports are coming in from various regions of the country that the presence of drug resistant bacteria is increasing daily, with conventional antibiotics being made useless. A major contributor to the problem is the ubiquitous availability of antibiotics as a result of unregulated 'over-the-counter' sales," Mathew wrote in 2017. Due to multi–drug resistant strains of plague like those found in Madagascar, the American Society for Microbiology wrote in 2006 that plague is a "reemerging disease."

But relatively cheap, low-tech public health programs aimed at preventing the spread of bacteria could rightly ease our minds about the first superbug outbreak destroying human civilization—if only they could be implemented. Such prevention takes many forms, and can be even more straightforward than rat collection.

For instance: You know those warnings at the bottom of restaurant menus telling you that maybe it's not a great idea to eat undercooked meat? Those might actually get your attention if antibiotics cease being an option for treating food-borne illnesses. Another great public health innovation—one that was implemented by the ancient Egyptians to prevent disease outbreaks—is what's known as "sick leave." Sick leave was once common, but it nearly disappeared from the Western world for thousands of years; it was rediscovered during the labor revolutions of the early twentieth century, but even then it wasn't rolled out comprehensively. When superbugs are a mundane fact of life, we may have to re-rediscover sick leave, because right now, we're not using it. According to a 2017 survey of Canadian health-care workers, 59 percent of pediatric physicians who had been sick in the past two months had come to work anyway. This "presenteeism" is a public health nuisance and can put people at risk for streptococcal infections like strep throat, according to a separate 2016 report.

Another example of a stupidly simple preventative measure for avoiding superbugs: condoms. Untreatable gonorrhea and chlamydia are becoming major public health problems, but condoms are much more effective at preventing the transmission of those diseases than you probably realize. Too bad, then, that according to a 2017 US study, only 18.2 percent of women and 23.9 percent of men reported using a condom during "100 percent" of sexual encounters in the past four weeks, which means a whole lot of unprotected sex is going on.

As for hospital-borne pathogens like MRSA, Rex told me the medical community has its work cut out for it when the drugs stop working. Outbreaks are becoming a persistent, nagging problem. Here's how: Let's say a patient touches a hospital railing with MRSA on it, then scratches her belly. So far, she'll probably be fine. But, an hour later when a surgeon's scalpel pierces her belly where she scratched it, those MRSA bacteria get pushed inside her, and now she has a potentially lethal infection.

"A lot of this infection prevention stuff is a matter of just being super-attentive to every little detail of the process, and it is always easier to be a little sloppy," John Rex, the Wellcome Trust researcher, told me. He then rattled off the thought process of an ideal, public health–conscious surgeon:

"I'm going to be sure that you're not currently colonized with a strain that I can't manage. Before I cut into you, I have the ability to decolonize you. I can use Phisohex [a powerful disinfectant that can kill MRSA, but has been banned in the US since 1972 after it was blamed for the deaths of thirty-nine French infants] and soap, and those sorts of things on the outside of you. I can do things to keep infections from occurring at the time I do your procedure. I can use things that are not drugs externally and just physical. Keep the air clean in the O.R." Rex also told me about how a simple operation like a hip replacement can be made less infection-prone via "really good process," aimed at avoiding "detectable signal" of an untreatable infection.

But surgeons aren't perfect, and superbugs *will* get inside of us—millions of us per year by 2050, according to British economist Jim O'Neill's 2016 report. And according to the CDC's 2012 report on MRSA, the mortality rate from MRSA bacteremia was 27.2 percent. But presently, doctors can still turn to some drugs in the hopes of treating MRSA, like the "antibiotics of last resort," such as vancomycin and daptomycin.

But these drugs aren't going to keep working on conditions like this forever, and reports of resistance to those drugs have begun to materialize—usually as hospital-acquired infections, since these drugs typically show up in hospitals. MRSA infections will give way to more advanced conditions called, perhaps, VRSA (vancomycin-resistant Staphylococcus aureus) and DRSA (daptomycin-resistant Staphylococcus aureus), and many more will die—victims of the worsening global epidemic of septicemia fatalities.

"Septicemia" refers to the body's inflammatory response to any infection, including MRSA, rather than a specific infection. A fatal septicemia incident can lead to a pretty swift death. To find out what people will experience as septicemia becomes more common, I talked to a guy who nearly died from his hospital-acquired staph infection.

On July 15, 2016, Christian Armstrong, a twenty-year-old construction worker in Tulsa, Oklahoma, accidentally deep-fried his arm in a grisly cooking accident. But it wasn't Christian's burned arm that came under attack from staph. It was his thigh, the donor site for a large skin graft, and a large wound in its own right. For comparison, 600 staples were used to close the wound on his arm, and 170 were used on his thigh, he told me.

"I left the hospital at 10 a.m., and by noon I had a 105 degree fever," he said. Somehow, the donor site on his thigh was in even more intense agony than the burn on his arm had ever been in. At one point, he told me, "I dropped to my knees, bawling, because I had never felt that kind of pain before."

"The best way I can describe the pain from [the infection] is if you pretend you're a toothpaste bottle, and you've run out of toothpaste but you forgot to go to the store. You know how everybody rolls that up and tries to squeeze out all they can, to brush your teeth that last time? That's what the pain felt like, it felt like my body was being rolled up and squished and crumpled. The more the infection set in, the more they would roll up that bottle."

After fourteen hours spent "sweating and losing consciousness" in the emergency room waiting room watching the news, he was once again admitted to the burn unit—not the emergency room. Over the course of two days in a painkiller-induced haze, Christian can recall, he told me, drifting in and out of consciousness, vomiting, collapsing on the way to the toilet, eventually being unable to move because of pain, along with his increasing awareness that intense heat was emanating from the wound dressing on his thigh.

At the end of the second day, Christian's medical team, including his surgeon, finally wheeled him into a bathing area to examine and clean his thigh. When at long last, the silver-lined dressing came off, Christian finally saw the monster. He says what he caught a glimpse of was worse than bloody, mangled flesh, or an angry red patch of inflammation. Instead, his wound looked like bright neon-green mold. And when everyone saw it, "All I could remember thinking was, *I told y'all so*," he told me.

As if by magic, the undressing of the wound seemed to trigger the telltale signs of sepsis. Now in the ICU rather than the burn ward, Christian's pigment had become a sickly swirl of green and yellow blotches. His fingers were blue and purple, since, much as in the final stages of hypothermia, Christian's septic body had begun instructing his vital organs to hoard blood, leaving none for his extremities. The hospital chaplain administered his last rites. Then, most dramatically of all, as if acting of its own accord, his IV sprang from his arm "like a Nerf gun."

Christian's veins had constricted—a sign that his kidneys were start-ing to fail. More hospital staff members were called in. He has a fuzzy recollection of a nurse screaming into a phone, "If you don't come get him now he's going to die!"

Acting quickly at long last, the surgery team broke into a run as they wheeled Christian down the hallway toward an operating room, where, somewhat puzzlingly, Christian remained awake. Patients with advanced sepsis generally lose consciousness, but Christian recalls asking everyone in the operating room, "Am I going to die? Am I going to die? Is there a chance I'm going to die?"

It was impossible to begin surgery, since Christian's tiny veins would no longer take an IV—meaning no drugs, no crucial fluids, and no blood transfusions. Christian estimates that seven people were trying to stick him, including one nurse using an ultrasound to detect a large enough vessel. "I'm hearing them say, 'Nothing, nothing.'" This was the moment Christian described with the most terror. "My body was in such pain but I could still feel the little sticks," he told me. He recalled being aware that they were running low on options. "They tried my feet, my legs, my calves, all over my arms, and my neck."

And should you ever find yourself in Christian's position, this is about the point where you slip into a coma and die. A 2012 survey of global data on sepsis published in the *Journal of Global Health* found that the fatality rates for severe sepsis and septic shock are as high as 50 and 80 percent, respectively. In other words, if five people were in the same condition as Christian at that same moment, the rest were goners. Christian is that lucky one-in-five who lived—doctors were able to give him an IV, perform surgery, and safely excise the infected tissue, and yes, they also gave him injectable antibiotics. If your septicemia comes from a superbug, that option won't be available.

When the injectable antibiotic drugs that are currently viable cease being recommended, it's a safe bet that a few doctors will know where to get unapproved injectable antibiotics, like fosfomycin. Injectable fosfomycin is just one patented antibiotic that's not widely available for IV use because, when it was developed, it had nasty side effects, and didn't perform as well as other drugs that had already been approved. According to a 2014 Greek report on problem-child drugs like fosfomycin, "the availability of novel genetic and molecular modification methods provides hope that the toxicity and efficacy drawbacks presented by some of these agents can be surpassed in the future."

Small amounts of other orphaned antibiotics can be found in university labs. Some, meanwhile, are languishing in the drug cabinets of the very hospitals where people are dying of infections, but they just won't be approved for IV use. But when there's demand for a drug that isn't legally available, markets have a way of sorting it out. It's called "drug trafficking," and it's been a booming business for centuries.

And once those sketchy, not-quite-legal antibiotics stop working, too, your best option will be to avoid vectors for infections like, well, the plague.

THE DAY THE LAST FISH IN THE OCEAN DIES

Likely in this century? > *Maybe*

Plausibility Rating > *4/5*

Scary? > *Yes*

Worth changing habits? > *Yes*

(Overheard in the University of California, Irvine, Biology Department. Office hours. Only one side of the conversation—a male student's excited voice—is audible.)

"I like surfing for the challenge, Dr. Peters.

"Standing up on the board? Kid stuff. Waking up early? Any tourist can do it once or twice. Catching a big wave? A lot of beginners get lucky and catch a decent five-meter dip in the curl for thirty seconds, boast about it later. That's great. I envy you. But you're not there yet.

"I wasn't really a surfer until I understood the daily grind. You have to get out there day in and day out, when the weather sucks, and the water's freezing cold—sometimes only twenty degrees Celsius! You may not be feeling it that day, but you do it anyway, even if your suit is old and leaky, and your face mask is hard to see through, or lets in water. If you shy away, just because you're that afraid to touch real seawater, or because the eutrophication is so bad you can see it and you're scared of a little bit of a rash and some diarrhea, you're going to miss the swell of a lifetime—the one that's maybe not the biggest, but it's yours. The wave that loves you.

"So before you even ask, that's why I was out there even though the water was red that day. No, I've never heard of 'karlodinium veneficum.' Who has? Haha.

"I was out there because I was going to be surfing *somewhere*, you know? I always read news about the currents, and it said there was a good chance the waves that week were going to be over fifteen meters, and the warnings about the red blooms sounded like the same warnings you always read: 'Oh, the water is full of phosphorus today!' Okay, dude, I know. 'The water is carcinogenic!' Yeah, that's why my suit's EN 61 331-3 rated. Don't leave home without it, you know? So yeah, I went right in. That's what I do.

"Like, FYI, a long time ago, there used to be these things called sharks in the ocean a few meters long, and they used to literally bite surfers' legs off, and dudes would still be out there in the surf, haha. I actually don't know if that's true, but it's a story surfers tell.

"Yeah, it was red. Like, bloodred out there. But that's not what I remember. I remember sitting on swells like twenty meters high waiting for one to feel right. And when it finally did, I guessed wrong, and when you wipe out on a wave like that, you get that tickling feeling in your heart, like dropping off a building or going over the edge of Niagara Falls, and then the lip catches up to you, and

it's just a nuclear explosion of water pushing you and dragging you in every direction, and you can hear your mask squeak sometimes under the pressure, like it's going to crack. And again, for the record, people used to be able to do this without oxygen tanks, just holding their breath under all that water. Can you imagine?

"So I was still in that swirl, just looking around, waiting for it to die down, and that's when I saw, you know, another piece of plastic, but a weird piece of plastic. Then on second thought I guessed it was just a dead bird, because you see those sometimes. But I reached out instinctively and grabbed it because I knew it was something pretty rare, and there you go. That's what I'm bringing in today, Dr. Peters. I didn't kill it, it was dead when I found it.

"You sound so sure all that red stuff in the water—'dinoflagellates' or whatever—killed it. But how do you know? Maybe that wave killed it, haha.

"'Sargassum fish'? Like I know what that is. It's cool-looking, though! I didn't know there were fish that looked like this.

"No, I didn't break into the university aquarium and steal your sargassum fish specimen just so I could—what?—be on the news? It was out there in the surf, man! You said the other day nothing can live in that water anymore except algae, but guess something was, and there it is.

"You going to put that fish in a museum, or can I keep it? I thought it might make a cool necklace."

When I spoke to Stanford University paleobiologist Jonathan Payne about the death of every fish in the ocean, he suggested I take things a few steps further: a completely lifeless ocean. "There are a lot of interesting environmental consequences of sterilizing the oceans," Payne said. "I don't think we have any evidence ever that prokaryotic life—the bacteria in the oceans—were ever meaningfully driven to low abundance or extinction in the last half a billion years," he said.

I was just asking about a mass extinction of fish. Why was his instinct to push it further and imagine *everything*—not just fish or marine animals, but plants, algae, and bacteria—all kicking the bucket, rendering the waters of our oceans deader than an over-chlorinated YMCA pool? Because, according to Payne, an expert in marine mass-extinction events, the notion of all the fish in the ocean dying is *far from science fiction*. That sort of die-off has happened before, and we're well on our way to seeing it happen again.

To get into Payne's frame of mind, we have to look at two areas of history. First, there's pre-dinosaur times, where we can find a precedent for the kind of huge-scale extinction we're seeing now. Then, we have to look at the past few hundred years, to understand why our fishless future kind of looks like, uh, the present.

We know that, about 250 million years ago, some extremely bad stuff happened, because almost everything on Earth that was alive at that time died *very* quickly, taking only a few million years to die off. (This event is not to be confused with the meteorite impact that happened 65 million years ago—the one that supposedly wiped out the dinosaurs. That was *nothing*. A lot of those dinosaurs never went truly extinct; they're now known as "birds," and quite a few mammals made it, and evolved into humans, in pretty short order.) This earlier event, the Permian–Triassic Extinction, is frequently called "the Great Dying," by paleontologists who like historical events to sound like Morrissey album titles. It made the Earth pretty quiet for a while—the oceans quietest of all.

In 2017, Payne and several colleagues looked into the source of the aforementioned extremely bad stuff that led to the Great Dying. They concluded that temperature-dependent hypoxia—loss of oxygen due to changes in temperature—caused about 70 percent of the losses. An oddly familiar culprit was fingered for this temperature change: "rapid and extreme climate warming." Payne and his pals weren't the first to draw comparisons between the events leading up to the Great Dying and the changes we're seeing today. A previous study had found that the Great Dying had resulted from rising carbon emissions—caused at that time by geothermal events—that occurred over sixty thousand years; in other words, the blink of a geological eye.

"The relevant thing we know from these recent results is that the patterns of warming, and loss of oxygen from the ocean that can account for the extinction at the end of the Permian, are the same features we're starting to see right now," explained Curtis Deutsch, a chemical oceanographer at the University of Washington and one of Jonathan Payne's colleagues on that 2017 study.

Thanks to our species's multipronged and comprehensive approach, humanity's present day "Kill All the Marine Life" project is going extremely well. Here's a quick cheat sheet listing our main strategies:

- We dump several million metric tons of plastic garbage into the oceans every year.
- Bottom trawling, or dragging fishing equipment across the seafloor, is turning "large portions of the deep continental slope into faunal deserts and highly degraded seascapes" according to a 2014 report on the long-term effects of this widespread practice.
- The planet is heating up really fast, and the resulting extinctions are happening in real time. (Although, for the record, at this rate it'll take a few more centuries for this effect to reach the life forms at the deepest depths of the oceans.)
- Ocean acidification—the other major side effect of CO_2 emissions besides global warming—is causing countless die-offs, most famously in corals, the backbone of coral reefs, the most biodiverse ecosystems on Earth.
- Fertilizer and pesticides poison the ocean, and when combined with the above factors, they help create "dead zones," nearly oxygen-free

patches of ocean where almost nothing can live. According to a 2018 paper published in *Science* magazine, dead zones make up four times as much of the oceans as they did in 1950.

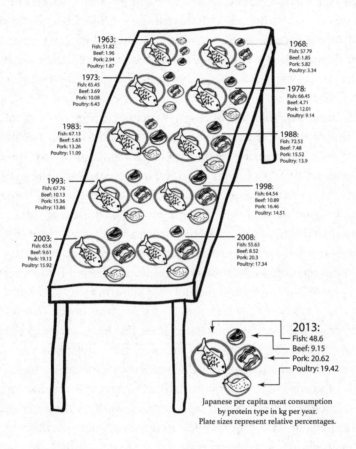

1963:
Fish: 51.82
Beef: 1.96
Pork: 2.94
Poultry: 1.87

1968:
Fish: 57.79
Beef: 1.85
Pork: 5.82
Poultry: 3.34

1973:
Fish: 65.45
Beef: 3.69
Pork: 10.08
Poultry: 6.43

1978:
Fish: 66.45
Beef: 4.71
Pork: 12.01
Poultry: 9.14

1983:
Fish: 67.13
Beef: 5.63
Pork: 13.26
Poultry: 11.09

1988:
Fish: 72.53
Beef: 7.48
Pork: 15.52
Poultry: 13.9

1993:
Fish: 67.76
Beef: 10.13
Pork: 15.36
Poultry: 13.86

1998:
Fish: 64.54
Beef: 10.89
Pork: 16.46
Poultry: 14.51

2003:
Fish: 65.6
Beef: 9.61
Pork: 19.13
Poultry: 15.92

2008:
Fish: 55.63
Beef: 8.52
Pork: 20.3
Poultry: 17.34

2013:
Fish: 48.6
Beef: 9.15
Pork: 20.62
Poultry: 19.42

Japanese per capita meat consumption by protein type in kg per year. Plate sizes represent relative percentages.

- We eat the sea's living creatures—which is the number one cause of their declining numbers. There are rates at which we can supposedly fish sustainably—meaning in such a way that we don't run out—but the fishing industry operates in volumes that meet, or surpass, the peak equilibrium rate. (Right now, we're hauling up 90 percent of fish stocks globally, according to the UN.) In other words, we're killing as many fish as we possibly can as a by-product of our industries, and then on top of that, we're also *eating* as many as we can.

*   *   *

To be clear, the Great Dying wasn't 100 percent caused by warming, either. But whatever the cause, 96 percent of marine species died off back then. All the trilobites and blastoids died, for instance. Every single one! But no one mourns the trilobites and blastoids, and that actually helps illustrate why we fail to grasp that we're annihilating life in the oceans. There's even a sociological term for this phenomenon: it's called a "shifting baseline."

"Shifting baselines" are our ever-worsening expectations about bio-diversity, or the sheer amount of wildlife around us. Your baseline for your hometown probably includes less flora and fauna than someone who grew up there a generation earlier. It also stands to reason that we perceive our own early experiences of ecology as more normal than what we see later in life, and from that we might conclude that things have gone to hell in a handbasket recently, when actually the downward slope has been much longer. To explain with a non-oceanic example, my own childhood memories of summers in California's Inland Empire include street gutters choked with thousands of California toads. Twenty years later, those toads are mostly gone in my neighborhood—likely deci-mated by chytrid fungus infections. Their loss leaves me with the false impression that the natural order in Southern California has vanished in a very *short* time, when actually, the damage humanity has caused here is of much longer duration and much larger in scale than the loss of one species of toad. Much more serious losses of biodiversity have been rolling out for centuries, but I don't miss animals like the Southern California kit fox, which went extinct more than a century ago, because my own *baseline* never included them.

Similarly, according to Deutsch, we won't collectively care about the death of all the fish, because when it finally happens, our baselines will have shifted so much that the lack of fish will seem normal.

So back to the first question I asked those scientists: What will the fishless ocean look like?

Aesthetically, it won't be very different, according to Payne. A point I came across again and again in my research is that crystal-clear blue waters are often relatively lifeless. It's rare to look at the ocean and see strong indications of life—even plant life. "It's not carpeted in green, there aren't cells everywhere photosynthesizing," Payne said. "The color you see is mostly just the physics of light absorption and water." So, in most places, you wouldn't actually see anything at all by looking at the ocean, just as a flight over the Great Plains doesn't tell you anything about the decline of the American buffalo.

Holistic accounting of the numbers of various species in the oceans have only begun recently, so it's hard to pin down exact numbers, but according to a 2015 report by the World Wildlife Fund, the oceans lost 49 percent of all vertebrates in just the time between 1970 and 2012. So rather, we should try to imagine the perspectives of people who saw the oceans when they were teeming with life, and Deutsch suggests reading accounts from the Age of Exploration. If they could time travel, Deutsch said, the Spanish explorers who first visited the New World would look at our ocean today, and say, *Wow, that's dead.*

"They would describe coming in on their ships through the Gulf of the Caribbean and not even being able to get to shore because the backs of the sea turtles were just so thick they couldn't get their boats in," Deutsch said. Indeed, when Columbus arrived, there were so many turtles, they thunked against the hull of his ship all night, keeping his crew awake. Today, spotting a sea turtle is momentous, because the number of sea turtles in the Caribbean is down to about 3 to 7 percent of what it was before Europeans arrived.

I have seen precisely one wild sea turtle in my entire life, and that was because I was searching for one.

I was off the northeast coast of Queensland, Australia, at the time, snorkeling in the Great Barrier Reef in the hopes that it might at least partially correct my own shifting baseline vis-à-vis ocean biodiversity. Even if you've never had the extreme privilege of visiting a coral reef, you've undoubtedly seen one, as magnificently CG-rendered in *Finding Nemo*, or majestically photographed for the BBC's *Blue Planet* TV series, which means you know the broad strokes of what a coral reef is—a place so teeming with life that it's one of the rare places for which the word "teeming" seems appropriate.

But don't picture a Technicolored Disney wonderland. Unless you have the right lens filters and the weather is just so, a coral reef just looks like what it is: a section of ocean with, well, a lot of life—like any part of the ocean you've ever seen, except with more brown and yellow (alive) stuff in there. When you look closely, there are the charismatic, photogenic animals down among the corals, and inside the anemones. Your expedition guide will call out when there's something to see. "Does anyone want to see Nemo?" they'll ask, and show off the clownfish, because clownfish are to the reef what the Eiffel Tower is to Paris. But the clownfish down there look pale and brown, and impossibly tiny, nothing like the bright red cartoon characters brought to you by Disney and Pixar. (I'm not implying that the Great Barrier Reef is anything other than breathtakingly beautiful; just that when you see it, it looks more "normal" than you might have thought.)

Meanwhile closer to the surface, thousands of indifferent, brownish fish dart around in schools that change directions in twitchy unison. In some parts, you can busy your hands at a coral reef by reaching out and gently closing them around a fish, feeling it squirm away, and then immediately grabbing another. The sheer density of "biomass" had a mounting emotional effect on me, particularly when my thoughts inevitably drifted to just how much below me had already died. Recently, 30 percent of the coral died in one year, bringing estimates of the total loss to about 50 percent. When I visited, in 2018, there hadn't been much coral bleaching recently, and lots of fish were around. The way the future is shaping up, though, finding a lot of life there is likely to become rarer and rarer.

After three hours spent touching what's essentially a closed-off memorial to the living ocean we once had, you inevitably leave, and this gives you an opportunity to test your original perception of the ocean against your fresh memories of a marine wonderland. Looking down at the seafloor off the coast of California, I saw the exact opposite of the Great Barrier Reef: *bupkes*. No visible fish at all. Not *all* patches of coastal ocean can be the Great Barrier Reef, but that doesn't mean they should all look like lifeless deserts. To assume they should be this lifeless isn't natural at all; that's just your already-shifted baseline talking.

If the Great Dying is our model, the process of environmental degradation wouldn't just mean dead marine fish, but massive die-offs in most of the plants and animals eaten by fish, meaning algae and kelp, along with many plankton, krill, worms, and everything else we tend to lump into "the bottom of the food chain." That carnage would, in turn, devastate species that rely on small fish, like most whales, dolphins, seals, penguins, and many humans.

It's a good time to pause and point out that some fish species, like the coelacanth, a deep-sea cave-dwelling monster fish, made it through the Great Dying and survived all the way to the present unchanged—so no, the Great Dying didn't kill *all* the fish on Earth, "great" though it may have been. It was just a very large-scale mass extinction. But as long as we're being pedantic, keep in mind that fish can't all be lumped into any single taxonomic category like phylum, class, order, or family. From a certain genetic perspective, a shark has more of an obvious connection to its fellow cunning predator the seahorse (look it up) than to a coelacanth, and a coelacanth shares DNA with a salamander that it doesn't share with a shark. So when I say "fish" I'm casting a very wide net (pun intended) that includes *all marine vertebrates with gills that aren't tetrapods—so no salamanders.* That might not mean much to you, but if any jargon-crazed biologists are reading this, they'll be glad I'm making this distinction.

And with the Great Dying as our model, we're imagining the disappearance of about 96 percent of all life in the ocean—not just fish, but just about everything down there with eyes (and a lot of blind species, too). What happens?

Well, in some ways this will be a *vastly* improved business environment for large corporations. Just as the overabundance of marine life in oceans around the New World was bad for business, today's ships also run into problems.

For one example, let's look at retailers that ship globally, like Walmart, Amazon, and Alibaba, which increasingly face regulations aimed at preserving marine animal habitats. The container ships—which are the size of a small town—that move merchandise currently have to plot out inconvenient routes to circumvent certain animal habitats and to avoid some forms of water pollution caused by their 100,000 horsepower diesel engines. And they must carve a path through the seas without making sounds that are too loud, or that fall below 100 hertz, because animals like whales use those frequencies to communicate. In the heated, acidified ocean that has killed all fish, baleen whales will have certainly starved to death long ago, obviating the need for any such regulations. The die-off will also allow for the easing of regulations against sewage dumping, and—needless to say—negate most of the public's antipathy toward oil spills.

That's not to say that businesses will make more money and that's that. Environmental remediation, a term that means "cleaning up after businesses that pollute," is currently a growing industry, with some market researchers claiming it'll be worth as much as $123.13 billion by the year 2022—an amount that's almost equal to Google's 2017 revenue. Some of those profits will obviously fall away when there's much less demand for oil spills to be cleaned up. But it's not clear how long the mostly dead oceans could be treated as free and open spaces to dump things.

We can safely predict one very large effect of all that dumping: the marine fishing industry will no longer involve "fishing." It may nonetheless survive with the help of fish aquaculture.

Fish farms appear to be a growing business. Just look at "bluefin tuna," the marketing term used to describe several giant silvery fish—all endangered or threatened—that we hoist onto ships and carve up by the thousands every day, to extract the fifteen-dollar morsels of fatty tuna we label on menus with the Japanese word "toro" and serve for the gustatory pleasure of the wealthy inhabitants of coastal cities around the world. Those morsels are about to become even more effective advertisements of wealth when the three or four species of fish they come from go extinct in the wild sometime in the next few decades and prices skyrocket.

To mitigate this inconvenience, projects exist today to grow bluefin tuna in tanks, like the ones at Yonathan Zohar's marine technology lab at the University of Maryland, Baltimore County. One way to use this technology would be to grow fish larvae, including bluefins, along with smaller species like sea bass, into viable juvenile fish that can be taken out in boats and tossed into overfished bluefin habitats to replenish the depleted population. More likely, Zohar's fish larvae could produce tuna for aquaculture systems—closed-off fish farms, essentially.

But if we move away from looking at the ocean as a business, it bears mentioning that *not eating any fish whatsoever* is decidedly not an option for a vast swath of humanity. "You'd be looking at a lot of starvation," Payne, the Stanford paleobiologist, told me. According to a 2016 op-ed in *Nature* magazine by public health researcher Christopher Golden, 845 million people—about a tenth of the global population—face some form of malnutrition in the near future when traditional fishing ceases to be a viable source of food for many of the world's poor.

We're also in for more big changes to the weather, Payne said. Part of the reason the oceans work as a "carbon sink" is that plankton consume carbon as a part of photosynthesis, turning them into organic matter. A reduction in photosynthesis means more carbon will just stay in the atmosphere and speed up warming, particularly in the vast dead zone around the equator—a probable cause of the extreme ocean temperatures of the Great Dying; areas that are now usually around twenty-eight degrees Celsius were forty degrees Celsius or more back then. Apart from heat, Payne said, "one thing you would see very quickly is the effect of storms on coastal systems would change, because with nothing living on the reefs, the reefs will start to fall apart. That will reduce their ability to protect coastal systems from waves during big storms." This means huge changes in the terrestrial climate near these coastal systems, particularly in places like Australia and the Bahamas.

But even with the combined ocean ecosystem more or less converted into a giant marine desert, there's a very good chance we'll always have a man-made oasis or two. A 2017 proposal by a consortium of tourism businesses and Australia's Reef and Rainforest Research Centre would protect six particularly profitable sites along the reef by literally pumping in cold water at a cost of millions of dollars to lessen the effects of climate change. The idea has been regarded as perverse, with critics noting that pumping cold water into a few areas of the Great Barrier Reef would be nothing but a Band-Aid, and that large-scale action is needed. But large-scale action isn't happening, and the mass die-off is proceeding.

Since it appears we lack the willpower to curb our worst impulses when it comes to the oceans, a few Band-Aids may be all we can hope for.

THE DAY THE US COMPLETELY BANS GUNS

Likely in this century? > *Doubtful*

Plausibility Rating > *3/5*

Scary? > *Surprisingly, yes*

Worth changing habits? > *Yes*

From an internal memo at the Western District of Pennsylvania Office of the Department of Justice.

NOTE: During the events of April 19, insurgents used a mobile phone app called Signal to coordinate. The messages were encrypted and impossible to intercept, which explains their silence and ability to coordinate during the ensuing manhunt. Only one conversation was recovered, from the mobile phone (exhibit 26-C) acquired during the apprehension of Suspect A (Eric Matthews). Later, a "disappearing message" option was turned on, and further transcripts were not saved.

DOJ was initially unable to access this phone, but as Suspect A is now cooperating with federal officials, he has provided necessary unlocking information and passwords. The two users in the conversation in addition to Suspect A are believed to be the deceased Bruce Edmunds and the suspect William Graves, and the conversation itself occurred between 9:15 and 10:21 a.m. Please review this evidence at your convenience.

Glossary of terms:

- **10/22:** A popular and durable small-gauge semiautomatic rifle made by Ruger.
- **3-Rs:** A survival rule of thumb stating that one can only survive three hours without shelter from severe weather, three days without water, and three weeks without food.
- **BOB:** Acronym meaning "bug-out bag." A prepackaged and stored rucksack or duffel bag, meant to be ready in case of a catastrophe.
- **EDC:** Everyday Carry. This term is typically used by gun owners to describe weapons and tools (not just firearms) they normally keep on their person.
- **Hellfire:** A type of air-to-surface ballistic missile.
- **Izzy:** Israeli bandage. An emergency bandage originated by Israeli military researchers, used to stem moderate to severe bleeding from traumatic injuries.

- **MilSim or MS:** A shooting hobby in which practitioners simulate contemporary military scenarios as closely as possible with "airsoft" weapons, essentially sophisticated BB guns.
- **MK-II:** Ruger Mark II, a small-caliber handgun, part of the Ruger Standard line. Like the 10/22, widely regarded by survivalists as a reliable and practical defense firearm in emergencies.
- **Molon labe:** Ancient Greek for "come and take them." A slogan among gun activists, spoken as a hypothetical taunt of those who would come to seize their guns.
- **Mozambique (verb):** From the supposed "Mozambique Drill" (probably apocryphal). To quickly deliver two shots to an adversary's torso and one to the head to ensure neutralization.
- **Reaper:** An unmanned aerial vehicle (drone) intended for combat.
- **SRT:** Special Response Team. For the Bureau of Alcohol, Tobacco, Firearms and Explosives (ATF), an SRT is the equivalent of a SWAT team in other agencies.
- **Tannerite:** A legal binary explosive typically used in small quantities for rifle practice.

Begin transcript:

Bruce Edmunds: Eric, you alive?
Bruce Edmunds: Eric?

William Graves: What's wrong with Eric?

Eric Matthews: I'm OK. Bleeding bad.

William Graves: What happened????

Eric Matthews: Got raided.

Eric Matthews: SRTs. It's happening.

Eric Matthews: The war is on.

Bruce Edmunds: They raided me, too.

Bruce Edmunds: I got 'em.

Bruce Edmunds: Molon labe, you ATF pieces of shit.

William Graves: Fuck. Should I get out?

Bruce Edmunds: YES. GO NOW.

Eric Matthews: Yeah don't wait. Grab BOB and leave now.

William Graves: My AR-15 is buried in the footlocker in my yard.

Eric Matthews: Take your EDC and go.

William Graves: Just an MK-II?

Bruce Edmunds: Nothing in your BOB?

William Graves: 10/22.

Eric Matthews: If you have ammo, you're lethal, just go.

Eric Matthews: GO.

William Graves: OK OK. Leaving. Talk later.

Eric Matthews: Godspeed.

Eric Matthews: Remember the 3-Rs.

Bruce Edmunds: Eric, you OK?

Eric Matthews: Izzy in place. Good to go.

Bruce Edmunds: In place where?

Eric Matthews: Eye.

Bruce Edmunds: Jesus.

Eric Matthews: You should see the other guy.

Bruce Edmunds: KIA?

Eric Matthews: Mozambiqued that ATF motherfucker.

Bruce Edmunds: Nice.

Bruce Edmunds: I think I got three.

Eric Matthews: No shit.

Bruce Edmunds: It was like Iraq. I swear it was like a whole company coming after me.

Bruce Edmunds: Think I might have got more than three.

Eric Matthews: You don't know?

Eric Matthews: That's not like you.

Bruce Edmunds: There was a lot going on!

Eric Matthews: That's not the Bruce I know from MilSim.

Bruce Edmunds: Yeah, but this wasn't MilSim.

Bruce Edmunds: No Geneva Conventions.

Eric Matthews: Does that mean what I think it means?

Eric Matthews: Bruce?

[Note: 11 minutes pass.]

Bruce Edmunds: I'm back.

Bruce Edmunds: Thought I heard helicopters.

Eric Matthews: What were you saying about the Geneva Conventions?

Bruce Edmunds: I had some tannerite traps set up in the woods back there, and I think they worked.

Eric Matthews: . . .

Eric Matthews: You maniac!

Bruce Edmunds: I definitely hear something coming.

Eric Matthews: No shit. You just blew up a whole SRT.

Bruce Edmunds: It was stupid of me to hide here.

Bruce Edmunds: Don't hide in a deer stand. They expected this.

Eric Matthews: Get outta there! Take cover.

William Graves: I'm safe. I'm in my foxhole. How's it going?

William Graves: Bruce, you OK?

Bruce Edmunds: OMG WHAT WAS THAT?

William Graves: ????

Bruce Edmunds: Fuck.

Bruce Edmunds: Never seen a hellfire missile from the target POV before.

Bruce Edmunds: Saw some from computer screen POV in Iraq.

William Graves: Reapers? On US soil?

Bruce Edmunds: They know my hiding spots.

William Graves: Run!

Eric Matthews: Get out of there.

Bruce Edmunds: Bill, you might want to go back for that AR you buried. You're gonna need it.

Eric Matthews: Bruce? You OK?

William Graves: Bruce?

[*Note: 4 minutes pass.*]

William Graves: Bruce?

Eric Matthews: I think they got him.

William Graves: I think so, too.

Eric Matthews: They're not getting me.

William Graves: Me neither.

Eric Matthews: Molon labe.

William Graves: Molon labe.

◆

On December 2, 2015, I scrambled out of my office in the late morning and drove from Los Angeles to San Bernardino to report on a mass shooting at a special needs education center called the Inland Regional Center. I'd never been so terrified about a story I was covering; it was happening in an area I knew well, just one town away from where I grew up; my cousin had been attending classes at the Inland Regional Center; rumor had it that this slaughter was terrorism-related; and worst of all, the gun-wielding homicidal maniacs were still at large.

The next few hours shredded my nerves even further as I ran around the cities of San Bernardino and Redlands trying to cover the story with one hand and reassure my loved ones via text that I wasn't in harm's way with the other. Before long, the shocking death toll from the initial massacre was announced: fourteen. And then police finally tracked down and cornered the SUV we'd all been told to watch out for. When they did, the occupants put their body armor back on, grabbed their rifles, and initiated a prolonged military-style gun battle along East San Bernardino Avenue. The cops brought in a tank. One of the shooters fled the SUV, took several bullets in the legs and torso, *and kept shooting*, wounding a cop before he finally died. His widow kept firing from the SUV, hitting another cop, and then died herself. About five hundred bullets had been exchanged, but the ordeal was finally over. It turned out the shooters considered themselves loyal to ISIS, so they were indeed terrorists. Nonetheless, their guns had been purchased legally.

That was one tragic, white-knuckle nightmare of a day, but I also knew San Bernardino was in the midst of an existing gun violence crisis at the time. San Bernardino is one of America's murder capitals—worse than the much more frequently maligned Chicago—and the following year, it would see a 41 percent increase in its total number of homicide deaths, above and beyond the tally from the Inland Regional Center massacre. That year only 44 percent of homicides in San Bernardino were ever solved; nationally, nearly two-thirds of homicide cases are solved.

When you look at America's history of gun violence, the question quickly becomes *How the hell hasn't a sweeping ban already happened?* Americans have endured heartbreaking mass shootings at Columbine, Virginia Tech, Sandy Hook, Aurora, San Bernardino, Charleston, the Pulse nightclub, the Route 91 Harvest Festival, the Tree of Life Synagogue, and the Borderline Bar & Grill. And that's just in the past two decades. But none have convinced America to outlaw guns. To accomplish that, what would it take?

It would take a Constitutional amendment banning guns, of course. But in the present-day United States, passing such an amendment would be political suicide, so America would have to be a drastically different place.

I can't overstate the importance of the role guns play in the lives of many American gun owners—particularly the 3 percent of American adults who own 50 percent of the guns. According to Pew Research, 74 percent of gun owners say owning a gun is "essential to their own sense of freedom," and half of all gun owners say owning a gun is "important to their overall identity." Moreover, in 2018, 58 percent of all Americans—

gun owners or not—said owning a gun makes you safer, according to an NBC/*Wall Street Journal* poll.

According to Jay Wachtel, a criminologist and former agent with the US Bureau of Alcohol, Tobacco, Firearms, and Explosives (ATF), a ban is a total nonstarter for this exact reason. "Your problem isn't just the gun enthusiasts. Your problem isn't just the people who have guns. An equivalent problem, and I think a far more intractable problem, is people who just think you're wrong. You generate a massive public reaction, and policing a reaction like that is extremely dangerous."

Indeed, the implausibility of banning guns right under the noses of present-day gun lovers is a challenge when writing about a gun ban. For starters it would be a little like banning pizza; it's a great way to not be an elected politician anymore. This may not feel true to some liberal readers, but gun-owner America would feel, to many of you who identify as liberals, like an entirely different country.

And once you take an interest in guns, you'll find yourself stepping across the threshold into that country involuntarily. The first time I shot a gun was at a place called the Los Angeles Gun Club, in the bright blue heart of one of the bluest states in America. Nonetheless, the clerk clocked my *Vice* T-shirt. "You work for *Vice*?" he asked. "I thought everyone there was anti-gun." Then, when I bought a bunch of rounds for the range, he told me I should probably stockpile because a California law requiring background checks for ammunition would go into effect at the beginning of 2019.

This cultural divide also made itself obvious when I picked up my own rifle. When I told the clerk I was interested in taking a marksmanship class, he suggested Project Appleseed, one of the cheapest and most popular ways to get a crash course in gun basics and—there's no other way to say this—a bit of low-key militia indoctrination. I took the clerk's suggestion, and during my Appleseed course I learned to hit a target standing, kneeling, and lying down. Much to my surprise, nothing like hunting was mentioned at all. We were *exclusively* taught to fight off theoretical invaders trying to rob us of our freedom. These situations would, judging from our training, involve hastily getting into position, hastily reloading, and hastily shooting a mind-numbing number of rounds. So many rounds that our fingers would become sore from loading our rifle magazines over and over (something I'm told you get used to in time). Our targets were red triangles referred to by my instructor as "Redcoats," which is what American colonists called British soldiers in the Revolutionary War.

More and more Americans now own firearms purchased specifically and expressly for the killing of other people. According to a 2016 study by the US Fish and Wildlife Service, only about 5 percent of Americans are hunters now, which is about a 50 percent decline since 1966. But a 2017 study from a team of researchers at Harvard and three other universities found that as gun laws have become more permissive over the past few decades, the number of concealed carry permits has grown from 2.7 million in 1999 to 14.5 million in 2016.

Simply put, guns in the US are largely weapons for (A) killing whoever dares to enter a gun owner's home, and (B) an eventual war. The enemy is whoever wants to rob Americans of their freedom, but since freedom—as we've seen—is defined as gun ownership, the logic is cyclical: "Stock up on guns so you can protect your guns when the Great Gun War kicks off!"

Let's contrast American attitudes with the attitudes of Australia's gun fans.

After a 1996 mass shooting killed thirty-five people in Port Arthur, Tasmania, sweeping restrictions on gun ownership went into effect in Australia, and the vast majority of personal guns were collected in a government buyback program. According to a 2012 paper published in *American Law and Economics Review*, "The buyback led to a drop in the firearm suicide rates of almost 80%, with no significant effect on non-firearm death rates." The drop in gun homicides is thought to be somewhere between 35 and 50 percent.

Despite the popular notion in the United States that Australia is now gun-free, the place still has some guns. I saw a few, actually, when I stopped by Kingston Brothers Gunsmiths, a gun store in Brisbane that seems to mostly perform repairs these days. But during my visit, there wasn't anyone there to tell me about guns—just a locksmith. (Most of the company's business these days comes from operating as a locksmith's shop under a different name, a switch the company made in 1996, shortly after the Port Arthur massacre.) Kingston Brothers had previously operated out of a much larger building just down the road. That building is now Brisbane's premier gourmet brunch spot, called Gunshop Café.

I sat down in Gunshop Café with a local lawyer named Oswald "Forbes" Norton, who was twenty-six at the time I spoke to him and is also a gun owner. "In terms of gun regulations in the world, ours are quite strict you might say, and I think that's a very good thing," Forbes told me. On the whole, Forbes felt, the Australian system had found a nice balance "between the rights and freedoms of responsible gun owners and the protection and safety of the community." Forbes walked me through the local legalities: if you're a farmer in Queensland, as Forbes and his family members are, you're eligible for a category "C" firearm license, meaning you have plausible reason to own a weapon, including a semi-automatic rifle, for killing feral animals. Most gun owners, who don't fit that category, have to settle for air rifles or, if they wade through a lot of government red tape, perhaps a bolt-action hunting rifle. "You get your firearms license by completing a firearms safety course," Forbes told me. A license, he said, is good for "a period of five or ten years, depending on the state."

Australia's outcome is the most useful model for this chapter, because insisting on a "zero guns" outcome rapidly makes hypothetical gun-free America impossible. So let's talk about how a ban would work, and then we'll discuss what will happen to America's biggest gun fans.

The fact that the foundational legal document of the country guarantees "the right to keep and bear arms" is a big deal, making it a lot harder for the US to change its gun laws than Australia. So how do you delete an amendment from the US Constitution? You add another amendment. This awkward, deletion-by-addition practice exists because we can't just draw over sections of the Constitution with a big Sharpie, according to Article V of, well, the Constitution itself. Such an amendment would have to be passed via a two-thirds majority in both houses of Congress, or two-thirds of the state legislatures.

This amendment could simply repeal the Second Amendment, and then leave it up to the states to actually ban guns. Almost nothing would change at first in that case, because forty-two out of fifty US state constitutions have the right to bear arms built in as a kind of gun rights backstop. A federal ban, then, would require the passage of a set of Australia-like regulations on gun ownership. This is a good time to remind you once again that *this would have to be very popular politically or it would never happen.*

But if it were to happen, then pop that champagne, American liberals, because guns are now illegal—kind of. Let's take a step back, though. When something gets banned, that doesn't always mean it's *criminalized.* For instance, here in Los Angeles, most uses of gas-powered leaf blowers are technically illegal, but a gardener comes by my apartment once a week with his, filling my home with noise and fumes for twenty minutes. (At such times, I turn into a crabby old man, and have to fight my instinct to run outside with a copy of the local municipal code in my hand.)

Most people I know have no clue there's a ban on the books, and since this equipment is legal to sell, just not use, my local Home Depot sells all sorts of gas-powered leaf blowers. But that would presumably all change if the LAPD started doling out harsh penalties for people who used leaf blowers. What I'm saying is, a law against guns wouldn't feel like much of a ban until the day a gun owner who didn't want to relinquish his gun had it forcibly snatched away.

None of this gun-snatching would happen in the moments just after the amendment won enough votes to achieve passage. Congress might, in theory, let the states devise their own methods and time lines for the seizure of everyone's guns rather than passing federal legislation detailing how to regulate firearms. But let's slow *way* down with all that gun-snatching. According to Wachtel, the former ATF agent, no matter what the public consensus is on guns, there'd be a different consensus among law enforcement types. "Not just every ATF agent, [but] every cop would know what the exact endgame was here," he said. "They've worked the streets. They know how people react. They've had to deal with relatively minor gun violence. They know what the consequences would be."

To that end, the early phase of the ban would probably be more along the lines of the one in Australia: big, heavily publicized, and, most important, *voluntary* firearm surrender events. Different US jurisdictions already provide different incentives for people who surrender guns, but the major one is cash. Americans have all seen this spectacle from time to time on local TV news: obedient citizens show up in droves and hand over their guns. The police in charge of the event disable the guns, mark them with zip ties, and arrange them in piles—rifles here, pistols here, shotguns over there. The former owners then collect cash or sign up for their tax credit. The cops get photographed with the piles. The chief gives a speech about a safer community. Snacks are served.

But banning *all* guns is lunacy. Few consumer items are ever banned so comprehensively that all legal uses go away altogether. Merck & Co. distributes cocaine hydrochloride, and the Danish drug manufacturer Lundbeck synthesizes legal methamphetamine; they call it "Desoxyn," and market it as a drug to treat both ADHD and obesity. Even during Prohibition, when you couldn't go to a bar for whiskey or buy alcohol at a liquor store, you could get a prescription for it. Doctors had prescription pads specifically for alcohol, with blanks where the doctor was supposed to indicate "kind of liquor," "quantity," "directions." (For that last one, a patient probably hoped the doctor would write "to be taken orally," because who wants to even contemplate the alternative?)

So an Australian-style permitting program would be established. Some Americans would still be able to get their hands on bolt-action rifles, and, if they're farmers, even semi-automatic rifles, as long as they had small magazines.

But that brings us to the government's big challenge: What about the people who *don't* willingly exchange their firearms? How do you get all those damn guns?

Currently, the ATF snatches guns all the time, including from felons, people convicted of certain misdemeanors, and the mentally incapacitated. According to retired ATF agent Thomas Faison, such people don't make much noise about guns being part of their God-given freedoms. If they do, "it doesn't last more than thirty seconds."

Presumably, once people have been given a few months, or perhaps a year, to voluntarily hand over their guns, that's when guns become an issue for whichever members of law enforcement haven't quit on principle. Wachtel remains convinced that at this point he and many other agents would bolt. "Say I'm ATF agent Jay when that moment happens, and my supervisor Jack comes in, and he's like, 'Hey guys, here's the deal: they went ahead and they passed a ban, so we're going to work on it.'

Everybody would be out the door. That wasn't our understanding when we signed up for ATF."

If he's correct, the ATF would have to rehire. It would certainly need to be beefed up. The ATF was originally created as a law enforcement agency called the Bureau of Prohibition, and was specifically for busting alcohol bootleggers. (The most famous Bureau of Prohibition agent was, of course, Eliot Ness, Kevin Costner's character in the movie *The Untouchables*—and Robert Stack's in the original TV series it was based on—a story inspired by the real team of high-octane crime fighters who worked as undercover agents and used advanced—at the time—surveillance techniques. That movie gives a good sense of what the vast operation to sniff out and seize guns would look like.)

ATF agents aren't all a bunch of Eliot Nesses, but they are still in the business of rooting out contraband, sometimes with tools the Untouchables didn't have at their disposal. "People post all kinds of pictures of themselves on Facebook if they've got guns," Faison told me. Or, he said, intelligence gathering can be low-tech in the extreme. "You could be arresting [a guy] for another crime, and you come in and there's guns there." And of course there are some illegal gun owners who give themselves away over the phone: according to Faison, "You make a recording, someone's on the phone saying that he's selling guns, and he's a convicted felon. That's enough for a warrant."

But despite having a centralized database for guns—the ATF's National Tracing Center in Martinsburg, West Virginia—a lot would have to change if the information in that database were ever going to be used to track down people who own guns illegally, because *it's not currently designed to trace owners*. It's designed to trace guns themselves, particularly if they're used in crimes. "I can't type in 'Mike Pearl' and find out how many guns he has from a federal database. No such database exists," Faison said. And the idea of such a federal database is a frequent sticking point in the gun rights debate. Gun fans often voice concerns that despite the 1986 Firearm Owners' Protection Act, which is supposed to prevent the ATF from having such a database, the agency is nonetheless still tracking their guns somehow. I'm not saying it's not, but if it is, that's still a government secret.

But it's reasonable to assume that the legal language of the ban would repeal the Firearm Owners' Protection Act, and that the National Tracing Center would become more useful. At the moment, it's famously a shambles. For the ATF to trace a gun that's been used in, say, an assassination, an official has to dive into a confusing jumble of records stored on various media. Such a trace reportedly works only 70 percent of the time. A large-scale gun ban would presumably also fund a revamp of the database, and perhaps, to the horror of the pro-gun crowd, make finding any gun owner in America as simple as a Google search.

It bears mentioning at this point that there's a real risk that the ATF's enforcement of these extreme restrictions would be uneven, and, well, racist. Anecdotally, it seems that as things now stand in the US, white violators of gun laws can expect leniency, and black offenders bear the brunt of enforcement. Michelle Alexander writes in *The New Jim Crow: Mass Incarceration in the Age of Colorblindness* that "virtually identical behavior is susceptible to a wide variety of interpretations and responses and the media imagery and political discourse has been so thoroughly racialized." Alexander quotes an anonymous US attorney who claims that an underling had requested that a white drug offender's gun charge be dismissed because "it's not like he was a gun-toting drug dealer"—and this was in regards to a defendant who stood accused of being just that: a gun-toting drug dealer.

Racist or not, the process of taking someone's guns is not usually hard, Faison told me. "You clear the couch. Sit them down on the couch—make sure there's no guns under the couch," and then you search. "Sometimes," he said, "they tell you where the gun is because they want you out of the house." Other times, he said it's necessary to use gun-sniffing dogs, but only, he said, "if it's in the bushes, or the grass or something like that," because "if it's a smelly house that can mess up the dogs a bit."

Back to those serious gun fans: assuming the folks who can't imagine life without them won't willingly give up their stockpiles, and won't respond to phone calls or strongly worded letters, the ATF has to start coming into people's homes with warrants. This is where the rubber meets the road, and the ban ceases to be a polite request.

"It would be disastrous," according to J. J. MacNab, who writes about the American militia movement for *Forbes* and spends much of her time researching other forms of extremism. "They see themselves as saviors of the United States."

American gun fans use the Second Amendment as a legal basis for defending their preoccupation, but don't make the mistake of thinking that without the Second Amendment, gun owners would collectively shrug and mutter, *I guess we no longer have a right to bear arms.* In 2012, Newt Gingrich, a right-wing political commentator and former speaker of the house, told a crowd at a meeting of the NRA, "The right to bear arms comes from our creator, not our government." He added that he wanted to tell everyone in the world—not just Americans—"You have that right. It comes from God." By Gingrich's logic, Second Amendment or not, banning guns would be a civil rights violation.

A ban would, of course, seriously hamper the ability of hard-liners to get their hands on more guns, assuming they didn't already have a healthy supply. But that might not matter much, as MacNab pointed out. "Now you have 3D printers and can make them yourself."

In 2018, after a legal battle that stretched out for years, Cody Wilson, owner of a company called Defense Distributed, won the right to "publish" guns as documents online that can be fed into 3D printers and allow any user to effectively manufacture their own gun at home. Wilson is another person who doesn't believe the Second Amendment is important in the grand scheme of things. He explained the ideological underpinnings of his work to *Vice Motherboard* in 2013, saying, "If we make a Second Amendment argument, it's all the way. It's to the limit. But I don't like to make it about the Second Amendment or gun control at all. It's more radical for us. There are people from all over the world downloading our files, and we say, 'Good.' We say, 'You should have access to this.'"

"It would be like a civil war," Wachtel told me.

When right-wing patriot groups in the US—which are always and without fail well armed—lash out against the federal government, it can sometimes be kind of funny (depending on your sense of humor). For instance, when Ryan and Ammon Bundy, along with other members of a loose collection of opponents to the federal Bureau of Land Management, occupied a visitor center in Oregon's Malheur National Wildlife Refuge, the internet called them names like "Y'all Qaeda,"

"Vanilla ISIS," and "Yee Hawdists." But then the whole thing ended in violence when one of the occupiers, LaVoy Finicum, was shot dead by Oregon state troopers.

These kinds of standoffs are over small slights, such as taxes and land use. If you're an American die-hard gun fan, "the feds are coming to snatch our guns" is a literal war cry. John Ross's 1996 *Unintended Consequences*, a hugely popular pro-gun novel, depicts a righteous war against the corrupt, gun-snatching ATF that culminates in the repeal of all restrictions on gun ownership when the president realizes the violence gun restrictions have inadvertently caused. Domestic terrorist Timothy McVeigh, who killed 168 people in the 1995 Oklahoma City bombing, suggested that *Unintended Consequences* had as much personal significance to him as the Bible.

So make no mistake: blood would be shed. It's only a question of how much. No one can positively say how many patriot groups are out there, and that's partly because, as we've established, they hate being tracked. The Southern Poverty Law Center, for what it's worth, placed the number of groups at 689 in 2017. If we assume each group has one hundred members (which is probably generous in some cases), then perhaps—back-of-the-envelope math disclaimer and all that—there are close to 69,000 bellicose gun nuts out there adjusting their gun sights.

But the pro-gun side in this conflict may well be even bigger, because it's not just militia members who might actually engage in literal battle with the federal government. Nearly every gun owner I talked to was horrified that I was writing about this, and told me they'd go down fighting if it ever happened. I received one particularly interesting note from a fifty-eight-year-old retired police officer from Arkansas. He wrote, "Everything in your scenario would likely lead to another Civil War." He concluded his email with "MOLON LABE," in all caps.

Maybe some of these folks are bluffing, but I see no reason to doubt that when the ban goes into effect, there'll be a large, violent uprising. And while that might sound like a joke to a lot of people—especially the same people who cracked the "Y'all Qaeda" jokes during the Malheur occupation—it seems as if the anti-government side would be able to do some damage. Many on that side, like Oath Keepers founder Stewart Rhodes, are ex-military, and have seen combat overseas. But when members of these groups show up at events, they look like a very mixed bag. Superficially, some appear out of shape, elderly, and far from battle-ready. Others are younger and leaner. They all wear body armor and camouflage and carry combat-style rifles with lots of extra ammunition.

And they can draw blood. Just look at the example of Eric Frein, a Pennsylvania man who, in his late twenties, came to see himself as a revolutionary who wanted to restore American freedoms, according to a manifesto he wrote in 2013. Frein had no military experience, but had tried his hand at combat as a MilSim hobbyist, becoming widely regarded as a strong competitor. Then on the night of September 12, 2014, he shot two Pennsylvania state troopers—killing one—with a sniper rifle and fled into the woods. What followed was a frighteningly intense forty-eight-day manhunt involving one thousand law enforcement officers. Frein repeatedly popped up, drew the attention of his pursuers, and then escaped, breaking into cabins for shelter and managing to keep himself alive and healthy the entire time, before he was finally arrested.

I don't think for a second that an armed uprising would work over the long term—that is, thwart a gun confiscation effort. If the government found it necessary to treat anti-government fighters as military targets, well, it's best to keep in mind that the US military is mind-bogglingly enormous. That said, another Civil War sounds like an incredibly dismal prospect. It's hard to imagine that the public would have a very strong stomach for it. It's worth noting that a 2013 Gallup survey found that the majority of Americans opposed drone strikes on American terror suspects in other countries. That being the case, it stands to reason that they'd be even more opposed to such strikes in, say, Michigan.

It seems incontestable that US law enforcement and the US military have the firepower necessary to successfully carry out a ban on guns. So the critical question becomes: *Would Americans still have the resolve to ban guns if they found out what it would really take?*

THE DAY NUCLEAR BOMBS KILL US ALL

Likely in this century? > *Could happen tomorrow, or never*

Plausibility Rating > *2/5*

Scary? > *This is the definition of scary*

Worth changing habits? > *Absolutely*

When the nukes started flying, the International Space Station was the best place to watch the show. As the deranged leaders of all the nuclear powers drew inexorably closer to war in those closing days of the standoff, the constant dread had become exhausting. When it finally happened, you could almost say it was a relief. Almost.

After the radio operators back on Earth were evacuated and all communications went silent, the crew just waited and watched, at first not sure if what they were seeing was forest fires or detonations. Then they caught a nuke going off as they drifted over Astana, Kazakhstan. For a split second, a blinding, white-hot spark turned everything white for hundreds of kilometers in every direction, and then it darkened, giving way to a little umbrella that opened fast, expanded, and then faded. Underneath the umbrella, a tiny little ring of dust rose up, and then grew and spread outward, starting as a perfect circle and then turning into a puffy cloud made of tiny apartments, cars, houses, roads, trains, offices, libraries, bicycles, parks, restaurants, people, museums, dogs, and cats. From the ISS, it was all just a little dot, and then a long chain of smoke—longer and thinner than the forest fires they saw from time to time—drifting lazily into the stratosphere.

The crew was simultaneously transfixed and horrified. Prokopyev, whose grandfather was from Astana, was inconsolable. But he wasn't alone for long. For the next forty-eight hours as the ISS drifted, unaffected by the bloodshed quietly unfolding beneath them, similar little clouds appeared over Seoul; Pyongyang; Tokyo; Honolulu; Los Angeles; Houston (perhaps worst of all for the American astronauts Gilford and Sanchez); Washington, DC; London; and on; and on; and on. And then the astronauts all felt nothing. The commander from NASA, who happened to be Canadian, thought his country might have escaped the carnage, but that notion didn't last.

At first, no one ate or drank. The Russians quietly inventoried their suicide pills. The Americans, lacking suicide pills, quietly contemplated opening the airlock. They all stared down in disbelief, knowing their families were down there, dead, or in agony. But after three days of this they resumed their routines: Meals on schedule; exercise. And occasionally, attempts to contact Houston and

Korolyov, all in vain. They lost count of the detonations at some point after three hundred.

And the view was never the same. The fires must have all just burned out of control, because the smoke clouds just hung there, and then linked up with one another, and swallowed most of the planet from sight. The clouds only allowed the crew occasional peeks at the darkened surface, and even then, usually just a glimpse of blackish blue ocean. After a week, most of the clouds dissipated, but they were replaced by a grayish brown haze that hung there, like a film that enveloped everything. At the horizon, where the crew could sometimes see the ghostly auroras of the ionosphere, now they could just see a line of smog where the sun illuminated a new layer of ash. Then the smoke thinned and they could make out enough detail to orient themselves again, but the view of Earth from space wasn't beautiful anymore.

On day forty, they finally crunched the numbers. The six of them could last about eighty-eight more days, give or take, depending on how toxic the recycled liquids got. Then slowly, it became a grim series of lifeboat thought experiments—"How long would it take you to eat me if I died?" "How much water could you recover from my corpse if you drained me?" It passed the time.

No one rationed. Why bother? On day eighty-eight of the countdown, they were all still alive and in good spirits given the circumstances. They had a final breakfast. And just as they said they would, the two most senior cosmonauts and the commanding officer took their suicide pills, and gave the extra pill to the American commander. They all said their good-byes, closed the curtains of their sleeping quarters, and expired, alone.

The Soyuz escape vehicle could only carry the remaining three, and it was time for them to try their luck on Earth. Prokopyev, Gilford, and Sanchez all piled in, and decided if possible that they'd aim for Korolyov. Just before the war, Roscosmos had prepped another launch vehicle. It seemed as if maybe their best shot at long-term survival might be to try to launch that, and come back to the ISS with supplies. They figured they could survive up here for about a year if they played their cards right. And didn't go mad.

Unfortunately, with no one down there to retrieve them from the water, they couldn't very well aim for the ocean. And with no line of sight to the Earth's surface, and no way to receive information from Mission Control about a safe landing point, it would all be guesswork. After a reasonably smooth reentry, the chute opened like clockwork and they all finally saw the land—nothing but yellow and brown— rush toward them.

Then they collided with it, bouncing at first like a tin can on a fencepost. Then they spun. The g-force compressed their guts and drained the blood from their brains until they blacked out, which was lucky, because next, they tumbled down a steep embankment, bounced again, and skidded to a stop in what used to be a forest.

Eight hours later, Prokopyev opened his eyes. It was pitch black. Gilford and Sanchez were limp.

Prokopyev took off his landing suit, and replaced it with his spacewalk suit, which came with two full oxygen tanks. He opened the hatch, and emerged in the early evening. He was home in Russia again, but it didn't feel welcoming. He knew from the dirt-colored evening sky and the black ash that hung in the air that this was an alien planet.

He opened his helmet, held his breath for a moment, and then sniffed. It burned his throat and lungs, and stung his eyes. He snapped his helmet back into place, knowing he might never open it again. Maybe he could breathe that air later when he found a bandana and some water. Maybe he didn't feel like it.

On the horizon Prokopyev could make out a town. Could anyone possibly be there? He laughed a little to himself at the thought of it. In truth, he hoped no one was alive in that town. That wouldn't be living.

◆

On Saturday, January 13, 2018, I got to thinking about what it would be like if we all were wiped out by nuclear bombs. I engage in these scary thoughts all the time actually, mostly in the shower, where I don't have audiobooks or podcasts to keep me from hearing my own thoughts. But in this case I thought about it because my parents were among the thousands of tourists who found themselves at the epicenter of the now-infamous Hawaii incoming missile alert false alarm.

My one big takeaway from False Alarm Day was that if the proverbial bomb (Why is "bomb" in this context so much scarier than "missile," which is probably more accurate?) was headed our way, most of us would have absolutely no idea what to do, even though we really could make ourselves safer.

As it was happening, the news informed me that Hawaii's Emergency Management Agency (HI-EMA) had activated their Commercial Mobile Alert System, blasting every mobile phone in Hawaii with a push notification saying "BALLISTIC MISSILE THREAT INBOUND TO HAWAII. SEEK IMMEDIATE SHELTER. THIS IS NOT A DRILL." In addition, the warning software sent similar messages out over TV and radio. The reaction online was half-scared and half-incredulous, which is to say, quintessentially American. It was immediately clear that either the United States president had finally lobbed one too many middle school taunts at North Korea's leader, or someone at the Mobile Alert System had accidentally pushed the wrong button.

We know now it was the latter. The FCC's investigation into the matter revealed that a comedy of errors had occurred. In a surprise "no-notice" drill, an HI-EMA officer had pretended to be a panicked military official notifying lower-level employees that a missile was on its way. The order of operations was to say "Exercise, exercise, exercise," followed by the warning, followed by, "This is not a drill."

When one staff member heard the "This is not a drill" part but not the "Exercise, exercise, exercise" part, he initiated a real alert, setting in motion a series of events that gave the world a thirty-eight-minute heart attack. The heart attack only subsided when a second push notification went out, announcing that the whole thing had been just a big, silly goof-up. So for more than a half hour, the people of Hawaii had it rubbed in their faces that seventy-six years after Pearl Harbor, they still had no clue what to do in the event of a surprise military attack.

Here's what it's like the day you're told the nukes are coming for you:

My parents only saw the alerts on TV—they didn't get the text. My dad's instinct was to find the nearest fallout shelter, but no guidance on where to find a fallout shelter was forthcoming. Meanwhile, my mom's instinct was to call my sister and me. She says it wasn't until that moment that she thought seriously about death. *I'm calling my kids to tell them that I love them, and I might not ever see them again*, she remembers thinking.

The alert was everyone's sole source of information about what was going on, and what to do about it: "seek immediate shelter." Everyone in the hotel would have loved to know *where the safest place to take shelter* was. (I reached out to this well-known hotel multiple times to ask if they've since formulated some kind of plan. They never got back to me.) So my parents skipped the elevator, and ran down twenty-four flights of stairs, not because they had a better shot at survival at ground level, but because their friend Lisa was down there, and "I didn't want her to die alone," my mom said. On the way, my mom recalls an elderly man struggling to make it down all those stairs. He eventually gave up and ducked into a hallway to sit down.

Once they met Lisa in the lobby, which my parents said was full of panicky people literally trembling with fear—and in some cases looking like they were showing signs of shock—they lingered in the stairwell. Finally, an all clear came in over the loudspeaker, but it was in Japanese—never in English—meaning everyone who wasn't Japanese had to get the all clear from someone who was, or just kind of notice that all the Japanese people looked at ease.

My mom shared some thoughts about why there was no plan: "They probably just thought we'd all be toast." Indeed, it's normal to talk as if *any* nuke going off *anywhere* will trigger the apocalypse, but when you get right down to it, that's a silly notion. It's also a dangerous one.

According to Brooke Buddemeier, a health physicist at Lawrence Livermore National Laboratory specializing in risk assessment and emergency response planning, members of several US communities have more or less just shrugged and said "I'm walking toward the light" when asked what they'd do if a nuke went off nearby. In 2008, Buddemeier collaborated with the US Department of Homeland Security to test American communities for nuclear attack readiness. "Really no community had any kind of coordinated response plan," he said at a 2011 conference, adding that, "there was a general lack of understanding of even what the response needs were."

The aftermath of the Hawaii false alarm showed that this was clearly still the case, so Buddemeier made the rounds of the news media, providing basic instructions to the clueless. Here are some highlights: Yes, *of course* you should take shelter. Specifically, you should get as far as you can toward the center of the building to avoid shock, incoming shrapnel, and broken glass. In fact, you should head to a structurally secure basement—or, hey, bomb shelter!—if you happen to have access to one.

We're talking about shielding ourselves from *an explosion* after all. We all love to laugh at old safety videos from the 1950s about hiding under a school desk from a nuclear explosion, because, LOL, of course a nuclear bomb would just vaporize all the children, and hiding under a desk can't save them. But that's needlessly cynical. If a nuke detonated above a major city, yes, the city could expect near-total destruction, but the destructive power of a nuke is not infinite. US researchers from the Atomic Bomb Casualty Commission discovered when they researched the effects of the Hiroshima detonation that victims who were low to the ground (ducking) or shielded from debris (covering) had a better chance of survival.

Decades of media representations of nukes have made them seem less like the extremely large bombs they are and more like the abrupt opening of a portal to hell, as exemplified by the slow-motion nuclear destruction of Los Angeles in *Terminator 2: Judgment Day*. That scene gets the destructive power just about right, but it makes the blast out to be some kind of epic Pandora's box, unleashing a roaring hellstorm of fire with a lot of low-pitched, cinematic whooshing and rumbling. This notion really seems to have embedded itself deep in our imaginations.

It doesn't help that the explosion sounds we hear in documentaries showing test footage of atomic bombs are almost always dubbed in by a Hollywood sound designer. Since almost no one bothered to capture audio recordings of 1950s and 1960s nuclear tests, filmmakers had no choice, and they've done their best to create ominous, bass-heavy soundscapes. But in 2017, *Atom Central*, a blog about the nuclear testing era, published some obscure film of an atomic bomb test from 1953 that happened to have been recorded with an optical soundtrack on the film strip—a real rarity, apparently. Someone recorded the sound of a nuke, and it turns out that sound is "bang." Yes, at the epicenter, it surely must be hell—whooshing and all—but if you're inside there, you'll likely be way too dead to notice. For everyone else, a nuke sounds like a very, very, very big dynamite blast, not Satan's speaker test pattern.

While the Hawaii missile warning was still active, my dad felt pretty sure he and my mom were about to be blown to smithereens, because they were near major targets. And to be fair, he had good reason to think this: Waikiki sits right on Mamala Bay, as do Pearl Harbor and Hickam Field, the location of the US Pacific Air Forces Headquarters—putting my parents' hotel in a target-rich environment, the destruction of which could soften the US counterattack. It makes sense that the second Pearl Harbor attack would have the same purpose as the first.

So given my parents' close proximity to a major air force stronghold, ducking and covering in the center of their building offered them very little peace of mind, even if they did it right. The blast, they reasoned, was just too damn close. But here's the funny thing about that: if a North Korean nuke had targeted Pearl Harbor that day, my parents would probably have been just fine in Waikiki, even if Kim had precision-targeted Hickam Field and scored a bull's-eye.

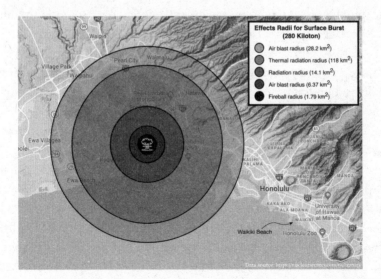

Let's deal exclusively with Kim Jong-Un's arsenal for a moment. The consensus of arms control bloggers and North Korea watchers is that Kim's most powerful nuclear test to date was the 280-kiloton, multi-stage thermonuclear warhead detonated on September 3, 2017. So if all North Korea's first strike prerequisites had been met—the missile was in shipshape, the launch went well, the warhead safely exited and reentered Earth's atmosphere, the guidance system worked as advertised, *and* the extremely flawed US missile defense system didn't intercept the missile on the way down—there's a really good chance my parents would *still have survived.*

To explain why, I'm going to call on my favorite website in the world: NUKEMAP, which is the creation of nuclear historian Alex Wellerstein of the Stevens Institute of Technology. NUKEMAP is a handy, and scientifically robust, tool for gaming out what I perceive to be the world's most edifying thought experiment: *What would happen if someone dropped a nuke, say, right over there?*

After tuning NUKEMAP to a 280-kiloton blast centered on Hickam Field, one sees a number of concentric circles spotlighting various kinds of death and destruction. The center circle is the deadliest, and from there, each circle becomes less and less deadly. The initial fireball would mostly just vaporize the air force base. The shock wave, and a devastating ring of lethal radiation, would annihilate Pearl Harbor, along with most of the military outposts on the island, and would lay waste to Honolulu's airport. But those effects wouldn't be felt by surrounding communities. A less lethal—but still devastating—blast of air would have knocked over houses as far away as Honolulu's Iroquois Point, likely killing numerous civilians, but that probably would have been the worst of it. Downtown Honolulu might not even have lost a building.

As for my folks in Waikiki, which is on the far side of downtown, "safe and sound" is probably too strong a descriptor; they would certainly have needed to worry about radioactive fallout, an electromagnetic pulse (EMP), and the spread of fires (more on these later), and maybe the tidal effects of the explosion and being in a city brought to its knees by massive destruction. But the point is that they were well beyond the perimeter of the initial explosion, assuming the missile was headed for the likeliest point of impact. Granted, NUKEMAP is a blunt instrument, and real nukes don't create perfect concentric circles of destruction—but the outer limit of the largest circle was 6.4 kilometers from their hotel. That's a pretty good sign, and that's what I told them.

Here's what I didn't say: *Congratulations! You're out of range! Let's not worry at all!* If the missile warning had been real, a major war would have most likely kicked off—maybe even the dreaded "World War III." And while losing a big chunk of Hawaii would be terrifying and tragic, the outbreak of a new and terrifying type of world war is what had the whole planet on edge that day, including my folks and me. A strike like that sets Earth on a path—we tend to assume—toward nuclear annihilation.

It would be nice if, in this chapter, I could just say "myth busted" to the whole idea of a nuclear apocalypse. I ran this by Seth Baum, executive director of the Global Catastrophic Risk Institute, a think tank concerned with matters of existential risk. I picked a random number of nukes that seemed too high to ever be exchanged—three hundred—and asked him if it was implausible. No such luck. In the event of a nuclear war, Baum told me, we should "definitely not dismiss the possibility of using large numbers of nuclear weapons."

Other attempts to find solace have failed as well. In 2017, when *FiveThirtyEight*, a paragon of data-based news analysis, asked a panel of experts in physics, diplomacy, and arms control what the chances were of a nuclear war, those who were comfortable answering proffered the following guesses: 20 to 25 percent, 5 percent, 5 percent, 1 percent, and less than 1 percent. But the exact framing of *FiveThirtyEight*'s question is important: they simply asked the group about the chances of any one nuke being dropped on any civilian target—so it theoretically wouldn't count if the US used a tactical nuke to blow up a North Korean missile launch facility. Specifying that civilians are being targeted suggests that things have really gone off the rails.

But even that doesn't necessarily mean we all die.

It would probably take multiple hundreds of nukes to kill us all, but we have way more than enough to do the job. And according to Baum, "the number of nuclear weapons that would be used in a nuclear war is simply not known." Some formal plans exist, and those must include exact numbers of missiles and bombs, but of course, Baum explained, only "the political and military leaders who would be involved in the launch decisions" are privy to those numbers. Further, he said, "They may only make the decision if and when the war has begun."

The International Campaign to Abolish Nuclear Weapons places the total number of nuclear warheads on Earth at 14,485. But even if nukes start flying willy-nilly, there are a lot of off-ramps on the road to the apocalypse. So let's talk about what would have to happen for world leaders to bypass them all.

Realistically, when we talk about Armageddon unleashed we're not talking about mushroom clouds over every single human encampment on the planet (but more on that in a minute). Instead, we're positing enough bombs that the secondary effects of their detonation kill everyone.

Arguably the most important, and damaging, secondary effect caused by a nuke is the ensuing firestorm. "Firestorm" is a term we use all the time as a metaphor, and it's come to mean anything from *the public outcry that follows a geopolitical misstep* to *people getting mad because someone tweeted something stupid.* Not to get all Merriam-Webster on you, but "firestorm" is a term for a very big fire. The firestorms after the bombs the US dropped on Hiroshima and Nagasaki were huge, damaging buildings up to four kilometers from the blasts. These types of fires are so big, in fact, that they count as weather—hence the "storm" part. The firestorm in Hiroshima caused "pyrocumulonimbus" clouds, and generated more than an hour of rain. So bear in mind, if every nuke is a meal, each one comes with a firestorm as dessert.

Stepping away from firestorms for a second, we're also, of course, assuming that a nuke dropped on civilians would trigger something called "massive retaliation"—also known as "nuking the enemy back to the Stone Age." But this isn't the only possible response a nuclear power could unleash after getting nuked. The US has the world's largest military at its disposal, and could effectively retaliate against a nuclear attack with conventional weapons. An overwhelming nuclear response to an attack has been criticized for decades. In 2009, arms control researcher Michael Krepon wrote that the doctrine of massive retaliation is a relic of a 1950s mindset—one formed during "the peak period of U.S. reliance on nuclear weapons."

The legendary nuclear tactician Bernard Brodie once wrote that he doubted the US would have the "brashness" to carry out a campaign of massive retaliation. In a paper he prepared for the RAND Corporation, "Strategy in the Missile Age," he wrote the following: "We are basing the argument for massive retaliation not on the military needs of concentration and on the evils of dispersion, but on an optimistic forecast of Russian or Chinese behavior in face of our threats. Military knowledge helps us only marginally in making such a forecast. It helps somewhat more in telling us the price we shall pay if we are wrong."

But let's go ahead and assume the US retaliates with nukes. Let's stay with the United States vs. North Korea model for this as we game it out:

We've established that we can't really be sure how many nukes this would be, but we do know some details. An early form of an on-the-fly nuclear retaliation plan was given the codename "Dropkick," and some version of it is still in existence today. There is probably a precise plan for a North Korean nuclear attack written down among the documents inside the US president's emergency satchel, also known as the nuclear "football." (Get it? Because the plan is codenamed "Dropkick"?) But the details of Dropkick are top secret, so we have to guess what they entail.

Let's say the plan calls for the deployment of five cruise missiles armed with W80 variable yield warheads (the US military has a ton of these lying around), and let's say they're all tuned to their maximum yield: 150 kilotons. *And* let's say those all hit various urban and military targets in North Korea in an attempt to regain the upper hand, cut off Kim's launch capability, and deter future launches—a ferocious, enormously lethal gesture, but not a full-on attempt to annihilate the North Korean population. North Korea might surrender! But we're not soft-pedaling here, so let's assume they don't.

The severely wounded North Korean military digs deep into its remaining nuclear arsenal, and responds with, let's say, five more intercontinental ballistic missiles aimed at the US mainland, and an additional five shorter-range missiles aimed at US targets in Japan, the Philippines, and Guam. And just for good measure, they also lob one at Seoul, and one at South Korea's second largest city, Busan, even though they're also shelling the hell out of them while this is going on, and using both chemical and biological weapons. Assume none of those get intercepted, and they all hit their targets perfectly. That's pretty awful, so the US retaliates *again*, with twenty nukes, in the hopes of annihilating the Kim regime and delivering a deathblow to North Korea's ability to wage war (and by the way, the odds aren't good that nukes alone would succeed at either goal).

But we haven't mentioned China or Russia yet! Let's suppose that those two countries, who at times seem closest to being North Korea's friends, choose to see America's response as an attack against their regional sovereignty. (It's not inevitable that they'd see it this way, but let's say they do.) They each throw caution to the wind and launch twenty nukes at the US. And let's further assume that the US—which has clearly lost its mind, too—impulsively responds with twenty more retaliatory nukes: ten for China, and ten for Russia, knowing full well that they have huge arsenals. We're now at a horrendous grand total of ninety-seven nuclear detonations. And, let's not forget, we're assuming each one sets off a Hiroshima-style firestorm and kills something in the neighborhood of one hundred thousand people.

We're well on our way to the apocalypse.

But let's go micro for a moment, rather than macro. We already know how horrific this day would be from the standpoint of someone at ground zero, because these horrors have already played out, and people have written about them. For instance, here's the account of Akiko Takakura, who was twenty years old when she survived the bombing of Hiroshima. The Atomic Archive records what it felt like to exist in that hell-on-earth:

> *What I felt at that moment was that Hiroshima was entirely covered with only three colors. I remember red, black and brown, but, but, nothing else. Many people on the street were killed almost instantly. The fingertips of those dead bodies caught fire and the fire gradually spread over their entire bodies from their fingers. A light gray liquid dripped down their hands, scorching their fingers.*

Yoshitaka Kawamoto, who was thirteen, described the last moments before a fellow victim died:

> *I found one of my classmates lying alive. I held him up in my arms. It is hard to tell, his skull was cracked open, his flesh was dangling out from his head. He had only one eye left, and it was looking right at me. First,*

he was mumbling something but I couldn't understand him. He started to bite off his fingernail. I took his finger out from his mouth. And then, I held his hand, then he started to reach for his notebook in his chest pocket, so I asked him, I said, "You want me to take this along to hand it over to your mother?" He nodded.

Multiply this suffering by about five million, and you can begin to picture the madness of global nuclear war. The parties involved will undoubtedly be able to watch this orgy of carnage play out in real time on TV news and social media. At the high point of the speculative scenario I've conjured, ten million people have died—the approximate population of Tokyo. And it's conceivable that the nuclear powers, having already brought about the most destructive event since the Chicxulub asteroid collided with Earth sixty-six million years ago, might want to call a truce and start talking things over.

But at that point would it be too late to save humanity? After all, radiation alone would finish off our species, right?

Fortunately—or unfortunately?—no. According to Dr. David Denkenberger of the Global Catastrophic Risk Institute, "Some people think that if there were a full-scale nuclear war, the radioactivity would kill everyone. That's actually not true." Radiation would be devastating near the sites of detonations during a nuclear war, and it would leak into nearby soil and waterways. But nuclear warheads are actually an inefficient delivery system for the kind of continent-sized toxic clouds of radiation people imagine when they picture a nuclear apocalypse.

Look at it this way: according to an International Atomic Energy Agency (IAEA) report on the Chernobyl disaster, "compared with other nuclear events: The Chernobyl explosion put four hundred times more radioactive material into the Earth's atmosphere than the atomic bomb dropped on Hiroshima." Unlike Hiroshima, which gave off one big blast of radiation, Chernobyl leaked nuclear material into the atmosphere for nine days, and still only caused an estimated thirty-one deaths at the time. Of course, that was followed by the slower rollout of Chernobyl-related cancer deaths, a scourge that still hasn't finished taking its toll. That number is expected to eventually reach about four thousand—horrible of course, but also something of a relief when you consider that the radiation from Chernobyl spread from Ukraine to Belarus to Austria to Finland to Sweden to perhaps other countries. And to be clear, thousands have died—and continue to die—from cancer as a result of the Hiroshima and Nagasaki bombings, but nearly all those individuals were very close to the points of detonation.

There's a reason bombs don't spread radiation all over the place, according to Denkenberger. "Most of the radioactivity is released in the lower atmosphere, the troposphere, and within a few days it would be rained out." In other words, unlike particles of soot that would rise up into the stratosphere, blocking out the sun, there's every reason to assume most of the radiation hanging in the air during and after a nuclear war would be brought down to the earth quickly as radioactive rain and snow—which wouldn't be great, but at least it would contain the problem.

But in my scenario there are still one hundred firestorms to worry about, so we'll have to worry about "nuclear winter," at least a "small" one. Climate models posit that the smoke and ash from those firestorms would enter the upper atmosphere and block out sunlight.

What's a "small" nuclear winter? On the optimistic side, it could just be a decrease of 1.25 degrees Celsius that lasts for about two to three years. (For reference, global warming has increased global temperatures by about 0.8 degrees Celsius since 1880, so the impact to the global climate would be catastrophic—far worse than the climate impacts we've seen as a result of global warming.) A 2014 paper published in the journal *Earth's Future* paints a dire picture of the winter resulting from one of these hundred-warhead "regional" nuclear wars (which, to be clear, mostly involve relatively small nukes). That paper predicts decades of cooling, ozone loss, and, paradoxically, increased solar radiation, which will worsen the impact on agriculture.

But once again, this type of nuclear winter doesn't mean humanity will just collectively give up on living and climb en masse into the grave. Instead, we'll suffer enormously to keep on living, spending a great deal of energy trying to feed ourselves just like we've always done. According to Denkenberger, who coauthored *Feeding Everyone No Matter What*, a book about situations like this, it takes 1.4 billion metric tons of dry food to feed the world each year. Denkenberger notes that our species doesn't store enough food to last even one year if there's an agricultural shortfall caused by nuclear winter. More gloomily, owing to the lack of sun for photosynthesis and the reality of reduced rainfall, agriculture pretty much collapses. A 2013 study by a group called International Physicians for the Prevention of Nuclear War asserts that two billion people would die in the ensuing famine. To give you a rough idea of what that number means, it's as if everyone in India, Japan, France, the US, Germany, and the United Kingdom all starved to death, but everyone else made it.

Denkenberger claims in *Feeding Everyone No Matter What* that humanity can avoid such widespread starvation, assuming we carry out a global campaign of social engineering that utilizes the mountains of decaying organic matter we'd suddenly have all over the world— converting them into nutritional slurries and using them as compost for growing edible fungi. This involves the production of mass quantities of mushrooms, and uses known processes to convert things like dead trees and bacteria into calories.

For a while we'd have to all stay indoors and keep our windows blacked out, to shield us from the increased UV radiation (at least until we all installed UV-protective windows). We'd have to wear protective clothes whenever we went out, or SPF 100 sunscreen every day of the week. If we took the risk of peering through our windows, we'd see darkened skies over a landscape of dying—and then later dead—forests and meadows. In the meantime, we'd derive most of our calories from leaf paste, mushrooms, and something akin to blue-green algae tablets. Eventually the UV rays would become less intense. An awful prospect, but better than our species ceasing to exist altogether.

So a hundred-warhead nuclear war likely isn't sufficiently lethal to end all life, but we're not stopping there. There are 14,485 nuclear war-heads on the planet in total, so the situation I've just described doesn't even exhaust 1 percent of the global nuclear arsenal. And clearly if *every nuke in every arsenal went off,* that would kill us all—no question about it. Right?

I may sound completely insane here, but I'm not so sure.

Sam Biddle, writing at the time for *Gizmodo*, gamed out this hypo-thetical back in 2012. It would take sixteen thousand copies of the biggest nukes in history to destroy every bit of Earth's landmass. That is to say, it would take 16,000 "Tsar Bombas"—Tsar Bomba is a one-off monster bomb created by the Soviet Union with a mind-boggling fifty-megaton payload. When it was tested in 1961, it sprouted a mushroom cloud fifty-six kilometers high. But the thing about that is that there aren't any more Tsar Bombas. And that 16,000 figure is a bit of a strain as well. There once existed 31,255 warheads, but as we've established, there are now thought to be only 14,485.

Further, many of those warheads are tiny. The American B61 warhead, for instance, can yield a blast of 0.3 kilotons. That means it would take 166,666 of them to equal one Tsar Bomba, assuming they were tuned to their lowest yield. What's more, approximately 5,000 of the warheads that exist are retired and slated for dismantlement, meaning there are about 9,600 warheads considered to be in active military use.

It's worth noting, however, that as I write this, the current US president has promised an expanded nuclear arsenal "far, far in excess of anybody else." What's more, the 2010 nuclear arms reduction treaty New START, which was intended to prevent the expansion of the US and Russian arsenals, is set to expire in 2021. So depending on a whole lot of political "ifs," the number of warheads could, sadly, have skyrocketed by the time you're reading this.

According to the Global Catastrophic Risk Institute's Seth Baum, "The main reason that a large number of nuclear weapons could be used [once a nuclear war started] is to attack the other side's military forces, including their nuclear weapons." This is called "counterforce" targeting, as opposed to "countervalue" targeting. The Hiroshima and Nagasaki attacks were primarily countervalue, meaning they mainly demoralized the enemy by destroying valuable things—cities, and the people living in them—instead of weakening that enemy's ability to use force.

For an example of a counterforce strategy, let's look at Pakistan. To protect its nuclear stockpile from India's conventionally superior military, Pakistan has beefed up its supply of tiny nuclear warheads, which are intended to be used on Indian forces attempting to destroy Pakistan's military installations. In a bizarre twist, India has claimed that, if necessary, it would call Pakistan's bluff, invade, and essentially force Pakistan to nuke itself.

So when you read about an ever-increasing raw number of nuclear warheads globally, keep in mind that many of these are part of a counterforce strategy. As much as I would still hate to be a soldier on the receiving end of a counterforce nuclear attack, it strikes me as slightly less terrifying than having my civilian community nuked while I'm taking my dog for a walk. Baum called counterforce "perhaps the main driver of nuclear arms races," as it sparks "one side to build more weapons, so the other side builds more to target them, and so on."

One can only wonder what it means for the prospect of nuclear annihilation if it's understood that many or even most warheads won't blow up "countervalue" targets. One aspect to consider is that once warheads are detonated at their "counterforce" targets, they'll start reducing the total number of warheads available to be detonated—one of the few upsides to a nuclear strike. But here's the point of this detour: Let's assume half of the world's active nukes, or about 4,800, are intended for counterforce targets. Many of those counterforce targets would be damaged early in a conflict, and that could seriously reduce the total number of nukes available for countervalue targeting. What's more, counterforce targets in the US include the locations of the country's nuclear stockpile—places like Malmstrom Air Force Base in Montana, Minot Air Force Base in North Dakota, and F. E. Warren Air Force Base in Wyoming. Those are rural areas, meaning the body counts from those strikes probably wouldn't approach those from countervalue strikes—though lush forests in those areas would provide a lot of fuel for firestorms.

But thanks to the global trend toward urbanization we can safely assume that if the nuclear powers unleashed all the nuclear fury at their disposal, they *could* wipe out just about everyone. As of 2016, about 54 percent of humanity lived in cities, and that number is climbing. We're at the point of vague guesswork now, but it seems that the 4,800 active warheads intended for countervalue targeting could kill *most* of the people in *most* of the populated parts of the world. And the ensuing fires, radiation, and what we can only imagine would be some sort of nuclear super-winter would surely take care of everyone else.

But it's arguably a bit bizarre to assume that the people who control whether these weapons get used would or could systematically try to blow up the entire world. Don't get me wrong, there are a lot of maniacs with nuclear weapons at their disposal (you can do your own calculations there), but when armies go to war they don't just open fire with every gun they've got until there's no ammo left. It's puzzling that we talk about nuclear war in this way all the time, but it's not actually inconceivable from a strategy point of view.

"Complicating the matter is a fundamental tension between the morality of launching more and more nuclear weapons once a war has already begun and the morality of threatening to launch the weapons to deter the war from starting in the first place," Baum explained. "In the best-case scenario, everyone is bluffing and everyone believes the bluffs." This is a mystifying best-case scenario, but it's also smart in a stupid sort of way. We all *theoretically* want to avoid total nuclear annihilation, so we can deter it as long as someone with nukes who is bluffing assumes everyone else with nukes is not bluffing.

See, one critical difference between nuclear and conventional war strategies is the concept of "mutual assured destruction," a term coined by Donald Brennan, one of the Cold War schemers who worked at the Hudson Institute, a conservative military think tank. The basic mutual assured destruction thought experiment goes a bit like this: let's say there's a conflict between two nuclear adversaries with large arsenals, and both parties know that the other party has taken a posture in which, if nuked, they've promised massive retaliation—specifically, nukes of their own. In that case the nuclear powers are forced into a clever stalemate, and peace is achieved through deterrence.

Unless, of course, someone flips their lid and goes through with that fateful first launch. . . .

According to Herman Kahn, Brennan's onetime boss at Hudson, this whole mutual assured destruction idea is madness. In his book *On Thermonuclear War*, Kahn wonders why the hell—even if you're attacked with nuclear missiles, and even if you've promised to end the world by counterattacking until Kingdom Come—anyone would actually go through with ending the world? To illustrate this absurdity, he offers up what would later become the central plot mechanism in the film *Dr. Strangelove*: the Doomsday Machine.

A Doomsday Machine is something that doesn't really exist, but if it did, it would be an automated nuclear launch system that detects attacks, and, via some irreversible triggering mechanism, launches tons and tons of nuclear missiles at the presumptive enemy. Once such a device is in place, whichever nuclear power controls it can make good on the promise of mutual assured destruction even if the humans who normally authorize reprisals get cold feet about killing everyone in the world. In other words, *any nuclear attack against me will kill everyone in the whole world, so no one had better ever launch a nuke, or else!*

In thinking about such a device, I'm reminded of the "Doomsday Clock," a symbolic clock that supposedly measures humanity's proximity to total destruction, as calculated by the bulletin of the Atomic Scientists' Science and Security Board. As of this writing, the clock reads two minutes until midnight, "as dangerous as it has been since World War II," says the security board. The previous "time" had been 11:57:30, so the clock seems to move in thirty-second increments. But it's tough to imagine what ninety seconds to midnight might be: a missile launch? After all, a launch wouldn't constitute doomsday. 11:59 might be a warhead detonating. 11:59:30 might be a retaliatory strike. Further retaliation might be doomsday, according to the clock, even if it wouldn't feel like doomsday to the majority of the planet.

In the end, it's probably good that thinking about all this—even the localized cases of nuclear incineration—makes us vow to never let it happen if we possibly can. Assuming that this is a common human reaction and that the world *isn't* filled with Hollywood villains who just want to burn it down and start over, we've got a chance of pulling through.

THE DAY A BABY IS BORN ON THE MOON

Likely in this century? > *No*

Plausibility Rating > *4/5*

Scary? > *If the cost of medical coverage doesn't go down, it's terrifying*

Worth changing habits? > *Absolutely*

"You may leave the delivery room at any time," Nurse Collins kept telling her. "It's your right."

But of course Alexandria couldn't just leave the delivery room. That made no sense. Sure, she could get up easily enough. That was the nice thing about the moon's one-sixth gravity. Tasks like getting out of a hospital bed while in labor were a whole lot easier than on Earth. But where would she go?

It wouldn't help to give birth in the hallway of Moon Base Hispaniola's med-ical center, since Collins would still be there, ready with all her forms. She and Francisco could dart out the automatic doors of the lobby and then what? Birth the baby themselves in the middle of Concourse A? Were they supposed to hop on the tram back to their residential block, fill the bathtub, and perform a water birth? That would have been a terrible idea for a million reasons, only one of which is that it would use up a week's worth of water.

Nope, she was stranded, and completely at the mercy of whatever these consent forms said. And they were long. According to the fine print in the Hispaniola Residential Compact, giving birth was considered elective medical care—never mind that once you're pregnant, there's nothing elective about giving birth. An abortion, unsurprisingly, would have been covered.

Alexandria had medical insurance, of course, through 3M, her employer. And 3M had never specifically mentioned anything about not covering the costs associated with delivery. Her brother Marco, a lawyer, had assured her that giving birth was technically legal on the moon. But the Hispaniola Council had convened, issued a non-binding resolution stating their preference that she abort.

Alexandria felt the baby move. It was almost time. It took all her strength not to instinctively push.

"They're making an example of us," Francisco said. "They can't make giving birth illegal, but they've found a loophole. They're making it too expensive."

"That's not true," said Marco. "This was codified years ago, before 3M ever put together these insurance policies with Aetna. They should have told you

more clearly. You can get them to cover this."

"What am I supposed to do? The baby's coming!" Alexandria exclaimed.

The whole situation made no sense. How can you prevent the creation of another mouth to feed on the moon? They'd promised before she left that the Residential Compact enshrined all the same rights as the US Constitution. But it looked like they had built in a big penalty for giving birth: crippling medical debt.

"Just give me the forms! I'll sign. I'll sign."

Nurse Collins handed Alexandria the clipboard, and she signed at the bottom. "And initial here," Collins said. She did. "And here," she added. Collins nodded to a gynecologist standing just outside the door, and she entered. A hospital administrator followed close behind with a very small camera.

"It's for the media. They'll want to see this back on Earth," the administrator said.

"Well well well," said the doctor. "Looks like we're making history today! Who's excited?"

Alexandria smiled without opening her mouth.

For most of my life, I naïvely imagined that if the moon were ever colonized, the colonizers would be benevolent pioneers, there on a mission of research and discovery subsidized by some union of nations working together for the betterment of humanity. But government organizations like the China National Space Administration and NASA are increasingly handing over the reins of space exploration to private companies like China's OneSpace, along with American companies like Elon Musk's SpaceX and Robert Bigelow's Bigelow Aerospace, both of which are formalizing plans for the first permanent bases on the moon in the first half of this century.

So when a moon base finally exists, residents will almost certainly be outside any country's social safety net but, in theory, still subject to laws. There aren't very many people who've thought about how this will work in detail, but American space lawyer Jim Dunstan has been pondering it for quite a while. His 1991 paper "From Flag Burnings to Bearing Arms to States Rights: Will the Bill of Rights Survive a Trip to the Moon?" gets right to the heart of it, at least from an American perspective. For example, will Americans on the moon really have the right to bear arms? Possibly, the paper says, though maybe strutting around with holstered guns can be forbidden, as long as there are enough firearms locked away somewhere in case a militia ever needs to be formed—to fight off an invading army of moon people, I suppose.

So what about reproductive rights on the moon? America's lower courts in the *Roe v. Wade* case argued that the Ninth Amendment ensures a right to privacy that shields women from reproductive interference. Dunstan agreed, stating in his paper, "The Ninth Amendment has been read to contain as a fundamental right the right to procreation and freedom of one's own sexual expression." He notes that as time goes on, "the essence of the Bill of Rights may be challenged," but asks "if one is not free in one's own bedroom, what is left of freedom?"

Dunstan is now the general counsel for the free market–centric think tank TechFreedom. When I spoke to him, he offered a more complete legal picture of life on a moon base, and what that might mean for the first moon mom.

When someone's giving birth on the moon, he said, "That would mean that there would have to be a law that allowed a woman to become pregnant on the moon." He foresees that before moon residents are allowed to reproduce, either a law or a contract would be put in place that says anyone who can get pregnant would have to take contraceptives, or that if they became pregnant, they'd agree to abort the fetus.

In his book *Building Habitats on the Moon: Engineering Approaches to Lunar Settlements*, Haym Benaroya, an aerospace engineer and professor at Rutgers University, writes, "Pregnancies in a low-gravity environment will be very challenging to women and their fetuses." The long-term effects of being in low gravity have been monitored in Valeri Polyakov, a Russian cosmonaut and medical doctor who was once in space for a record-smashing fourteen months straight, and they don't sound fun for someone already experiencing the joys of childbirth. They include the upward shifting of blood and other body fluids, which can result in a blood pressure decrease, which can in turn cause blood loss and cell death in the brain, conditions that can lead to headaches, fatigue, and sleep disorders.

Other effects of time spent in space are all but certain to hamper the development of a healthy fetus. According to Benaroya, bones become less dense and astronauts experience the slowing of biological growth. "Microgravity," he writes, "results in an annual one to two percent bone loss in astronauts in weight-bearing areas such as the pelvic bones, lunar vertebrae and femoral neck. As bones in the lower body atrophy due to lack of use, upper body skeletal regions grow in density."

Benaroya also notes that muscles atrophy in low gravity. More to the point, among the residents of the moon who'll inevitably have to spend a significant amount of any given day performing intense muscle workouts akin to the brutal exercise regimens the residents of the International Space Station are subjected to, there'll be a very well-grounded fear that a child born and developed in one-sixth gravity will never develop enough muscle mass to atrophy in the first place. That includes the child's leg muscles, which, it goes without saying, won't stand much of a chance if the child ever has to fly to Earth, though they might recover with physical therapy. But we can't breathe without muscles (the thoracic diaphragm), nor would our hearts be able to beat (another word for the heart is "cardiac muscle"), and we don't yet have any way of knowing whether these will properly develop on the moon.

That concern may sound overly cautious. Why, after all, would heart and diaphragm muscle development be hampered by low gravity if astronauts' hearts and lungs seem to work just fine? But the research we have about animals born and raised in space and returned to Earth gives reason for concern. According to a 1994 paper in the journal *Advances in Space Research*, animals that begin their lives in space are sometimes okay, and sometimes very much not. Pregnant guppies that spent five days on board the Russian spacecraft *Cosmos 1514* "tolerated space flight conditions well," but the paper's author, Dorothy B. Spangenberg, noted that the "female allowed to bear young gave birth to twenty-five normal young and two anomalous and underdeveloped embryos." Only six of thirty-five Japanese quail eggs hatched without help after incubation on the Mir space station, but those that did appeared perfectly normal. In fruit flies, researchers noted "a decreased [egg production] rate in females and a shortening of male life."

Spangenberg also experimented with jellyfish polyps, allowing them to reproduce in space. The results were a mixed bag. Unfortunately for the space polyps, some experienced defects stemming from, ahem, "abnormal development of the graviceptors, the neuromuscular system, or a defect in the integration between these systems in apparently microgravity-sensitive animals." In case you're not following the science lingo there, they responded badly to gravity, and had a hard time moving around.

Does this mean a mother can't have a healthy baby in space? No. It just means we have reason to worry she *might* not.

Before her baby's due date, there's a good chance a mother will have been subjected to long periods of gravity simulation in the hope that the baby will have a better chance of an ideal outcome. "Research has been performed on the utility of artificial hypergravity in countering these effects," Benaroya wrote in *Building Habitats on the Moon*. But he thinks that as time goes on, we might give up the ghost in this area and just allow ourselves to transform into creatures of the moon instead of Earthlings. As he put it, "Our lives will be lived on the Moon and beyond. We may need to become prepared to see subsequent generations with less development in their lower bodies."

All that's to say it'll probably be a long time before the lunar community feels comfortable adding a newborn. As troubling as it would obviously be, making all moon residents—male and female—sign a contract barring them from reproducing might be a smart move for at least the first few decades, while the lunar base is a hardscrabble outpost.

It stands to reason that the first moon birth won't happen until the "base" is more of a complete moon community with creature comforts and medical facilities. Even then, live human births would still be a risk that the corporate overlords who'd likely run the outpost wouldn't be thrilled about. Dunstan told me he can envision animal experiments happening well before that. Still, people love to reproduce, so it's easy to imagine, as I did at the start of this chapter, someone getting pregnant when it's possible but still in the "less than ideal" phase.

By then, the questions will be much more bureaucratic. Would the moon baby be able to list "Moon" as their nationality on forms? In Dunstan's opinion, no. It's more likely that whatever country the mother is a citizen of would "make a claim that the child is a citizen of that nation, because otherwise, you begin to lose your population, and your ability to tax them." That checks out if you ask me.

If the baby's parents are American, there wouldn't be any problem issuing a Social Security number, since that process is already electronic. The time on the birth certificate would be, well, lunar time. But will the moon have clocks and calendars that reflect lunar time intervals? Well, moon "days" are about twenty-seven Earth days long, or arguably—thanks to the complexities of the lunar-terrestrial-solar relationship—about twenty-nine Earth days long, depending how you do your space math. But given our human tendency to carve life into twenty-four-hour cycles, citizens of the moon will almost certainly simplify things by just syncing up with the time on Earth. Most likely, according to Dunstan, "whoever fires up the first computer on the moon base and has to sync it to a clock back on Earth—that would be your time zone."

But here's a brain buster: assuming the baby's parents would have a lunar mailing address, they might be tempted to put the baby's lunar address on the birth certificate. That probably wouldn't be a great idea if the baby might ever move to Earth; it might create proof-of-citizenship issues. Assuming the parents maintain an additional address in their home country, it might be wiser to use that.

But back to the lunar delivery room. What about those astronomical medical bills for using it? They make sense, according to Dunstan. Looking ahead from the present, we can safely assume the moon will follow the American economic model, including the economics of the medical industry. And as Dunstan put it, that implies someone will probably pay for "the most expensive forceps in the galaxy."

THE DAY THE ENTIRE INTERNET GOES DOWN

Likely in this century? > *Yes*

Plausibility Rating > *4/5*

Scary? > *About as scary as it gets*

Worth changing habits? > *It would be a disaster. How up-to-date is your disaster preparedness kit?*

Note: These police dispatch records are normally entered into a web-based application for cloud storage. Today, due to the outage, they're being hand-written.

5:30 a.m., Manhattan, 111 Eighth Avenue: Shots fired inside 111 Eighth Avenue data center building. Possible explosive device. Crime scene being established. Situation ongoing.

8:58 a.m., Brooklyn, Marcy Ave. & Broadway: Shots fired. NYPD called a level 1 mobilization when a taxi driver became aggressive toward a nonpaying customer and opened fire. (Appears to be a citywide pay-service problem. Several nuisance-type calls relate to the same issue.) No injuries reported.

9:00 a.m., Citywide: NYPD visits all media outlets, requests that they publish statement from mayor requesting that all NYC residents "Relax at home." Mayor also notes, "We'll get through this. It's just the internet. We've been through worse."

9:10 a.m., Manhattan, 11 Wall Street: NYSE requests police presence as internet outage will not permit trading. Officers unable to respond to non-emergency call. Small disturbances reported. NYPD will monitor the situation remotely.

10:45 a.m., Brooklyn, 669 Lefferts Ave.: Officers assisted NYFD in containing a flood after a water main breakage. DEP reports system-wide emergency. All automated services have switched to manual, and DEP is understaffed in regards to DEP officers. NYPD officers standing by to assist further.

11:15 a.m., Queens, JFK Airport: NYPD mobilizing for crowd control as all flights grounded. All further airport patrons are requested not to enter the area.

11:45 a.m., Brooklyn, 132 S. Oxford St.: NYPD calling a level 1 mobilization

in response to a large gathering. Activists calling for political action against unknown business. NYPD making multiple arrests citing curfew violation. Situation ongoing.

12:20 p.m., Brooklyn, Stillwell Ave. & Boardwalk: NYPD calling a level 1 mobilization after an unknown disturbance resulted in a Verizon truck being overturned.

12:55 p.m., Brooklyn, Broadway & Gerry St.: Pedestrian struck by a car. Officers responded and administered CPR. Other first responders report problems responding to large volume of walk-in complaints at emergency dispatch (note: this is also occurring in my location) and other communication problems due to internet outage. Ambulance services report inability to respond to high call volume and request NYPD assistance.

1:20 p.m., Manhattan, 125 E. 54th St.: Level 1 mobilization requested in response to a bank robbery at an empty bank—all staff had gone home, and private security had been preempted by another emergency. Only one officer could respond due to call volume issue.

2:10 p.m., Brooklyn, 132 S. Oxford St.: Ongoing protest situation. After multiple arrests, crowd has grown significantly in size. NYPD requests assistance from state and federal agencies. State and federal agencies report that they cannot fulfill requests at this time. (Internet-related problems appear to be in all known jurisdictions.)

2:45 p.m., Brooklyn, 132 S. Oxford St.: Nearby intersection has become a citywide hub for protest activity. NYPD requests that all protesters remain peaceful, and withdraws police presence.

3:35 p.m., Manhattan, Statue of Liberty: NYPD Harbor & ESU responding to protest activity. A crowd has gathered inside the statue, despite closure.

Multiple officer-involved shootings reported.

4:10 p.m., Citywide: Mayor announces restoration of 80 percent of internet service.

4:55 p.m., Manhattan, Statue of Liberty: State and federal agencies responding. Multiple fatalities reported inside statue.

Note: Web-based record-keeping has been restored. This written account will be digitized at a later date. For further dispatches from today, please see digital records.

◆

What you just read might sound unusually dramatic, but I promise it's not. Losing the internet would be very, very bad.

I know the cliché: "Kids these days . . . They can't do anything without their Snapchat and their Fortnite. They should relax and read a book or play outside." Undoubtedly a whole lot of people in a position to do so would simply view Internet Blackout Day as an "internet cleanse," a large-scale version of that self-care trend where you turn off your phone, unplug your Wi-Fi, and spend your day taking bubble baths, gardening, and enjoying quality time with the kids. That's lovely and everything, but it's also naïve in the extreme.

The world would come to a dead stop if the internet clicked off—particularly in extremely wired countries like China, India, the United Kingdom, and the US.

Let's start with your job. There's no clear measure of exactly how much the internet has penetrated the working world in any country, but I put it to you: Could do your job without the internet? I did a quick inventory of my own career stops:

I've worked at a video store, and that whole industry no longer exists because its business model was annihilated by, well, the internet. It's worth noting, however, that this was simply a retail job, and these require point-of-sale (POS) systems. Modern POS systems like Oracle's Hospitality Simphony are cloud-based, and when they lose their internet connections businesses that rely on them can't function. (In 2015, the Oracle system Starbucks uses went down and all the stores had to just close or start handing out free drinks.)

I've worked as a substitute teacher, and while the classroom experience would be lovely—no kids on their damn phones!—I'm not sure I'd be able to get jobs, because without online portals like ReadySub most of the schools I know can't request substitutes. They'd have to make a quick ad-hoc switch to a phone call–based system, and both mobile phones and voice over internet phones (VOIP) would be either spotty or useless. What's more, on Blackout Day, I'm sure the front offices of schools would already have their hands full.

I've been a private ESL tutor, and I relied on smartphone apps and downloadable material for curriculum, but I could probably adapt, assuming my lessons that day were all scheduled in advance, and were all at familiar addresses. I always relied on GPS apps to get to where my students were, and unlike dedicated satellite navigation devices, GPS apps generally don't work without the internet.

I've worked at an eBay store and an online marketing company, and needless to say, neither of those could operate at all, on any level. Everyone would just have to go home.

Finally, I've worked at an international news publication, and while I could theoretically compose stories offline, that was just a small part of my job. Without the internet, it would be tough to gather leads—I find probably 75 percent of my story leads on the internet—and almost impossible to reach sources. It would also be impossible to file or publish any of my articles, since the vast majority of my work was only ever published online.

But as a member of the Coastal Elite, I worried, in pondering the repercussions of Internet Blackout Day, that I might have blinders on regarding how workers would be impacted, so I went in search of whichever kind of job was furthest from my own personal experience, and I found truckers. In my mind, they drive loads from point A to point B, and if they need to communicate, they use CB radio. What use could they possibly have for the internet other than maybe phone-based GPS?

"I'm almost about ready to say we'd be fucked," said Jim March-Simpson, a fifty-two-year-old Alabama-based long-haul trucker. "I get my job assignments over the internet. Could be email. Could be Google Hangouts, depending on the company." He said other truckers are independent owner-operators who use websites called "load boards" to find loads and plan and coordinate trips.

In fact, almost every aspect of trucking is saturated with internet connectivity. Upon receiving a shipment, March-Simpson told me, "I get a physical paper in my hand. I put it on my steering wheel, photograph it with my phone, and send the picture back to home base so we can get paid on it." If he uses email for this, then during the blackout he could try to switch to text messaging to send the photo, but that's just the beginning of his worries.

March-Simpson also uses the internet for his expenses. "There are financial instruments that we use in trucking that you don't see anywhere else in the world." These include cards from a company called Electronic Funds Source, LLC, that can only be used to pay for trucking-related expenses, such as fuel at the pump and roadside repairs. And to use the card, he said, "I get a quote. I tell the boss. 'Okay it's gonna be $237 to fix the tire.' He emails me something called a 'money code.' It's a long string of numbers. It turns into that amount of money."

All that being the case, as soon as March-Simpson needed to stop for fuel, he'd run into an almost insurmountable problem. "*Could* I use my own cash to pay for more gas? Yes, I could. Would I *choose* to . . . ?" he said, trailing off. The trouble is that if you're a trucker, spending several hundred dollars of your own money to buy fuel is a huge risk, when you have no idea if you'll be reimbursed. Instead, there'd more likely just be thousands of truckers stranded on the side of the road. "You'd have to commandeer every Greyhound bus in the country to do nothing but get truckers home," March-Simpson said.

But that's easier said than done because the problem wouldn't be limited to truckers. Bus companies like Greyhound, along with planes, trains, and automobiles—particularly app-based companies like Uber, Lyft, and Gett—would all be in holding patterns. Some of this would no doubt be dire—operators of public utilities and those who staff emergency services can't suddenly take a day off because there's no internet (more on these people in a moment), and neither can companies that process payments. Stock exchanges would absolutely be brought to their knees, leaving markets to go haywire. At this point, it's probably quicker to name the very few sections of the economy that sound like they'd still function than to name the ones that would be forced to shut down. Most jobs dealing with plants, like landscaping, gardening, and small-scale farming, seem like they'd be unaffected. Businesses that dispense food, like restaurants, would be a mixed bag because kitchens aren't digital, but their point-of-sale and concierge systems often are. Nearly everything else in the industrialized world is too saturated with digital information to keep chugging along without a hitch.

So billions of us would suddenly be unable to access, transmit, and store information the way we're used to.

But let's not be so literal, or practical. The internet is more than just your job. It's your life. No one thinks about how they're moving ones and zeroes around while they're using the internet. If you're old enough, there was a time—1997?—when you might have fired up your computer and said to yourself, "All right! Time to log on to the web, so I can access and transmit some data!" but those days have long passed. Today, taking away the internet means taking away a superpower that billions of people take for granted. All at once, everyone on Earth basically goes from wizard to Muggle. The actual impact is hard to fathom.

The only thing that compares was in 1998, when PanAmSat Corporation's Galaxy IV satellite went haywire, knocking out most pager connectivity in the United States. Even then, the pager network was small potatoes compared to the internet. But in those days, millions of Americans, including ER doctors, actually did rely on pagers for cheap, easy, and, most of all, reliable communication with their families and employers. Still, much of the reaction at the time was glib and more or less about being relieved not to hear any annoying beeping sounds.

"How's that for a picture of bliss?" *Los Angeles Times* columnist Shawn Hubler wrote at the time.

But all that came about because of *pagers*, which just make a few numbers appear on a bulky device in someone's pocket. If you think *that's* bad, imagine about four billion people suddenly without intra-office communication, public safety updates, calendars, weather updates, medical records, driving directions, most phone calls, movies, answers to urgent questions, study materials, music, currency transfers, breaking news, games, photo and document storage, reminders, along with—let's just acknowledge it—procrastination, dumb jokes, and porn.

Could the result of losing all that really be as terrifying as the introduction to this chapter?

Yeah, it could.

In my days at *Vice*, I used to seek out and research some of the reasons the entire internet might theoretically go down. Two biggies were solar flares and electromagnetic pulses (EMPs). Both are just big floods of electromagnetism with the potential to fry electronics and, just maybe, break society—the internet, the power grid, a country's defense infrastructure, you name it. But in the end, I didn't find much there to worry about. The biggest solar storms can certainly futz with radio reception and GPS, and they've caused local damage—including knocking out all the power in Quebec in 1989. But since the Earth is shielded by a magnetic field, and a lovely thick atmosphere, solar storms simply aren't strong enough to knock out our internet infrastructure (although someday we'll move more of our telecommunications infrastructure into space, and when we do, solar weather will become much more of a life-and-death concern). Meanwhile, EMPs in their current form aren't really much of a danger, either, because only a tiny one can be generated with present-day technology; to take down the internet with an electromagnetic pulse you'd have to do it with the help of dozens of nuclear bombs. If either one of these catastrophes befell us humans—a record-shattering solar storm or a huge EMP—we'd have *much* bigger problems than the internet going down.

But when I corresponded about this topic with Stuart Schechter, a former security researcher and now an entrepreneur based in Seoul,

South Korea, he joked that the whole thing might come crashing down when "OK Go and Psy collaborate on a video together." His joke wasn't completely a joke. This is where we get the cliché "break the internet." A sufficiently viral piece of content with international appeal can cause an outage at a major website—this is why *PAPER* magazine boosted its server infrastructure, making it capable of handling eight thousand requests per second instead of the usual maximum of two thousand requests per second—in the days before the magazine's website published a now-famous photo of Kim Kardashian's oiled butt. What's more, this effect can be simulated with distributed denial of service (DDOS) attacks, in which an army of users keeps accessing a site in order to overload it.

So let's follow that thread: Can overloading the internet break it?

It would take an absolutely gargantuan DDOS attack, requiring (and this is my own conjecture here) perhaps millions of human participants, to temporarily disable even just the top ten websites in the world: Google, YouTube, Facebook, Baidu, Wikipedia, Yahoo, QQ, Taobao, Amazon, Twitter. Individually, any one of these sites is designed to handle *hundreds of millions* of requests per day. Google.com alone performs millions of web searches per *minute*. So overloading it would require an unimaginable amount of computing power.

But cyber-weapons can temporarily kill a Google-sized website, as we saw in 2016 when hackers used the Mirai botnet—a collection of compromised "internet of things" devices (the eponymous bots) around the world whose owners had no idea they were infected with malware—to attack servers that connected people to Twitter, Reddit, Spotify, and CNN, preventing many users from accessing them for several hours. It's important to note that this isn't a perfect comparison because the Mirai botnet didn't attack specific popular sites; it attacked one popular name server that connected people to those sites.

But in my top ten scenario, there'd be alternatives to most essential sites, and that could keep the internet going. Even if Baidu, Google, and Yahoo are down, Sogou, Bing, and DuckDuckGo would enable web searching to carry on as usual, more or less. Twitter and Facebook could go down and we'd still be able to post on Instagram (assuming it doesn't share too much server space with its parent company, Facebook). Wikipedia would be down, but Wikipedia is an open-source project, so authorized copies of the entire site, like the one at TheFreeDictionary .com, would still be around. Shoppers on Taobao and Amazon could, well, go to a store.

I don't mean to downplay the impact these attacks might have on people's lives—undoubtedly, there'd be unforeseeable and, most likely, dire problems—but as far as I can tell, for the average person, the worst DDOS imaginable would mostly just be annoying. So a DDOS super-attack—or probably *any* software-based attack—could only be a small part of a multipronged strategy to take down the whole internet.

Nonetheless, there are some frightening vulnerabilities in the system that keeps our ones and zeroes flowing.

See, the global internet as we know it exists thanks to something almost stupidly low-tech: a network of transnational communications cables—pretty much the same system we've been using since the telegraph days. As of 2018, just under four hundred of these cables spanned the Earth's oceans, just like those old telegraph cables did. When you email a photo, it may feel like that data is traveling through the air—perhaps into the majestic *cloud* you've heard so much about—but really, that data travels along cables, just like the electricity that powers your house does. If you're sending that data internationally, a fiber-optic cable essentially shoots it across the ocean in the form of a laser beam. And this is how the "World Wide" part of the World Wide Web works.

These submarine internet cables are made of several protective layers around the gossamer-thin optical fibers in the middle. Some of the outer layers insulate the signal from the elements, and others are just armor, keeping the fibers from being damaged by the many undersea slings and arrows of outrageous fortune. The whole thing is about as wide as a garden hose, but less flexible, because it has to be tough enough to withstand a lot of abuse. Up until 2006, according to a memo from the International Cable Protection Committee (ICPC), less than 1 percent of submarine cable failures were caused by shark bites. But if you read that memo differently, it means that some failures *were* caused by shark bites. (For the record, the ICPC says the shark situation is fully under control.)

But unlike a shark, a human can destroy an undersea cable without much trouble. In fact, someone already has. In 2011, seventy-five-year-old Hayastan Shakarian was hunting for scrap metal in her village outside Tbilisi, Georgia, and accidentally severed a fiber-optic cable, knocking out internet services to 90 percent of Armenia and much of Georgia for five hours. Press photos of Shakarian show her holding a hand saw—a pretty rudimentary tool for such high-tech sabotage. That means Shakarian accomplished her dastardly feat accidentally, and without modern tools.

But what if a motivated individual, or more likely a terrorist group with state funding, went on an intentional seek-and-destroy campaign?

First of all, they wouldn't have any trouble at all with the seek part. No, there aren't any big signs or markers showing passersby where the cables are (on the flip side of that same coin, there aren't any security outposts protecting them), but the paths of all the cables are public information, and the landing points have even been comprehensively mapped by groups like TeleGeography. That would make it pretty easy to deduce their rough locations and hunt them down. Some cables, like the one I scouted out in Singapore, are hard to spot without scuba gear because they start out in fenced-off seaside facilities and jut out into the murky depths beneath busy harbors, but others run into the ocean via public beaches, where crews just leave them exposed without so much as kicking sand over them—a fact that cable contractors don't bother to hide in promotional materials.

And even if a cable is several meters underground at its landing site, it can be easily detected with handheld tools. And once someone finds a cable, that person can hack into it with anything sharp until the work is done—like Shakarian did—or, if the individual has deeper pockets, spend money on a high-end hydraulic cable cutter, which can sever an armored fiber-optic cable in about three seconds.

So in case I haven't made it perfectly clear, the global internet is a big, messy tangle like kudzu vines. And just like kudzu vines, killing a huge mass of it only requires a few well-placed cuts. But exactly how to cut cables to ensure a global internet blackout would be slightly trickier to work out, not least because the internet is so dispersed. Depending on where you are, there's a good chance your internet service provider

(ISP) doesn't depend entirely on a single transnational cable like the ones in Georgia, and even if it does, your information isn't all in one place.

For instance, if you use Google products, the Google Cloud help page says your user data is distributed among its many data centers, thus "eliminating any single point of failure and minimizing the impact of common equipment failures and environmental risks." Google says it has sixteen such servers spread internationally, including eight in the United States and just two on the entire continent of Asia. This sort of dispersal is the internet's strength—and also one of its weaknesses, given that we know the bridges between these data centers are extremely vulnerable to an intentional attack.

Such an attacker would need to sever the connections that enable some of the core features of the internet, and in 2012, *Gizmodo*'s Sam Biddle wrote that there were eleven such crucial cable landings. They're located in Singapore, the Southwest of the United Kingdom, Tokyo, Hong Kong, South Florida, France, and Sicily, along with two in India and two in Egypt. In 2017, I asked Andrew Blum, author of *Tubes: A Journey to the Center of the Internet* and Biddle's technical advisor for that article, if the crucial pressure points Biddle identified in 2012 were still the ripest targets, and he said the article still held up in that regard.

Once those points were severed by an international cable-chopping task force, most internet functions would be localized to each individual country—so no more World Wide Web. So clipping international cables won't finish the job, because local data will still be accessible. To make sure there's still no usable internet, the anti-internet terrorists would need to attack the Domain Name System (DNS). Without DNS to provide directions, we have no ability to "navigate" the internet. If you're such a geek that you know that the IP address 216.239.32.10 corresponds to Google.com, that's great; you can still get that site to load. But even if you know that, if there's no Domain Name System, the links to all the websites in a page of search results will be worthless.

DNS is operated not by any one government but by a Los Angeles–based nonprofit called the Internet Corporation for Assigned Names and Numbers (ICANN), and security around DNS is pretty insane—like something out of *Mission: Impossible*. Fourteen people in different countries around the world hold physical keycards that open one of two physical boxes—one on the East Coast of the US and one on the West Coast—containing a digital master "key" for the DNS system. The seven key-holders for each master key have separate meetings every three months for a kind of confirmation ceremony involving invasive security screenings and retinal scans, according to a 2014 report by the *Guardian*. After their identities are confirmed, the key-holders all crowd into a small room and confirm that the IP addresses and names still correspond to one another.

Whether you find all these complex security procedures comforting is really up to you, but for what it's worth, I don't readily see how the system can be infiltrated—but then again, my name isn't Danny Ocean.

But there are vulnerabilities in the DNS system that don't require you to indulge your heist movie fantasies. The numerous name servers that do the actual work of handling the billions of DNS requests that happen every day are just machines made of silicon, sitting in brick-and-mortar buildings, and that makes them inherently vulnerable to an attack, just like everything. These spots aren't altogether unprotected, like the undersea cables. But while staff members at the buildings that house the name servers are well aware of their importance, they're less like the intense key-holder security officials at ICANN, and more like security guards at a particularly fancy apartment building.

Now, to be clear, no one's going to damage these servers without committing acts of violence against humans, so while I'm comfortable telling you about the vulnerabilities of the undersea cables, you'll just have to use your own imagination to work out how some nefarious group could harm one of these buildings. There are thirteen of these servers, along with a vast number of redundant backups. As of this writing, there were 948 individual "instances" of the thirteen name servers—with "instances" meaning both originals and backups of each server—according to root-servers.org. We know knocking out one instance would do next to nothing, and knocking out all 948 would be overkill. This is far from an exact science, but after asking a few IT people about this, it seems to me that, if someone managed to disable forty or so instances of root servers, that would put a serious dent in the usability of the already-hobbled internet.

Let's also imagine that the terrorists, saboteurs, state-level attackers, neo-Luddites, or some combination of the above performed similar feats at about ten or so of the most important data supercenters. Services we've all come to trust would be offline, and data would be destroyed. And, by the way, according to Biddle's research the most critical buildings can be found in five cities: Miami, London, Paris, New York, and Los Angeles.

But as I mentioned before, all that digital carnage might not be necessary if an attacker were playing a long enough game with servers themselves, according to Schechter, the former security researcher. For all we know, there could have been already a "catastrophic security breach" that just isn't being exploited yet. Schechter pointed out that servers are just computers, and they're often constructed piecemeal from retail hardware. To be absolutely sure our data is safe, he said, "you'd have to be sure no state actor had ever touched the bios code in your hardware before you bought it." If you build DNS servers, you no doubt take these security considerations very seriously, but as we saw in 2018 when a team of researchers including the cryptographer Paul Kocher found a twenty-year-old vulnerability in Intel microprocessors, and revealed that most of the world's servers had been fully exposed for years, there can be huge weaknesses in extremely sensitive areas that can cause untold damage if the wrong actor finds them. If such a vulnerability had been intentionally added to a server component, it could lie dormant for ages, only to be activated and exploited as part of a coordinated global attack.

So let's say there *has* been an attack. Crucial data centers have been taken offline, DNS has been compromised, a large number of routers made by some popular brand like Linksys have been disabled via some exploit no one knew about until it was too late, and the most critical undersea cables have been cut. The internet is now effectively dead.

Let me be absolutely clear: this is a *lot* of effort, and not every IT expert I asked was willing to go along with this hypothetical. Some thought there was simply no way the internet could ever, ever go down wholesale, even if someone attacked it this comprehensively. Others felt that there was simply no way to execute the attack I've outlined. So take comfort in that.

The US Department of Homeland Security, however, also wouldn't game it out with me. I reached out several times, and was told my emails were being forwarded to the necessary official, but eventually the emails stopped, and my follow-ups were ignored. There is, of course, a great deal of mystery about to what degree the US government controls and scrutinizes the data we all move around online, and whether the US government can simply flip a switch and kill the internet.

There is, however, an eighteen-page report on the DHS website about this. It's called "Risk Management Strategy—Internet Routing, Access and Connection Services," compiled by the DHS's two IT-focused "coordinating councils," which are independent organizations that meet to advise the government about security. They include representatives from hardware manufacturers and the major US telecom companies, according to the DHS website. According to the report, "there must be a comprehensive incident management plan in place that can be followed to respond to incidents, even if unforeseen events or circumstances block or delay the response to an incident." But since DHS ignored my interview requests, I don't know if any such incident management plan exists.

While the actual step-by-step procedure in the US for getting the world back online is cloaked in mystery, it's hard to imagine that an internet blackout would last long—figure less than a day, if that. If researching this chapter has taught me anything, it's that the idea of knocking out the internet is impossible—incoherent even—but a constellation of disruptions could make it *seem* knocked out. Each disruption would be spotted quickly, and a massive, global effort to fix it would inevitably commence. Companies like Orange Marine would spring into action, repairing undersea cables in a process that can take up to sixteen hours. Emergency server repair companies around the world, no doubt smelling money, would rush to the sites of the biggest potential problems and offer their services. In many cases, data would be lost. Some cables might be harder to repair than others, meaning some areas would probably be without connectivity for weeks or longer, but after a short time there's little doubt the internet would be *mostly* up and running.

I say "little doubt" here because the blackout itself would be the biggest obstacle in the way of repairing the blackout. So since most forms of telecommunication rely at least partly on the internet, many of the disruptions would have a cumulative effect, which would compound the damage, and prolong the chaos.

For instance, I hear you saying, "But businesses still use landline phones!" but go ask your office IT team if those would still work without the internet. They probably wouldn't, because they're voice over IP (VOIP)–based, meaning the data transmits via internet providers, rather than via the traditional circuit-based model.

Worse, mobile phone calls are in trouble, too. While on one hand, "the network transmits zeroes and ones that represents those analog signals," said Murat Torlak, a professor of electrical engineering at the University of Texas, Dallas, if you're a mobile phone provider "you don't have to actually use a dedicated line, per se." Mobile phone companies bill separately for data and voice, but in reality it's all data now. The companies move the packets of data corresponding to the sound of your voice using whatever method they want, and since the internet is a fast way to move data around, that's an increasingly cheap option for them. "What's happening is all the base stations—basically radio stations—that provide wireless connections to cellular phones [are] also connected to each other through a main switch, through the internet as well in some cases," Torlak said. "There's a conversion going on." In an email, he told me, "The backbone connections between towers are mostly becoming IP (internet protocol)–based. The trend is towards full IP network."

If you were born before the 1980s, losing the ability to make calls probably sounds like a bigger deal than losing the ability to use the internet. But according to a 2017 report published in the UK by the auditing firm Deloitte, you're probably making fewer than you even realize. Only 32 percent of respondents were using their phones for business calls, down from 33 percent in 2016, and an earlier Deloitte survey from 2015 found that a quarter of UK smartphone users don't make any calls whatsoever in any given week. Still, phone calls are the go-to procedure for urgent situations: when a car has broken down, a loved one is in the hospital, or a landlord demands to know what a smell is.

Worse than the loss of calls, however, would be the loss of smart infrastructure. At the moment, the internet-based automation that keeps the utilities running normally can mostly be switched into manual mode if the internet blinks off, and workers can be sent out to fill the gaps. For instance, a small water utility operating in Southern California most likely has an IP-based telemetry system. If the internet went down "workers would have to operate the wells and fill the tanks," according to former general manager of Mesa Consolidated Water District (and my dad) Lee Pearl. In a worst-case scenario, tanks could empty out if wells weren't pumped, and pipes would go dry, but utilities have "redundant systems," he told me, which should keep such emergencies in the realm of the unlikely.

But utilities, including energy grids, are relying more and more on automation like this to keep them running smoothly. Cities as big as Chicago have internet-enabled smart grids keeping the lights on, and the US Department of Energy is urging utilities to automate even more. As of this writing, most of these systems are relatively new, and the staff at such a facility probably still has sufficient institutional memory to switch back to manual operations. But in a few decades, that won't be true anymore—staff members will only be used to the automated systems, not the manually operated antiques that are kept around exclusively as back-ups. So the loss of automation caused by an internet blackout wouldn't necessarily kill any given utility, but there inevitably would be failures, which would beget other failures. A water utility would lose power, and switch to backup power, at the same time it lost its automated features, and workers would lose their ability to communicate with one another.

This gets even darker when you consider what else is in the process of being smartened up. That list includes traffic lights; emergency dispatch, which has already seen multiple outages due to internet failures; fire monitoring; and triage at mass casualty events. In short, much of the work that goes into keeping cities running and people from not dying is being handed over to internet-connected machines. If the manual backups for only a few of these systems fail, those failures run a serious risk of compounding one another, and there's little doubt that the result will be thousands of tiny catastrophes.

The only good news is that some people and places would probably emerge relatively unscathed. When Egypt deliberately killed its internet in 2011 in the early days of what would become known as the "Arab Spring," documentary filmmaker Parvez Sharma told CNN there wouldn't be much of an effect on Egypt's lower class since they're "not Twittering and Facebooking and emailing. They've never even heard of the damned internet, most of them." The blackout cost the local economy $18 million per day according to *Forbes*—pennies compared to what an internet failure would cost the United States. To this day, Egypt has barely increased its reliance on the internet—with only 50 percent of Egyptians online in 2017 according to a report by Northwestern University in Qatar, and those who are online in Egypt use the internet much less than in other Middle Eastern countries.

On Blackout Day, perhaps the luckiest country of all will be North Korea, where, according to the Colombian market research site Internet World Stats, there were only fourteen thousand internet users as of 2017, which corresponds to about 0.05 percent of the population. Then again, most of North Korea's internet use seems to be tied up in its notoriously effective international hacking sector, famous for the fateful 2014 infiltration of a Sony Pictures email server. So even North Korea would lose one of its signature exports.

THE DAY THE LAST SLAUGHTERHOUSE CLOSES

Likely in this century? > *No way*

Plausibility Rating > *2/5*

Scary? > *No*

Worth changing habits? > *Have you not gotten the memo about eating less meat? You should do that.*

Moongchi is four months old. His soft, fuzzy coat is mostly white, but his face is brown with black around his muzzle. He was also the last dog smuggled out of the Namgu dog meat production facility in Gwangju, South Korea, and he's looking for a loving home.

Moongchi is thought to be the last survivor of a slaughterhouse anywhere in the developed world.

It might surprise you to learn there was still a slaughterhouse operating in South Korea at all. It's been decades since most citizens of industrialized nations ate meat from a slaughterhouse, or, as it's usually called these days, "dead meat," apart from the occasional flamboyant chef determined to draw attention to a new restaurant by shocking the public with dead meat—usually citing some claim about it tasting better. But perfect, factory-cultured replicas of Kobe beef medallions and grass-fed Australian lamb cutlets are a bargain at any supermarket these days, and they're every bit as tasty as the dead meat versions of those products that the same meat companies used to produce.

Appeals to give up all meat no longer come from animal rights activists, but from doctors.

And that paradigm shift was exactly why the stealth dog meat industry in South Korea stayed alive for so long—the mainstream supply chain for meat simply hadn't included dog. It slipped through the cracks.

Korean food companies like Pulmuone began by buying industrial meat-culturing equipment from American companies like Tyson, factory-calibrated to produce the big three types of American terrestrial meat: beef, pork, and chicken. The Korean super-conglomerate companies, known as Chaebol, generated their own versions over the next few years, with a focus on selling new and improved versions of the technology back to the United States, and in the meantime, putting cultured meat on every Korean table.

But ever since Korean dog meat moved underground in the 1980s, the production and enjoyment of *bosintang*, or dog soup, had been an open secret in most Korean cities, consumed by an ever-shrinking minority of Korean citizens. The slaughtering operations were usually small, and since the soup was really only popular in the summer, they usually only operated for half the year. Most of these—technically illegal, but still tolerated—dog meat markets, such as Namgu's tiny shop, operated far from the prying eyes of the federal government.

Gwangju, where Namgu was located for all these years, was way down in the southern tip of the country, shielded from scrutiny, and churning out three thousand dogs per year into a solid local food business for a handful of local restaurants—even after the rest of the meat in South Korea shifted away from the slaughterhouse model. Korean animal rights activists occasionally took notice of a dog meat operation during this time, and made a stink on social media, but getting a slaughterhouse closed down somehow didn't keep the meat out of those *bosintang* bowls, as many of the restaurants simply started their own slaughtering operations.

It was probably inevitable that a dog meat culturing business would flourish in the Korean market, but the sharp regulatory backlash was harder to predict. Banning the practice of slaughtering dogs in the twentieth century was seen as a necessary step toward becoming a modern society, and the older members of the country's leadership feared that reviving the dog meat industry at all might look a bit like backsliding. Fortunately, the regulatory efforts failed, and cultured dog meat became a sensation. Most Koreans had never tried dog meat, and—alongside legions of curious foreign visitors—they finally got to have a taste.

That should have been curtains for Namgu's business model, but as is so often the case, an old folktale passed around by practitioners of traditional medicine kept it alive: you get a burst of red-hot, mad-dog energy by eating dog meat on the hottest days of the year, the story went, but only if that dog was angry when it died. For eons, it was a known—if not entirely common—practice in rural corners of Korea to abuse dogs during captivity, beat them just before slaughter, singe off their fur, and generally force them to die in a fit of rage. You couldn't get the purported energy boost effect from cultured meat.

So it was with Namgu: sticking to an old tradition most Koreans had forgotten. Moongchi, who was born in that hell-on-earth, was discovered when agents from the group Korea Animal Rights Advocates (KARA) snuck in, took video footage, and rescued him.

But KARA didn't simply call for Namgu to be shut down.

The video KARA released was "hosted" by Moongchi (voiced by the star of today's highest rated TV drama), and it didn't rely on footage of the slaughterhouse. Instead, it was a bright, cheerful, family-friendly, TV-ready production featuring a taste test followed by a test of "energy." A group of Namgu's most loyal customers unwittingly tried cultured dog meat on camera, believing all the while that it had once been an angry, tortured dog. They confirmed that it was "*mashita*"—delicious—and reported the greatest surge of energy they'd ever felt. The video was a viral sensation, and the public pressure that ensued resulted in Namgu's voluntary closure.

Moongchi still doesn't like loud noises, and he'll nip people's fingers if they approach without warning, so families without children are strongly encouraged to apply to adopt him. He's still a very good dog—a hero even—and he's been neutered and vaccinated.

◆

Most people I know, no matter their attitudes toward animal welfare, can, if they try, conjure a pretty accurate mental picture of a crowded "intensive animal farm," also known as a "factory farm." Some can even describe the killing procedures in a modern meat-packing plant without much trouble, but of course, they'd rather not do any of that if they eat meat. It appears that the silent majority of food consumers isn't thrilled about the methods that put meat on its plate, but is hesitant to make drastic dietary changes. These "ambivalent omnivores" are, if not the silent majority, a silent plurality of food consumers.

As the Dutch philosopher Cor van der Weele wrote in 2013, "Ambivalence is unpleasant and it comes with various (subconscious) mechanisms to reduce it, such as strategic ignorance. The result is that attitudes toward meat look more unequivocal than they really are." In short, meat eaters and non–meat eaters have more in common than they might like to admit: meat eaters are capable of feeling empathy toward animals, and meanwhile, 86 percent of animal-loving vegetarians eventually get tempted back to eating burgers, and, in my experience, they usually rationalize their decision with a hearty "my doctor told me to." (I cannot find any studies, incidentally, to defend the position that a nutritionally complete omnivorous diet is healthier than a nutritionally complete plant-based diet. The key to healthy eating appears to be balance and variety, not the presence or absence of meat.)

We all know why people become ambivalent about eating meat in the first place: farm animals have big wet eyes and soft fur; thinking about them being sliced open so they can be made into sandwiches is a drag. To pretend there's nothing to this, or that worrying about it is childish, seems objectively wrong. A series of psychological studies carried out at the University of Oslo went to great pains to prove the obvious: it turns out that—big surprise—exposing people to realistic images of the specific species of animal that died for a particular food tends to make people temporarily unwilling to eat it. The key word there, however, is "temporarily," because according to the University of Oslo's study, "culturally entrenched processes of dissociation found in the way we produce, prepare and talk about meat and animals sustain people's willingness to eat meat as they make it easy to ignore the meat–animal link."

It's perhaps this capacity for empathy that gives ambivalent omnivores a hidden desire to—get this—jeopardize their own eating habits for the benefit of animals. A puzzling 2018 US consumer survey from Oklahoma State University, partially funded by the US Department of Agriculture, demonstrated that while 90 percent of respondents eat meat "regularly," 47 percent nonetheless agree with the seemingly contradictory statement "I support a ban on slaughterhouses." So these meat eaters are willing, it seems, to be thrown into a meatless world in which their diets would suddenly need to change drastically—that or they literally don't know how meat gets onto their plates.

So assuming this ambivalence turns into a global movement, when a sufficient number of world governments take the surprisingly popular step of banning slaughterhouses our world will go topsy-turvy. "Normal" people as we define them today will be considered strange brutes. They'll be "carnists," to use the term coined by psychologist and vegan activist Melanie Joy. Meat will be rare (by which I mean "in short supply"), or impossible to find. Sounds pretty unimaginable, right?

I have been to that world—or at least one version of it.

The town of Pushkar, in the Indian state of Rajasthan, is almost certainly the global center of vegetarianism, because 100 percent of the town's twenty-one thousand inhabitants are vegetarians. All the restaurants in Pushkar advertise themselves as "pure veg" and none of the shops have meat counters.

Pushkar is meatless by decree because it's a major pilgrimage site for Hindus, particularly those from the sect known as Shaktism, who are often—though not always—lifelong vegetarians. The town is located by a stunning holy lake that hosts hundreds of gurus in waterfront temples and ghats, where visitors can take part in a *puja*, which is a sort of Hindu micro-ceremony carried out in exchange for a small donation.

So does a lack of meat in a municipality transform it into some kind of hippie paradise, full of touchy-feely people who reek of patchouli and weed smoke?

I'm not sure when the transformation happened in Pushkar, but yeah, it looks like it does. To a greater degree than any other tourist site I've visited in India, Pushkar is absolutely *overflowing* with stoned, dreadlocked, unwashed hippies. These foreigners—many from Israel, for some reason—meditate by day, eat zero animal flesh at every meal, and then, perhaps because of the kumbaya-type atmosphere thus created, gather in vast drum circles each evening to dance, play with poi and devil sticks, and take part in various other Burning Man–esque forms of self-expression.

Pushkar probably isn't a reliable microcosm of a meat-free global future, but it's an awful lot like the fictional meat-free world imagined by British comedian and filmmaker Simon Amstell in his 2017 mock-umentary *Carnage: Swallowing the Past*. In that film, the world has finally attained enlightenment vis-à-vis animal slaughter, and everyone has become a vegan. Life after meat in this satirical world looks like, well, Pushkar: full of placid, smiling young people gathered in meadows to eat plants and gently caress one another. In the film, meat is part of humanity's brutal history, and its characters have a hard time reconciling that history with the present. "Why would anyone eat a baby? Just a little baby. A little baby lamb," pleads one of the film's innocent denizens.

If an act of carnivory happens in Pushkar, the consequence couldn't be further from a drum circle: "Beating," said Kamal Pathak, the chairman of Pushkar's municipal board—essentially the mayor—when I asked him to explain the repercussions. He punched the air, clarifying that the beatings aren't delivered with a flyswatter (flyswatters are tolerated in Pushkar). "You're going to be six months in hospital, 100 percent."

From 2015 through 2017 there were more than a dozen killings in India carried out by lynch mobs who believed they'd identified individuals possessing or selling cow meat. This followed the rise of current Indian Prime Minister Narendra Modi and his Hindu nationalist Bharatiya Janata Party. Modi seemed to tolerate these attacks for several years, until he finally condemned them in 2017, telling the public, "Violence is not a solution to the problems."

I was astounded that defenders of seemingly compassionate customs were so violent, but according to Suryakant Waghmore, sociologist at Mumbai's Tata Institute of Social Sciences, "the Western vegan idea is very different from the Indian idea." "Hindu vegetarianism is not about compassion towards animals," Waghmore, whose research focuses on power dynamics among the Indian castes, said. "It's more about distinguishing [oneself] from other beings who may eat meat, just to claim moral ground or purity, and just to call these people untouchables." Often, Waghmore told me, the fierce reaction against meat eating is a thinly veiled form of bigotry toward Muslims.

Indeed, I spoke to an anonymous Muslim slaughterhouse worker who told me that he lived in fear of attacks by members of the Hindu majority. Shiv Sinha, a Hindu real estate agent who works in the conservative Hindu city of Jaipur, told me his Muslim clients routinely experience discrimination when they look for homes. "There are some people who believe that they should give their property to vegetarians only," Sinha explained.

So in a world without slaughterhouses, what about other forms of slaughter—particularly as they pertain to religion? Would an animal rights utopia provide dispensation for Muslim practitioners of the Islamic Eid al-Adha animal sacrifice custom? What about American practitioners of Santeria? If these practices are still legally allowed, will practitioners nonetheless be made into pariahs?

Let me put a finer point on this: if you're a militant vegan, you probably find it annoying enough when your movement gets co-opted by hippie-dippie, sandal-wearing types. But if veganism starts catching on, you need to be even more careful about it getting co-opted by anti-Islamic neofascists and other kinds of people looking for yet another excuse to discriminate against groups they don't like.

On that note, let's just table the whole idea of an all-vegetarian world for a second, because I'm not convinced everyone has to become a vegetarian per se in order for the last slaughterhouse to close.

According to Joshua Tetrick, CEO of the vegan food start-up JUST, Inc.—formerly known as Hampton Creek—and a vegan himself, vegans shouldn't assume their worldview is winning just because Western supermarkets and restaurants are beginning to offer meat alternatives. "In the world today, because of higher per capita income and urbanization, there's a meat revolution, not a plant-based revolution," Tetrick told me.

A 2017 report from *Our World in Data*—an online publication by researchers at the University of Oxford—shows that since 1961, the rate at which animals die to become our meals has skyrocketed. "Growth in per capita meat consumption has been most marked in countries [that] have [undergone] a strong economic transition," the report says, noting a fifteenfold per capita increase in meat eating in China and a fourfold increase in Brazil. So while Americans *have* been scaling back their beef consumption since about 2005, humans actually kill more than twice as many cows for food as they did in 1961. We also slaughter four to five times as many pigs, and twelve times as many birds.

That immense scale makes a quick shift away from meat—say, over the course of one day—totally impractical, and is why we're not talking about one big, global come-to-Jesus moment in which the entire world shifts away from meat. Such a shift has actually already been contemplated in plenty of "What if everyone went vegetarian right this second?" articles.

In 2016, for instance, the BBC asked agricultural zoologist Ben Phalan about this magic-wand scenario, and, unsurprisingly, he said it would be really, really awful for humans. Three-and-a-half billion grazing animals around the world would suddenly be toxic assets along with a comparably mind-boggling number of economically pointless pigs and poultry. We could expect the overnight monetary losses to be over a trillion dollars, a surefire recipe for a global recession that would be worsened by the ensuing chaos as all those animals were massacred and burned en masse, or set free to roam the countryside, eating freely as they went, clogging roads and reproducing without regard for local ecology, before eventually dying and decomposing in inconvenient places.

Another thing that would happen in the "everyone joins PETA on the same day" fantasy is that huge swaths of rangeland in the developing world would be rendered essentially worthless, because much of it physically can't make the shift to crop-based farming. Nomadic pastoralist cultures like the ones in the Sahel region of West Africa would be impossible to maintain. And pretty much everyone in places like Mongolia, where meat and dairy are the primary sources of calories—simply because little else can be farmed there—would starve to death.

But despite these now-familiar arguments about how meat, unpleasant as its origin may be, is the Jenga block that would cause the whole tower of global civilization to topple over, there's a growing awareness of the cruelties visited on animals. The problem doesn't seem to be as simple as "meat equals death," but instead seems rooted in the slow churn of exposés proving time and again that *the way* those animals die is incompatible with an increasing number of people's value systems. Bestsellers like Eric Schlosser's *Fast Food Nation* and Michael Pollan's *The Omnivore's Dilemma* aren't pro-vegan screeds, but they touch on the shortcomings of today's meat industry, from the animals' lives in cramped, fetid concentrated animal feeding operations, to their terrifying and grisly industrialized deaths.

At the prompting of animal welfare activists like Temple Grandin—a Colorado State University professor of animal science who works with the cattle industry rather than attacking it—many slaughterhouses around the world have taken measures to make conditions more humane, like building more comfortable restraints and purchasing more reliable stunning equipment. Cows, Grandin says, should rarely moo in distress, or fall down, or show signs of pain, if slaughterhouse workers are doing their jobs correctly. But according to a 2013 article in *Modern Farmer* magazine, which is largely sympathetic to the cattle industry, even in facilities where Grandin's techniques have been adopted, cows moo prodigiously just before metal bolts break their skulls. In the next few seconds, the animal will be chained by its back legs to a hoist so that it can be sliced open and drained of all its blood; one sincerely hopes the captive bolt stunner fully anesthetizes the animal before that happens.

But as was extensively documented in *Slaughterhouse* by Gail Eisnitz, these sorts of measures fall miserably short. Grandin acknowledges that bolt stun guns are tricky to use, and prone to failure if improperly maintained, leading to animals being sliced open after being improperly stunned, or not stunned at all. It's not clear how often bolt guns fail in this way, but if the number ranges as high as even one-tenth of 1 percent, that would add up to frightening, agonizing deaths for thousands of animals each and every day.

In Europe, similarly industry-friendly reforms have been more far-reaching. Switzerland has gone as far as banning the practice of boiling lobsters alive. And in some countries, including Denmark and Belgium, laws (with disturbing civil rights implications) have banned kosher and halal slaughter, mandating that all animals at least be stunned before they're killed. Even so, a 2018 video report from the Swiss activist group Pour l'Égalité Animale (For Animal Equality) portrayed the circumstances of legal European slaughter in these newly regulated conditions as a savage and somewhat slapstick affair. The report showed workers literally chasing terrified cows and lambs around killing floors with electric probes and bolt guns, having mixed success at best with the actual stunning, and frequently slicing animals' necks while they're quite obviously still alive and sensitive to pain.

So the bleak picture of the meat industry painted by Upton Sinclair in *The Jungle* more than one hundred years ago has largely been sanitized, and conditions have improved for the workers, but the situation has changed very little for the animals. (Contrary to popular belief, Sinclair was not a vegetarian, but was, according to his book *The Fasting Cure*, an ambivalent omnivore.)

On that note, let's get back to Tetrick, the CEO of JUST, Inc.—the guy who manufactures and markets vegan food for a living. He isn't expecting the developed world to give up meat in huge numbers just because the circumstances it's derived from are unsettling. "I think the probability of that happening in the next century is somewhere less than 1 percent," he said. One major obstacle, he says, is people's unwillingness to associate themselves with labels like "vegetarian" and "vegan," even if they have no objection to the (rather commonplace) foods most such self-identified people eat.

"It becomes more than a food choice. It becomes an expression of one's identity," Tetrick said. "It means whining. It means complaining. It means all sorts of, like, quinoa issues. It means you're annoying people. It means you're throwing blood on people. It's not a good look."

But however you feel about killing animals, the meat industry is just plain bad for the planet. Livestock animals generate more greenhouse gases than driving, according to a famous 2006 United Nations report. Cows, for instance, are powered by a process just as complicated as any factory, and with more exhaust fumes. That famous four-chambered stomach you've heard about is just the beginning. Cows only eat grass, and after initially chewing and swallowing all that tough, indigestible cellulose, they feed it to microbes called methanogens that live inside their digestive tracts. When those microbes feed on all that grass, they turn it into something you've no doubt heard of called "cud," a substance cows can much more readily eat, which is why they regurgitate it back into their mouths for a second chewing-and-swallowing session.

But when the methanogens inside cows digest grass, they produce methane. Cows and other ruminants (animals that chew regurgitated cud) produce about 37 percent of global methane emissions, and methane has twenty-five times the warming potential of carbon dioxide. So pastures laden with cattle may look nice and natural, but on a large enough scale (and 3.5 billion ruminants in the world is a pretty large scale), this is one giant grass-to-methane conversion operation, and it's warming the planet very quickly. The Union of Concerned Scientists also notes that cattle are the number one driver of deforestation.

So, as tired as you probably are of reading reports about this, it just keeps getting truer and truer: the end of animal agriculture will be a huge win for the environment. But that win won't come easily; even if the disproportionately damaging effects of raising beef cattle are eliminated, poultry and pork are still ecologically disastrous compared to vegetables, according to a 2011 study by the Environmental Working Group. To cite some examples from the study, a kilogram of turkey emits 10.9 kilograms of carbon dioxide over its "full life cycle," while a kilogram of broccoli emits 2 kilograms of carbon dioxide, and it just gets more damning from there. A kilogram of pork produces a whopping 12.1 kilograms of carbon dioxide, and a kilogram of lentils, only 0.9 kilograms.

But Big Meat isn't one big monolith. When it dies, the people who will lose their livelihoods aren't who you might think. What I'm referring to as "the meat industry" can roughly be divided into two industries with significant overlap. On one side you have Industry A, a handful of vast corporations, like Hormel in the US, JBS S.A. in Brazil, and WH Group in China, that trade in and market meat. You could sum up the way they make their profits as "converting animals into edible products and then selling them." On the other side is Industry B, which makes its profits by converting land and animal feed into animals, and selling those to Industry A. This makes Industry B a largely separate and far less profitable industry. Industry A, therefore, can get its raw materials from Industry B—or someone else if there's a better offer.

Slaughter may disappear, in other words, but according to Tetrick, "meat companies are going to be more critical to that happening than people would think," he told me.

See, right now, the "Story of Meat," if you will, starts in a grassy field, moves to a feedlot, then goes to a slaughterhouse, then a manufacturing facility, and then a store. The new story might go like this: Meat starts in a manufacturing facility where meat cells are grown and packaged, then goes to the store. The end. The finished meat product is theoretically the same, but the story has no death in it. PETA not only approves, but has been investing in this process for years.

JUST, Inc.'s sprawling, multistory San Francisco office and head-quarters contains a lab where—at least while I was visiting—chicken cells were being cultured by agitating Erlenmeyer flasks full of reddish liquid in the hope that the cells would eventually divide into the elusive death-free McNugget. According to JUST's press materials, the company's representatives traveled to a farm, purchased an exceptionally winsome hen, and extracted from her an exceptionally photogenic feather. JUST claims to have already processed from that feather a meal of actual chicken meat, enjoyed al fresco by JUST, Inc. staff as the chicken from whom the meat was derived scratched and clucked happily in the dirt next to their table.

And so began the process that Tetrick is confident will lead to one of the world's first marketable cultured meat products, a category of products I've also seen referred to as "in vitro meat," "lab grown meat," "clean meat," "test tube meat," "shmeat," "technomeat." When it gains acceptance, Tetrick claimed, we'll just call it meat. "I think you won't call it 'clean *blank*' or 'vegan *blank*.' You would just call it the thing." He compared it to a smartphone. "We don't say, 'I left my smartphone in my car.' We say, 'I left my phone in my car.'" And whatever it's called, 65.3 percent of US consumers say they'd definitely or probably try the stuff, according to a 2017 survey of US consumers conducted by the University of Queensland.

While that idea might eventually sit just fine with meat business juggernauts like Hormel, it's clearly not going to work for farmers, who have a vested interest in making sure the word "meat" remains synonymous with "dead animal." In February 2018, the US Cattlemen's Beef Association—the lobby that represents ranchers—declared war on cultured meat by filing a petition asking the US Department of Agriculture to "exclude products not derived directly from animals raised and slaughtered from the definition of 'beef' and 'meat.'"

But Tetrick seems to have allied himself with the Industry A side of Big Meat, and potentially against the ranchers. "I've spent a ton of time with the world's biggest meat companies," he told me. The meat industry and a vegan food company may be strange bedfellows, but according to Tetrick, they're both in "the business of selling animal protein, as opposed to being in the business of slaughtering animals."

In other words, companies like JUST, Inc. and its main competitor, Memphis Meats, seem to be positioning themselves to be the meat producers of the future. If they can generate meat in high enough volumes at low enough prices, they can deliver it to companies like Hormel, where it can be processed into anything the firm wants, from hot dogs to sliced ham. Hell, if it's cheap, they can even mix it with actual, slaughtered meat if they feel like it. If the dollars and cents work out for the buyer and seller, who cares?

Well, consumers might care. Cultured meat cells emerge from labs as strands of muscle fiber, arranged into pinkish lumps, which have, through sheer culinary wizardry, occasionally been fashioned into shapes resembling food items. The present configuration will probably suit many consumers just fine as long as the dish calls for lean, ground-up meat, but fat still has to be added during cooking—for now, anyway. In 2018, Tyson Foods invested $2.2 million in an Israeli biotechnology firm called Future Meat Technologies, which says it's developing cultured animal fat in addition to muscle, so with any luck, we'll one day be able to eat cultured meat that doesn't taste like it comes from animals that starved to death.

And in time, cultured meat lumps will have to be arranged into objects that look like they came from a butcher shop, assuming cultured meat is ever going to pass for anything close to a "steak." As of this writing, lab-grown meat hadn't yet been made into a plausible can of Spam, which means descriptors like "gamey" or "grass-fed" or "marbled" are still light-years off. And even if cultured beef becomes tasty enough to pass a double-blind taste test, if the finished product is being sluiced from a dispenser, rather than carved like a Sunday roast, some consumers will still reject it.

But one can probably focus too much on "meat labs." As I recall, when this concept started being publicized in about 2006, news reports about cultured meat still usually featured newscasters scrunching up their faces and asking if viewers would eat "meat grown in a lab." But consumer-grade cultured meat won't come from a lab. Like most industrially produced foods, there'll be a lab phase, and then the product will start to originate in factories, and then be sold to other factories for processing—not much different, really, from the way we get our slaughtered meat today.

Here's another way cultured meat is no different: You know the old-timey farm imagery printed on the food you're buying today—grassy fields, barns, and lovable farmers—none of which have anything to do with the rasher of bacon in your hand? Expect lab-grown meat to use the same imagery. At least, *some* of these items will be stealthily packaged by familiar meat companies, and given innocuous names like "Farmer John's Sunshine Sausages." This stuff won't be marketed as "lab-grown." Instead it'll be awarded some comforting, agreeable product label, like "mercy meat," or it'll come with a "certified slaughter-free" sticker. And just as with existing meat products, as long as the stuff tastes good, consumers probably won't spend too much time agonizing over how it got in the package.

And while adopting a new process sounds more expensive for meat companies than just maintaining the status quo, it's worth noting that mollifying ambivalent omnivores is getting expensive, too. In 2017, for example, McDonald's announced that its chicken suppliers would have to phase out the industry-standard process for killing birds: stunning them with electricity, shackling their feet to an upside-down conveyor system while they're still alive, and then slitting their throats just before butchering them. Now soon-to-be McNuggets have to be enclosed in a gas chamber full of inert gases for several minutes until they lose consciousness and die, and only then can they be butchered and nuggetized. Converting to a new system like this costs a facility $3 million, according to the *New York Times*, and comes with additional maintenance costs, and it obviously slows down the killing floor, reducing productivity.

Ginormous-scale operations like McDonald's, which stereotypically show no interest whatsoever in animal rights, are getting curious about cultured meat at a faster rate than you might think. Ahead of the 2018 Sino-American trade war—which saw tariffs in China on US beef—the Chinese and Israeli governments struck a $300 million trade deal to bring Israel's cultured meat technology to China as soon as it becomes available, according to the *Times of Israel*.

So assuming slaughterhouses spend eons on the slow conveyor belt that leads to their own eventual bolt to the brain, when the big day finally comes, we've firmly established that fewer animals will die, but what effect will that have on people—apart from needing to breed domesticated cows, pigs, and chickens in zoos so that those original animals won't just go extinct?

For starters, the transition will have slowly put millions of ranchers and farmers out of business. According to the National Cattlemen's Beef Association, there are 662,394 small, family-owned beef farming operations in the US, averaging forty heads of cattle each. So that's one part of the American meat industry that more or less conforms to the myth—yes, American beef financially supports a lot of ranchers who favor horses and cowboy hats.

While that's fewer than a million operations, the degree to which their closure would transform the landscape of the US "flyover states" is impossible to overstate, because when you look out the window on a flight from New York to Los Angeles, what you're seeing below you *is* the cattle industry. This isn't an exaggeration. According to a 2018 Bloomberg survey of land use in the US, pasture and rangeland takes up 264,664,410 hectares—that's an area slightly larger than Mexico. In other words, ranching, combined with ranching-adjacent uses of land like animal feed farming, accounts for 41 percent of land in the contiguous states.

But I'm not convinced the global closure of all slaughterhouses would change much for the majority of livestock farmers around the world. Globally, most of the individuals who raise animals are among the world's two billion subsistence farmers, who by definition raise their livestock for personal use, and even when those animals are slaughtered, they never see the inside of an actual slaughterhouse. (That said, some of these farmers also generate supplemental income by raising extra animals, so they would subsequently lose that revenue stream.)

Still, the decline of large-scale animal agriculture will inflict extra economic pain, because just taking meat out of the equation still doesn't remove the animal by-products from seemingly animal-free areas of the economy.

After all, we humans do *a lot* more with dead animals than eat them.

As Michael Pollan famously wrote in *The Omnivore's Dilemma*, a policy of vegetarianism for all has downsides for vegetable-lovers, because "it is doubtful you can build a genuinely sustainable agriculture without animals to cycle nutrients and support local food production." He's referring, of course, to the manure we derive from cows that are destined for slaughter. Ironically, ceasing the slaughter of cows would leave us with a whole lot less food for our plants. We *can* replace manure with a mix of synthetic nitrogen fertilizer and human feces (also known as "night soil.") That process isn't unheard of, but it comes with ecological and safety risks. Recycling our own, ahem, contaminants and putting our waste anywhere near our food is such a basic civilization no-no it comes with its own idiom: "Never shit where you eat."

But the shift away from slaughter would also disrupt the supply of rendered by-products, which are scattered across seemingly every industry in the world. Since only a little more than half of an animal is of any use to the meat industry, the rendering industry takes the rest—about twenty-seven billion kilograms of spare animal parts per year, according to the National Renderers Association. Rendering plants take in mountains of revolting animal carcasses, and process them into slightly less revolting usable products. Some, such as tallow, are edible, but many are industrial products like glycerin—which is in many soaps and cosmetics—and the ubiquitous lubricant stearic acid, which is also in cosmetics, and countless factory processes. (Stearic acid is found in just about everything produced through modern manufacturing, from laptops to plastic bags, so if you're such a hardcore vegan that you really plan to live without even the *by-products* of the meat industry, I hope you enjoy making your own textiles and living off gathered berries.)

Losing the existing animal agriculture system means commodities like fertilizer or stearic acid will vanish or become hard to acquire. But the world doesn't end when something like this happens. Whaling by-products all vanished when the commercial whaling industry was shut down in the 1980s, and in more contemporary economies, a widespread recall of some commodity, or the depletion of a mine, or a stoppage of production can interrupt a supply chain as well.

We always manage to get through it.

Some of the by-products of animal death can absolutely be replaced with synthetic or plant-based alternatives, but not all can. Reliable synthetic collagen, for instance, was only invented in 2011 and is still in the iffy stages of development; collagen is vital for applications like organic heart valves. The process of developing mass-produced collagen would have to shift into overdrive. Longer-lasting (synthetic) replacement heart valves can be manufactured without collagen, but they don't perform as well as pig valves. Cardiac patients, cut off from a fresh supply of pig hearts, might start hunting wild boars to steal their heart valves.

Without animal collagen we would have to somehow replace one of the most versatile materials in the world: leather. Leather is mostly just animal collagen, and it's everywhere—not just belts, shoes, wallets, and handbags; have you looked at the grips on the tools in your toolbox? They're most likely animal skin. Have you ever wondered what that cheap vinyl-type stuff labeled "bonded leather" is? That's real animal skin, too. Plasticky patent leather? Yes, that's real animal skin. Dime-store watchbands with that dubious "genuine leather" tag? Pig leather. So thanks to the food industry, leather is cheap, cheap stuff. That will change drastically when slaughterhouses are all gone.

Then again, maybe by-products like leather and collagen don't have to be chemically synthesized at all. Maybe they can be cultured like meat. In 2017, a company called Modern Meadow announced that they'd begun to "biofabricate" leather in a lab by culturing a specific strain of engineered yeast that produces a film of collagen. They call their product "Zoa." The Zoa website claims the product is "able to be any density. Hold to any mold. Create any shape. Take on any texture. Combine with any other material. Be any size, seamlessly. A liquid. A solid." Offhand, I don't know why I would want my leather to be a liquid, but maybe that's so it can be molded into the shape of a heart valve.

If a Zoa leather belt sounds like an exciting novelty, I've got more good news for adventurous people like you: the era of cultured meat will usher in an age of genuinely exciting—if slightly macabre—culinary experimentation. I'm talking, of course, about eating the sort of char-ismatic animals we normally object to because we're uncomfortable slaughtering them. Returning to that University of Queensland survey, none of the respondents were willing to eat slaughtered horse meat, but 5 percent were willing to eat horse if *it came from a lab*. Three percent were willing to eat cultured dog or cat meat. (Only one respondent was willing to eat slaughtered dog or cat.)

But lab-grown cells unlock our ability to guiltlessly devour animals most people have never dreamed of tasting—opening the door to flavors and textures we never knew we craved. Maybe panda liver is more delicate and juicy than the finest foie gras. Maybe filets of spider monkey have been crying out to be made into Reuben sandwiches. Since it's taboo to slaughter these animals, we won't know what recipes to try until culinary geneticists start culturing their meats in their labs and hand them over to molecular gastronomists.

But as long as we're breaking taboos, why stop at endangered species? If the reaction to the guy who, in 2016, invited his friends over to have tacos made of his own amputated leg was any indication, there's a market for slaughter-free cannibalism as well. A Dutch infotainment website called Bistro In Vitro jokingly proposes serving cultured celebrity meat. But joke or not, I don't mind telling you, I'd absolutely try cultured meat made from human cells if it were available.

But here's a puzzling piece of trivia about the end of slaughter: American vegans and vegetarians, according to the University of Queensland study, are more aware of the benefits of cultured meat, but somewhat puzzlingly, are also less interested than any other category in the survey in tasting cultured meat when it becomes available. Maybe those respondents were just assuming a posture of superiority and plant-based purity. But then again, maybe it's because once meat is truly in your rearview mirror, it loses its appeal.

But if you're one of the people who, for whatever reason, considers synthesized meat cells to be a nonstarter, I still wouldn't worry too much about the slaughter-free future. First of all, you're probably more of a vegetarian than you think you are, which will help make the switch feasible. Americans—famous for our prodigious meat consumption—only get about 30 percent of our calories from animals. Compare that to the 36 percent of food calories currently produced by farmers that go directly into animals' stomachs. That means that, calorie-wise, we're most likely already producing more than enough plants to make up for the loss of food animals—and that's if you assume that synthetic meat never makes it to market.

So it could happen and it should happen. But a decision by everyone in the world to cease the slaughter of animals is one of the *least* plausible scenarios I've worked with. That's simply because in spite of it all, *we just don't wanna.*

THE DAY HUMANS GET A CONFIRMED SIGNAL FROM INTELLIGENT EXTRATERRESTRIALS

Likely in this century? > *Maybe*

Plausibility Rating > *4/5*

Scary? > *Only if they're scary extraterrestrials, but that's possible*

Worth changing habits? > *No*

ThomasLuvr69 @RachelRogan1998 · Jun 28

Yes. I admit I'm sexually attracted to Thomas the Tank Engine, but I would never act on it because I'm in a committed relationship with Lightning McQueen

💬   ⟲ 1   ♡ 1   ᵢₗ

The AP ✓ @AP · Jun 28

BREAKING: Team of scientists confirms a signal detected earlier this month is extraterrestrial in origin, proof of alien life

💬 14K   ⟲ 9.2K   ♡ 10K   ᵢₗ

Jasonnnnnn @JasonJWurster · Jun 28

@NYTimes, carrots do not EVER belong in quacamole. I can't believe I'm even typing these words

💬   ⟲   ♡   ᵢₗ

Leon S. @LeonSchwarts · Jun 28

Wait, Seriously?

> **The AP** ✓ @AP · Jun 28
>
> BREAKING: Team of scientists confirms a signal detected earlier this month is extraterrestrial in origin, proof of alien life

💬 14   ⟲ 1   ♡ 7   ᵢₗ

The New York Times ✓ @nytmes · Jun 28

Peer-reviewed paper calls signal from 13,000 light years away comes from an "intelligent extraterrestrial species," and says findings meet "any reasonable standard for certainty"

💬 8K   ⟲ 12.4K   ♡ 14K   ᵢₗ

Heatherly @HeatherDaly21 · Jun 28

Is the real life?

> **The AP** ✓ @AP · Jun 28
>
> BREAKING: Team of scientists confirms a signal detected earlier this month is extraterrestrial in origin, proof of alien life

💬   ⟲   ♡   ᵢₗ

Neil deGrasse Tyson ✓ @neiltyson · Jun 28

Quite possibly the biggest story of my lifetime. Maybe anyone's lifetime

> **The AP** ✓ @AP · Jun 28
>
> BREAKING: Team of scientists confirms a signal detected earlier this month is extraterrestrial in origin, proof of alien life

💬 8K   ⟲ 2K   ♡ 6K   ᵢₗ

BBC Breaking News ✓ @BBCNews · Jun 28

Intelligent extraterrestrials: Where are they? How do we know? And what's next?

> **First Contact**
>
> Everything we know so far about the discovery of aliens 13,000 lightyears away

💬 11K   ⟲ 1.5K   ♡ 7K   ᵢₗ

CNN ✓ @CNN · Jun 28

Meet Kathryn Anderson, the UC Berkeley astronomer who made today's discovery thanks to the radio telescopes at the Arecibo Observatory in Puerto Rico

💬 5K   ⟲ 9.2K   ♡ 10K   ᵢₗ

The Battle Info News Network @BattleInfoNews · Jun 28

BREAKING: Globalist news provides so-called "proof" of alien life to distract from leftist push for gun control, possible marshal law situation. Story developing...

💬 644   ⟲ 967   ♡ 1K   ᵢₗ

Leon S. @LeonSchwartz · Jun 28

Should we be building a giant space laser? I mean… The aliens might want to kill us, right?

💬 1   🔁 2   ♡ 10   ᵢₗᵢ

Kat JK Anderson, Ph.D. @KathrynJKAnderson · Jun 28

Just to be clear: We at Berkeley believe this was not a communications signal. As our paper says, this signal was almost certainly produced accidentally by some large and powerful piece of alien technology

💬 7K   🔁 11.2K   ♡ 19K   ᵢₗᵢ

Annie @TheAnnie_Gray · Jun 28

So about this "large and powerful piece of alien technology"... precisely how soon should I expect it to melt my face off?

💬 1   🔁   ♡ 3   ᵢₗᵢ

Jeffffff @JeffMartin8850 · Jun 28

Have we notified the aliens that we have nukes? I don't want them invading, thinking they can get the upper hand. I'm serious. We have to move fast here. #GalacticShowOfForce

💬   🔁   ♡ 1   ᵢₗᵢ

Casey Swain @CaseySwainLester · Jun 28

Bye guys. Off to OGLE-2016-BLG-1195Lb to become the human emissary to our alien overlords. Enjoy being enslaved in the zinc mines of Earth

💬   🔁   ♡   ᵢₗᵢ

Sarah tweets @sarahcruddas · Jun 28

Seeing a lot of misconceptions about today's big news:

-Alien signal was not a deliberate "hello"

-We probably will never decipher it

-13,000 light years is FAR

💬 455   🔁 1.3K   ♡ 3K   ᵢₗᵢ

Frank 🏴 @FrankHatesFakeNews · Jun 28

@KathrynJKAnderson so I'm just supposed to believe this "announcement" without you presenting your evidence? Nice try 🌚

💬 2   🔁 9   ♡ 22   ᵢₗᵢ

NASA ✓ @NASA· Jun 28

An introduction to OGLE-2016-BLG-1195Lb, the only known star (apart from the sun) known to foster intelligent lifeforms

> **A New Dawn**
> Meet our new neighbors, the creatures of the OGLE-2016-BLG-1195Lb solar system

💬 1.2K   🔁 2.4K   ♡ 8.3K   ᵢₗᵢ

Leon S. @LeonSchwartz · Jun 28

So if I'm reading these stories the signal was sent about 13,000 years ago, so that makes these literally:

ANCIENT. FUCKING. ALIENS.

💬 14   🔁 115   ♡ 223   ᵢₗᵢ

Kat JK Anderson, Ph.D. @KathrynJKAnderson · Jun 28

@FrankHatesFakeNews, actually, my colleagues and I included all of our findings in our paper. And our colleagues at ASU posted a sister paper explaining the review process. Feel free to perform your own review if you'd like

💬 234　🔁 101　♡ 503　📊

JJ Wurster @JasonJWurster · Jun 28

Heads up: if you're headed to the supermarket today, the hoarders are out in full force. I can't imagine the scene at the gun stores…

💬 3　🔁 9　♡ 10　📊

Frank 🏴 @FrankHatesFakeNews · Jun 28

@KathrynJKAnderson, Right. I'm sure you worked just as hard on your little paper as you did on your latest grant proposal 🌝

💬 4　🔁　♡ 7　📊

Elon Musk ✓ @ElonMusk· Jun 28

Glad I invested in a 2500 kilowatt radio transmitter! I'll be broadcasting a 1420 megahertz signal to the OGLE-2016-BLG-1195Lb solar system later today. Watch live as I say "wubba lubba dub dub" to our new alien friends!

💬 14K　🔁 9.2K　♡ 10K　📊

Sarah tweets @sarahcruddas · Jun 28

A few more points of clarity about these findings:

-There's no "alien audio"

-It's a series of elecromagnetic pulses in patterns akin to a coding language

-No we can't translate unless you have the Alien Rosetta Stone handy

💬 141　🔁 233　♡ 982　📊

La Luke @LucasTReines · Jun 28

@FoxNews It's not an "assertion." We're not alone. It's a fact now. Not that you know anything about "facts"

💬　🔁　♡　📊

GlenS @GlenSalsbury · Jun 28

@sarahcuddas Any idea how the signal was sent? What technology was used? cc: @KathrynJKAnderson

💬 33　🔁 29　♡ 103　📊

Kat JK Anderson, Ph.D. @KathrynJKAnderson · Jun 28

@FrankHatesFakeNews, I'm so sorry that you only see the world—excuse me, WORLDS, plural—through a lens of avaricious self-interest. I feel sorry for you!

💬 199　🔁 348　♡ 633　📊

Sarah tweets @sarahcruddas · Jun 28

@GlenSalsbury, Unfortunately not so far. We may never know. No decipherable information in the signal.

💬 74　🔁 9　♡ 109　📊

Kat JK Anderson, Ph.D. @KathrynJKAnderson · Jun 28

@GlenSalsbury, We've made all the data available, but like @sarahcruddas said, we might never know anything about the device that sent it. Just that it uses something like computer code.

💬 32　🔁 92　♡ 138　📊

Katie Mack @AstroKatie · Jun 28

@ElonMusk, NOOOOOOOO! Please don't do that. We Earthlings need to be very careful and democratic with our next steps

💬 122　🔁 77　♡ 430　📊

The Guardian ✓ @guardian · Jun 28

BREAKING: At least 300 dead on religious compound outside Okayama, Japan. Authorities say mass suicide "likely" but investigation is ongoing.

💬1.3K　🔁3.2K　♡ 13K　📊

GlenS @GlenSalsbury · Jun 28

@sarahcruddas, So... we can never go there, and we can never know what's in the signal, and we have no idea what they are, or if they know we're here?

💬 1   ♺ 2   ♡ 7   �᠁ᴵ

AFP news agency ✔ @AFP · Jun 28

International Astronomical Union Sends Urgent Appeal to Elon Musk: "Please immediately abort your effort to contact these beings. Our survival as a species may depend on it."

💬 331   ♺ 292   ♡ 1.2K   ᠁ᴵ

Sarah tweets @sarahcruddas · Jun 28

@GlenSalsbury, that's about right, yes.

💬 23   ♺ 12   ♡ 93   ᠁ᴵ

Elon Musk ✔ @ElonMusk · Jun 28

A lot of people seem worried about me sending a signal to the aliens. Grow up! It won't get there for 30,000 years. Besides, I already sent a test pattern. Whoops! LOL

💬 801   ♺ 452   ♡ 1.3K   ᠁ᴵ

Kat JK Anderson, Ph.D. @KathrynJKAnderson · Jun 28

Again, I agree with @sarahcruddas, except it looks like they'll know we're here in 13,000 (not 30,000) years thanks to @ElonMusk. I hope they're friendly!

💬 66   ♺ 98   ♡ 209   ᠁ᴵ

🐦

Back to top ↑

Funnily enough, contact with intelligent extraterrestrials is one of the most plausible topics in this book. It used to make people sound unhinged if they said they believed in space aliens, but these days it's not risky at all to go out on that limb.

Probabilistically speaking, it's pretty insane to believe that there *aren't* aliens. One in six stars, according to NASA, has a planet the size of Earth orbiting it. And okay, not all planets have water, magnetic fields, atmospheres, or pleasant temperatures—let alone all of the above—but in his analysis of a 2016 Princeton study looking at the habitability of known planets outside our solar system, Eric Berger, a space journalist for *Ars Technica*, found that there were probably tens of billions of habitable planets.

The more we learn about the universe, the higher this number gets. For instance, in the months after that Princeton study, another 2016 paper, this time from physicists at the United Kingdom's University of Nottingham, used a few known data points like the number of known galaxies and the age of the universe to figure out the total number of galaxies, "as a function of time and mass limit," and concluded that there are about two trillion—ten times the previous estimate.

So a reasonable updated estimate might show that there are actually *hundreds* of billions of habitable planets, but let's be conservative and say there are one hundred billion habitable planets. (For reference, if we assume 120 grains of rice together have a mass of ten grams, there are then 120,000 grains of rice in a ten-kilogram sack. If each grain of rice were a habitable planet, you would have to individually inspect every grain of rice in 833,333 sacks to determine conclusively that we're alone in the universe.) My point being: there are probably aliens.

Keep in mind, though, that space is really enormous. There's one potentially habitable exoplanet practically in our backyard, orbiting around Proxima Centauri, "just" four light-years away. But aliens from Proxima Centauri would have to travel at the speed of light for four years just to abduct one of our planet's isolated farmers and perform experiments on them, which hardly seems worth the trouble. The next closest potentially habitable exoplanets are orbiting around Tau Ceti, twelve light-years away. In short order, the distances—and accompanying travel times—become immense. If they weren't from our Milky Way galaxy, that would mean they'd have to travel at the speed of light for 2.537 million years minimum just to get here from Andromeda. If they were from most galaxies, they would have to travel for billions of years or more.

Distance aside, as you've probably noticed if you ever watch daytime television, people can, and do, talk in extremely serious tones about aliens, often referencing "Search for Extraterrestrial Intelligence" (SETI) research. For instance, Chris Impey is a British astronomer based at the University of Arizona whose primary research is about cosmology, yet he still finds himself roped into SETI. He finds the topic a little too short on results for full-time study, and speculates that it "wouldn't sustain me through a career." But even though SETI research is "a low-probability side bet," according to Impey, "the implication of succeeding in this a priori, very low odds experiment make it worth doing."

I sought out Impey because compared to people who dedicate their lives to SETI research, he's, well, a bit of a bummer, and it seems to me that when a very exciting signal comes in from what seems like an intelligent alien species, the full-time SETI people might need their enthusiasm taken down a peg. Impey feels this way as well. "When people—radio astronomers, say—see something that, to an average one of them looks pretty emphatically like an artificial signal, it is still going to be true that the two most likely explanations for it are that it's something that the universe does naturally—that we haven't predicted or understood—or that it's fake," he said.

Dan Werthimer, the director of the University of California, Berkeley, SETI program, is one of these radio astronomers, who—despite staying fully grounded in the realm of the rational—will happily recommend science fiction novels to illustrate a point. He explained to me that while we might find primitive life forms—organic slime stuck to a rock, maybe—in the next few years, "if we're going to detect advanced life, we have to find [it] from technology."

Our current tools for seeking out alien communications are pretty much what you'll see in the book or movie *Contact*: arrays of giant radio telescopes like those at the Arecibo Observatory in Puerto Rico. The telescopes in this case are essentially big antennas capable of monitoring billions of frequencies at once, and they can either scan the sky bit by bit, or be aimed at a particularly interesting corner of the galaxy. In 2017, when astronomers discovered TRAPPIST-1, a star with seven potentially habitable planets, Werthimer and his team took notice. Though they've done targeted searches of this newly discovered solar system, they haven't found anything yet, he told me.

Precisely what we're looking for is not clear. In the end, radio "may be a little too anthropocentric," Werthimer said, because "some civilizations might be a billion or two billion years ahead of us." We're operating based on what we know: signals that travel at the speed of light; but what ultimately gets beamed to Earth might bear no relationship to our communications technology. "We know there's physics that we don't understand," Werthimer said. "We have no clue what dark matter is, [or] what dark energy is. So maybe there's something even better than electromagnetic communication."

Whatever it is, for the time being, to get our attention, it'll have to either show up as visible light or give off signals that get picked up by radio, and it'll have to be so unprecedented, and so unambiguously artificial, that it can't possibly be anything but aliens. Werthimer told me that the normal rules of science apply to a SETI discovery: peer review. "Reviewers come back, and say 'Oh, you didn't understand this,' or 'You didn't understand that,' or 'What you got is bogus.' Or they might say, 'It's great. Publish it.'" Then again, he told me, "We might skip over those steps—because that takes a long time—if we're very confident." ("I don't think that's how it's going to happen," Impey told me, "because the egg-on-your-face of being wrong is too great and the stakes are too high.")

Indeed, if it's Berkeley's SETI department that lands the big discovery—and it's reasonable to assume that it may be, since it's on the large side with no fewer than eighteen scientists and an army of volunteers numbering in the millions—there's an established set of nine protocols to follow. The first two are about submitting the evidence for a thorough peer review. This means that all the scientists involved might discover what they're pretty sure are intelligent aliens, write about them, and then twiddle their thumbs and wait for the information to be published in a journal, and hope it doesn't leak. Then, once the discovery is determined to be ready for prime time, things would escalate quickly.

According to protocol three, the discoverers must next send their findings to the International Astronomical Union and a bunch of similar organizations, and also "inform the Secretary General of the United Nations in accordance with Article XI of the Treaty on Principles Governing the Activities of States in the Exploration and Use of Outer Space." Then it's time to alert the media. If it's Berkeley, Werthimer predicted that the press release would be written by one particular person: Robert Sanders, a science journalist.

Logically, the next step is a press conference, and according to Berkeley's list of protocols, the discoverer gets to appear on TV. If you don't already have a sense of what press conferences in the science world are like, the phrase that leaps to mind is "pulse-deadening." In 2014, when the European Space Agency landed a probe on an asteroid—a groundbreaking achievement—the announcement was completely overshadowed by a particularly garish shirt worn by the mission's head scientist, Matt Smith. The shirt was covered in illustrations of scantily clad women, which, yes, made the faux pas a newsworthy act of tone deafness at best, or misogyny at worst, but should that have really been more newsworthy than the landing itself?

More likely, the cable news reports will be livelier, and according to Impey, that's where things might just slide off the rails. "What's going to be hugely fun as a scientist or an astronomer having spawned this, is just to watch the world go batshit over it for a while," he told me.

"Even though we're joking, that actually is a significant concern," Impey said. "It's possible that just the frenzy and the turmoil, and the ferment that results in the popular culture, will actually lead to some world-changing events." He added that "our tribal world culture is fairly unstable already, and this will just be another destabilizing element coming out of science, which we sort of don't need."

Then again, people might be pretty reasonable about the discovery of aliens. In 2018, psychologist Michael Varnum and his team at Arizona State University asked 501 people to predict their reaction to the announcement of aliens, as well as the reaction of humanity as a whole, and then Varnum performed a mathematical breakdown of the emotional content of what the subjects wrote, based on affect. The paper accompanying the study says that, overwhelmingly, "people believe that they will react positively to the discovery of extraterrestrial microbial life and that humanity as a whole will do the same," although it notes that "people anticipate that their own reactions would be more positive than those of humanity as a whole."

And they'd be right to not freak out. According to both Werthimer and Impey, the whole thing would get old pretty fast, because actual interactions with the aliens will almost certainly be off the table.

If a signal came from, say, the TRAPPIST-1 solar system, that would be pretty close to a best-case scenario in terms of communication. "Radio waves or light waves can get there in seventy years," Werthimer told me. That means, he said, "you could send messages, but you'd be dead when you get the message back."

"There's no immediacy to any of this," according to Impey. Most likely the signal would be "already centuries-old by the time you received it." If we actually wanted to send a reply, it would involve transmitting our message across hundreds, or thousands, or hundreds of thousands of light-years, meaning we'd be engaging in what Impey called a "millennia-long conversation" in which generation after generation would wait for a reply. "So that sort of takes some of the heat and excitement out of the discovery," he said.

It's conceivable that there could be some readable content in the signal. "If it's intended for us, I think they would make it cryptographic with lots of pictures and language lessons. And then I think earthlings could be pretty confident that we've intercepted a deliberate signal," Werthimer ventured. This might take the form of "prime numbers or a Fibonacci sequence, or something like that."

Or, Werthimer said, the signal might just be "information that we know is artificially generated by some kind of technology," but something that "wasn't really intended for us." This may take the form of waves or photons given off by some unknown piece of space infrastructure. This sort of idea sent imaginations soaring in 2015 when the Kepler Space Telescope detected a seemingly unexplainable dimming effect that was *thought*, for a time, to be caused by a distant star, perhaps one shrouded by a giant, energy-capturing megastructure. When I say "thought," I mean, mostly in the fevered imaginations of sci-fi fans. The idea was later debunked, but if an alien society is millions or billions of years ahead of us in terms of development, they might be capable of building immense things that, for all we know, might accidentally result in light discrepancies or radio waves that reach Earth.

It's conceivable that we might be able to definitively prove that such a signal came from aliens, Werthimer said, "but we can't decode it."

By the end of the first day, humanity could very well have gone from elated to deflated. Impey told me to imagine that I'm a European in the Dark Ages, and some piece of evidence washes up on a beach proving that there's another advanced civilization on another continent, but in Europe everyone is still learning to grow carrots so they won't starve. This other land, he said, becomes "this huge continent of unknown possibility and unknown creatures and resources and so on, but it's not like you would know how to build a ship and go there." That civilization, he said, "very quickly just becomes this little abstract factoid you hold in your head because it doesn't have any use."

The first seven protocols mostly consist of confirming the signal's extraterrestrial origin, and distributing the news of its existence to the world in an orderly, rational, and hopefully fair manner. That brings us to Berkeley's eighth protocol: "No response to a signal or other evidence of extraterrestrial intelligence should be sent until appropriate international consultations have taken place. The procedures for such consultations will be the subject of a separate agreement, declaration or arrangement."

The trouble with responding is, quite simply, that the aliens might murder us if they found out we were here. By telling them we exist, we'd also be telling them we have the resources necessary to foster life, and they might reasonably want something of ours—be it water, air, or the minerals in our spinal fluid. "I think they might think of us kind of like ants," Werthimer told me. "When ants are in our way, we kill them. And so I can imagine civilizations a billion years ahead of us, [and] if they want something on our planet, they can just grind it up and not think much about whether we're intelligent or not."

But of course, sending the aliens a reply without international consensus is not illegal, nor is it a violation of any international treaty. Weak signals are pretty easy to shoot into space, and an individual with enough money to build a powerful transmitter could, without any real consequences, invite the aliens to come and eat us for breakfast. There probably *should* be some international laws about this, but there aren't.

"I think that this, right now, would be the time to start thinking about these consequences and get international bodies to work together," Werthimer told me. "It could actually bring countries together to think about these kinds of big problems that might confront us."

THE DAY THE NEXT SUPERVOLCANO ERUPTS

VOLCANIC THUNDERSTORM.

Likely in this century? > *No*

Plausibility Rating > *5/5*

Scary? > *Very*

Worth changing habits? > *Building giant, national food vaults is probably something we should think about*

You're in Billings, Montana, about two hundred kilometers from the north entrance of Yellowstone National Park. Eighty-eight years, seven months, and six days since the last Yellowstone eruption. From the rickety balcony on the second floor at Harry's Cabin in Bill- ings, you can see the sign they installed on the tenth anniversary of the eruption: "Welcome to Billings: Yep, it's still here!" And behind that, you can see the cone of ash.

The evacuation order came a few weeks ago when the earthquakes started.

Then there were several explosions, but like just about everyone else in Billings, you took it as a good sign that there was never the one "big boom" that you assumed would signal a supervolcano eruption. But now you're starting to worry. Is this ash ever going to stop?

With your ears still ringing from those last explosions yesterday, you ask your friend Harry to tell you the story of the other eruption one more time. He's pushing one hundred years old, and he loves to tell stories.

"The last eruption was just like this one," he says, "and I'll be damned if I'm leaving because the feds say so."

He tells you again about that cold night in January eighty-eight years ago, when there was that explosion near Canyon Village over in Wyoming. "All those rich folks in Jackson Hole evacuated their ski lodges. Hell, people in Los Angeles took off south of the border into Mexico. Idiots."

The ash came down, a few centimeters deep, all over Billings, Harry tells you. Then came the "basalt," they called it. Red and black lava that started leaking out, and just didn't stop. Everyone knows about the basalt flow. It lasted for eight years. It destroyed forests, wiped out towns, but in slow motion. Never made it to Billings. "Billings will still be here in a thousand years," Harry says. "Relax."

You step out onto the balcony again, with a handkerchief over your face, and sneak another peak, but to your surprise, you step down into a layer of ash as deep as your foot, like a layer of freshly fallen snow. It's 10 a.m., but the sky is dark. The ash is really starting to come down, covering the ground in a thick layer, filling your field of vision like a hot blizzard. And judging from all the cars, it looks like no one's evacuating.

The wood from the balcony creaks eerily. Is that your weight doing that, or is the ash out here getting heavy?

"How long did it go on last time?" you ask Harry.

"Just until morning," he says. "Your beer's getting warm," he adds with a laugh. "Drink up." The creaking from the balcony sounds like it's everywhere.

"It's been almost a day, though," you say. "And it doesn't look like it's letting up. You saw the news: that whole family in Big Springs over in Idaho died from breathing the ash."

"You tryin' to scare me, too?" Harry asks, still managing to laugh over the intensifying creaks of some seriously stressed-out wood. "This'll pass. They always pass."

Harry cracks open one more Miller High Life, but he doesn't get to take a sip. You feel the roof come down on you first, then you hear the sound of the cave-in, a hundred wood planks all snapping at once, like a fireworks show. And then, for a second, you're blind and deaf as all that ash fills your senses. The whole world is ash. You gasp, and the ash fills your lungs. It stings. You try to cough and it's more of a sputtering choke. You catch your breath, and then wipe your face with your hand, then your sleeve, but neither works. You try wiping it away with your shirt collar, and that does the trick. You can see light. You keep your shirt pulled up. It's your gas mask now.

"Harry, you okay?" you sputter, grasping in the dark.

You find him. He got the worst of the roof collapse. A beam landed on his shoulder and pushed him to the floor. "Harry, you alive?" you ask, but he doesn't respond. His chest is still moving up and down.

You know help's not coming. A tow truck can't get through this mess. But you also know St. Vincent Hospital is down the hill sloping behind you. You tie your handkerchief around your face and wrap your jacket around Harry's whole head. "What are you doing?" he asks, as you pick him up—all ninety pounds of him—and drape him across your shoulders.

After an eternity of walking, snow-blind through the ash—*ashblind* you think—you make it. "We're here," you say to Harry. But he's not responding anymore.

You finally notice the flashing lights and sirens from multiple emergency vehicles. And then you get close enough to the building to see why there are so many: St. Vincent is a pile of rubble. You're close enough to a firefighter to see his face through the protective glass of his face mask.

He just shakes his head. You know what he means.

You lower Harry to the ground, and sit down. Through a break in the cloud of ash, you get a look at the woods: no more leaves or bark. Just sticks. Beyond that, you see something even worse: no more Billings, either.

◆

When you think of Yellowstone National Park, "supervolcano" proba-bly isn't the first thing that comes to mind. Bison and geysers, sure. Massive seismic things that spew lava and ash? Not so much.

It perhaps goes without saying that the terms we use for supervol-canoes can be confusing. You might be surprised, first of all, to learn that there's a giant network of pressurized magma chambers underneath Yellowstone, a wonderland of geothermal oddities northwest of the Great Plains of the United States, let alone that those magma chambers are capable of turning into a volcanic cataclysm beyond measure. Some reports about the volcano, termed the Yellowstone Caldera, skip the word "volcano" and use "hotspot" in its place. Similarly, a better word than "eruption" might be "ashpocalypse."

Whatever you want to call it—the Yellowstone Caldera, Yellowstone Hotspot, or Yellowstone Supervolcano—this thing is really colossally huge. There's something called a Volcano Explosivity Index (VEI), and anything, including the Yellowstone Caldera, that rates an 8/8—meaning it's known to be capable of expelling more than one thousand cubic kilometers in deposits—is considered a supervolcano.

But that doesn't really tell you all that much, so let's compare it to other volcanoes.

Remember the 2010 eruption of one such mountain with a crater on top: Eyjafjallajökull, an Icelandic volcano that grounded planes for the better part of a week? That's not even close to Yellowstone's capacity. They might have taught you in school about the 1883 eruption of Krakatoa, located in what is now known as Indonesia—famously, the loudest sound ever documented (multiple sounds, actually, because it involved multiple explosions). The story goes that Krakatoa deafened people as far away as sixteen kilometers. Kid stuff compared to Yellowstone.

Instead, let me draw your attention to the even larger Mount Tambora, which is also in Indonesia. That went off in 1815, and spewed so much sky-darkening ash and sulphates that a persistent veil hung in the stratosphere for over a year, cooling the entire world and causing food shortages as far away as the United States. Legend has it that the skies were so dark in the months following the Tambora eruption that the ensuing global gloom prompted Mary Shelley to sit inside and write *Frankenstein* while her friend Lord Byron wrote the short story that gave us today's vampire myths. But that was still nothing compared to the damage the Yellowstone eruption will cause.

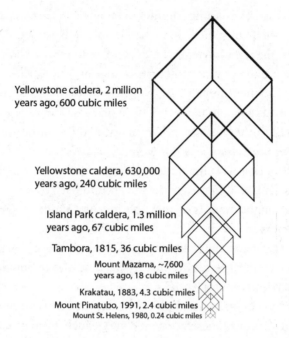

Yellowstone caldera, 2 million
years ago, 600 cubic miles

Yellowstone caldera, 630,000
years ago, 240 cubic miles

Island Park caldera, 1.3 million
years ago, 67 cubic miles

Tambora, 1815, 36 cubic miles

Mount Mazama, ~7,600
years ago, 18 cubic miles

Krakatau, 1883, 4.3 cubic miles

Mount Pinatubo, 1991, 2.4 cubic miles

Mount St. Helens, 1980, 0.24 cubic miles

Now are you getting just how big Yellowstone is?

Calderas like Yellowstone are flat, so instead of the Mount Fuji–shaped stratovolcanoes you probably recall from elementary school science projects, picture a giant, rather formless crater. If you stand out in the open on a hill in the middle of the Yellowstone Caldera, with its seventy-kilometer diameter, you most likely won't see all the way to the outer edge of the crater because the caldera is so big, the edge is beyond the horizon. So yes, it is a volcano, but it looks like nothing more than a big flat section of the national park, because if you're just looking at it from the surface, that's exactly what it is.

But assuming you're still standing on that little hill in Yellowstone, if you could somehow burrow a couple dozen kilometers straight down, it would be quite a different story. You'd burn to death first of all, because you'd have just found the volcano's magma chambers, two enormous masses of molten rock. The upper magma chamber is about ninety kilometers long and forty kilometers wide. The lower chamber has much less liquid rock—and thus is less active—but is thought to be about four and a half times as big as the upper chamber.

We don't need a volcanic eruption to know there's magma down there. Heat has to vent constantly, and when it does, it blasts jets of water and steam from the famous geysers all around Yellowstone National Park.

But those underground structures change over time, allowing magma to move, and when the hot magma is less dense than the surrounding rock, and it has room to move, it will. Worst case scenario: what geoscientist David Rothery of Open University, and the author of *Volcanoes, Earthquakes and Tsunamis: A Complete Introduction*, calls the entire "ring fault" will break as lava finds the surface—which will take the form of explosions. That will in turn cause the ground itself to turn into a giant sinkhole as huge amounts of rock fall into the suddenly empty upper magma chamber.

When that happens, according to Rothery, "We're not all going to die, but we could lose twenty or fifty percent of our population." He means the population of *Earth*.

Why would it be so catastrophic? The day the super-eruption becomes a major threat, your experience would vary widely from others' depending on how far you are from the caldera. If you were a few states away, you'd have to come to terms with the lingering environmental effects— some of which would be devastating for years to come. Meanwhile, if you were within a few hundred kilometers of the eruption, you'd be in immediate peril.

To get a sense of how all this would work, I asked Rothery to walk me through the inevitable worst day in some future Yellowstone geologist's career.

He set the stage by describing what it would be like to be there during the ominous lead-up to a super-eruption. After noticing the seismic signs and changes in the terrain—perhaps swelling of the ground that goes on for centuries—you'd see some major geological drama as gases seeped out of the ground. Since, as Rothery informed me, "carbon dioxide escapes from solution in magma at a greater depth than sulfur dioxide does," a sudden large volume of carbon dioxide would be relatively benign, suggesting perhaps a bunch of magma just hanging out twenty kilometers below the surface. This would be notable, but would probably happen many times without being followed by anything disastrous.

But, Rothery said, "if you then found [that] rather than getting carbon dioxide, you're getting the *sulfur dioxide*, which escapes at lower pressures when a magma has to be close to the surface. You'd think *oh no!* [Although he used a few dirtier words here.] *The magma is a lot closer to the surface now because the sulfur dioxide is escaping!*"

Cut to: Billings, Montana, the nearest major city to the caldera, where everyone would probably be pretty blasé about the whole "eruption" thing. By the time a super-eruption becomes imminent, the area would have a history of volcanism, which the residents would have survived. Upon noticing the escape of sulfur dioxide, "you'd be on the alert—'Hey, this could be heading towards the big eruption!'—and more often than not it's going to just subside away, and not build up with catastrophic eruption," Rothery said.

Once there have been false alarms, declaring that the sky is about to fall becomes a risky judgment call, because, as Rothery said, "the economic losses for evacuating a large number of people, and the social consequences, are pretty dire." And even when the ground is rumbling and the magma is getting close to the surface, "maybe it's a fifty-fifty chance it will subside and nothing major will be erupted."

According to the United States Geological Survey (USGS), if we think only in terms of a possible super-eruption, we're missing the potential for other types of disasters. Yellowstone is more likely to start experiencing other types of volcanic events, including "a rock-hurling geyser eruption" or "a lava flow." So geologists will likely want to wait on predicting the apocalypse. Getting too frantic without the antici-pated dire things really happening just creates problems for emergency management later.

Someone from the USGS or FEMA might tell everyone to evacuate not just the city of Billings, but the whole state of Montana, along with perhaps Idaho and Wyoming. People would be directed to camps in Utah, Colorado, and North and South Dakota. But having experienced their share of earthquakes and minor eruptions, many people in Billings might not be inclined to get out of town. It's human nature to assume that if past events haven't harmed you, future events won't, either.

How much of a false sense of security will people near Yellowstone start to develop? Well, think of it this way: according to a 2018 study by University of Illinois geologists Haley Cabaniss, Patricia Gregg, and Eric

Grosfils, the eruption will have been telegraphing its arrival for eons. When the volcanic system gets a fresh supply of magma, there'll be a huge change in seismic activity that won't go unnoticed, which can be observed "on timescales of centuries to thousands of years."

This is why the future residents of Billings who do actually see the eruption will have grown up with a baseline understanding that the volcano is in super-eruption mode, but that it's never happened. Geologists will be in the same boat: they'll be seeing all sorts of red flashing lights and menacing bleeps and bloops when the big day has finally arrived, but they still won't be absolutely positive it's the big day until they have proof in the form of hundreds of cubic kilometers of ash.

So if you're a non-evacuee in Billings, here's what it will be like when the super-eruption kills you:

You'll look up at the sky and see what Rothery calls a "sixty-kilometer-high column of ash"—at which point the ash will be higher than the stratosphere. "Okay. Now you've got a supervolcano eruption in progress," Rothery said. That column of ash will, at some point, collapse, and the ensuing cloud will be called a "pyroclastic flow," which will turn the whole area into a hellscape of hot, gray shards of ash known as ignimbrites, traveling at hundreds of kilometers per hour away from the volcano. Rothery estimated that this will consume everything within "many tens, possibly a few hundred kilometers."

Let's say you're within those few hundred kilometers, and the ignimbrites are coming toward you.

How a pyroclastic flow works is that "if you're caught in the open you're dead," Rothery told me. But you can get lucky. A pyroclastic flow looks a little like an avalanche, or a cumulus cloud rolling along the ground, and if you see one coming, and you happen to have access to a sealed-off basement, or an emergency shelter, you may be able to hide. In some cases, Rothery told me, it's been possible to survive a pyroclastic flow just by getting behind a sturdy wall. Then again, he said, the flow "could be meters thick, in which case you're going to get cooked." But the point is, try to let the pyroclastic flow pass over you, and "don't breathe in while the really hot air is rushing by," and you might make it through this part.

Now your challenge is to try to survive with ash hanging in the air and covering every surface. Keep in mind, Eyjafjallajökull spewed out ash for six days in 2010, and this is going to be much, much worse than that. So expect a snowstorm of ash that lasts for perhaps several weeks.

Volcanic ash isn't like the dusting of soot that clings to you at a summer bonfire. In fact, "ash" is maybe not the right word for it, given that it's more like a fine sand. According to a 2017 study from the *Journal of Geophysical Research*, volcanoes produce all different types of ash, but they "consist of glassy juvenile components, crystals from multiple mineral phases." In other words, volcanic ash is a fine powder full of tiny bits of glass that will sting your eyes, lungs, and skin. And the shards in the ash aren't the only breathing hazard. Volcanic emissions also include gas and aerosol, which means those who weren't toasted by ignimbrites, or simply blown apart by the initial series of shockwaves, will have to worry about acute respiratory problems as well.

So the situation is that you can't breathe or see when you go outside, which you obviously shouldn't do. But staying indoors isn't entirely safe, either, Rothery said. The weight of the ash will collapse the roof of your house if you don't sweep your roof clean. So if inside is almost as dangerous as outdoors, it seems the only logical response is to flee. According to Rothery, that's not an option, either—try finding safety when car engines won't work, he challenged me.

And as we learned from Eyjafjallajökull, planes and helicopters can't fly through plumes of volcanic ash, so search-and-rescue operations are going to be tricky, assuming they can be performed at all. But if you're prepared—by which I mean if you have a few weeks of food and water stored somewhere, a good air filtration system, and a very sturdy roof—you might be able to batten down the hatches and get through it. But obviously it's much more likely that if you're within a few hundred kilometers of Yellowstone, you'll just die. Sorry.

But there's so much more to worry about than just what will happen to the area around the volcano. Yellowstone's location, about a thousand kilometers from the Pacific Ocean, and three thousand kilometers from the Atlantic, means very little ash will blow into the ocean—as much of it will next time the Lake Toba supervolcano in Indonesia erupts—but will instead coat a huge swath of land. Since weather ordinarily travels west to east in the United States, we have every reason to fear that, geographically speaking, most of the US and Canada will be crippled by the ensuing shower of ash.

In 2014, the USGS issued a report designed to illustrate the extent of the ashpocalypse. They noted that "lack of reliable information left the door open to speculation and fanciful depictions of the effects of supereruptions, which are easily found on the Internet." According to USGS, "ash accumulation, while widespread and substantial, is far less than in most of these 'doomsday' scenarios." Nonetheless, when they mapped a worst-case version of this—the result of a monthlong super-eruption—it was still pretty doomsday-ish:

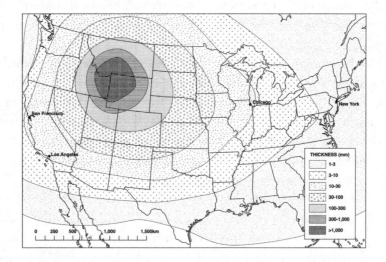

As you can see, every inch of Billings will be devastated by a meter-thick blanket of ash. But every major city in the US except Miami will get at least a nice dusting.

Yellowstone's three known super-eruptions in the past 2.1 million years appear to have coated much of what is now the United States. For reference, the 1980 Mount St. Helens eruption took place in Washington State and dumped a considerable but non–life threatening layer of ash on Montana, Idaho, Wyoming, North Dakota, South Dakota, Colorado, and Oklahoma. One single Yellowstone super-eruption is thought to have produced 2,500 times that much ash, according to the USGS.

A snowstorm of ash shouldn't be our number one concern, though, since the people who get dusted will be able to just brush it off their clothes. The real trouble starts when all those volcanic deposits reduce the opacity of the atmosphere. In a 1992 paper published in *Nature,* geologist Michael R. Rampino and volcanologist Stephen Self pointed out that the Toba supervolcanic eruption about 73,500 years ago caused a "volcanic winter," which is a little like a nuclear winter, resulting in "a few years with maximum estimated annual hemispheric surface-temperature decreases of 3–5 degrees Celsius." This in turn would have caused drastic environmental change, losses of vegetation, and general chaos for living things. For a while, it was believed that this era of dark skies and cooler temperatures nearly wiped out our early human ancestors, but a more recent scientific consensus is that it didn't. A 2018 study looking for geological evidence of a volcanic winter found that early humans in east Africa most likely faced little to no adversity. And a 2018 archeological study in South Africa found evidence that humans were having a lovely time being alive in the years just after the eruption, possibly because they happened to be in a resource-rich location, or because they were technologically advanced enough to have survival tools.

Nonetheless, there are a lot more of us now, and while many of us will certainly survive the day of the super-eruption come what may, it will cause food scarcities—particularly in the ash-covered breadbasket of the United States—and economic shocks. And what's more, we'll have no ability to stave them off as the ash continues to fall. "All we can do is prepare to survive the effects, and that will be quite hard to do," Rothery said.

THE DAY THE LAST
SLAVE GOES FREE

Likely in this century? > *I'm optimistic*

Plausibility Rating > *4/5*

Scary? > *No*

Worth changing habits? > *The sooner everyone learns to spot slavery the better*

On a sunny spring morning in Lusaka, Zambia, the heads of state from Angola, Namibia, Rwanda, Uganda, Zambia, and Zimbabwe pose for a photo with the special guests: the president of China, the secretary general of the United Nations, and the newly elected President of the Democratic Republic of the Congo (DRC), along with representatives from warring nations. The decades-long regional peace process has been leading up to this.

In the back of every photo is Sifa Okitundu, a woman who deserves credit for striking the final blow against slavery. But it's the peace treaty that's on everyone's mind, not slavery. So instead of sitting at the table with the dignitaries, Sifa sits off to the side, with a group of recently freed slaves, whom she guided through the foreign ritual of sitting down and eating a formal meal. Two were missing hands, and none had ever eaten with a fork and knife prior to their invitation to this event.

Sifa, now in her sixties, started her career in 2021 as president of the regional chapter of Break the Chains, a multinational NGO that has been fighting to end modern slavery since the topic rose to prominence in the 2000s.

The UN's original plan to end slavery by 2030 didn't quite pan out, but it's better late than never.

As the wars wound down over the past few years, Sifa sensed an opportunity. She contacted UN peacekeepers and notified them that a collection of warlords was about to receive mining contracts in exchange for ending hostilities, despite their track record of relying on slave labor. The Lusaka Conference was announced a few weeks later—and a $12 million development grant aimed at establishing a paid labor force was on the agenda. It was toward the bottom, but there it was.

Now, at Lusaka, the warlord generals keep avoiding Sifa. She has, after all, spent her life campaigning for them to be arrested and taken to The Hague for crimes against humanity. But when the cameras start snapping, they shake her hand. There's a brief chat, and then out comes the Lusaka Agreement, which, among other provisions, divides up regional mining rights and outlines pay structures for miners, ensuring them contracts for years. The agreements will terminate instantly if signatory leaders are found to be using slaves. Everyone signs.

With that, they all pose for a second round of photos. At Sifa's insistence, the warlords shake hands with her new friends: the freed slaves. Things get a little embarrassing when the warlords struggle to shake hands with people who have only stubs where their hands should be. The warlords won't go to The Hague, but Sifa gets the last laugh.

◆

This is going to be a little bit of an ice water bath. It's impossible to say this without sanctimony, but I'll just go ahead and let you call me sanctimonious: slavery could easily end if everyone suddenly gave a shit, or it could keep going for centuries if we continue to ignore it. More or less every slave in the world has to be freed individually, and every situation is different. But this problem isn't like climate change in that the most powerful people in the world will fight tooth and nail to the bitter end to prevent it from being solved. Slavery's beneficiaries are relatively easy to vanquish. They're just hard to find.

To start with, we need to recognize the size of the problem, so here comes the ice water: it's estimated that five out of every thousand people on Earth are enslaved. In the words of Zoe Trodd, director of the Rights Lab at the University of Nottingham, the emancipations of slaves around the world were all "botched emancipations." Consequently, she hopes that "on the day when we can finally say we're in a slavery-free world, that it's sustainable freedom and it's done the right way."

When abolition was *en vogue* back in the eighteenth and nineteenth centuries, the practice of slavery just carried right on, often in the form of debt bondage, and transmogrified into what is arguably its ugliest form ever—*modern global slavery*, which comes in two major flavors: forced conventional labor and forced sex work.

According to the most recent estimate from the International Labour Organization (ILO), the world's slaves are essentially divided into twenty-five million people being forced to do backbreaking work without pay and fifteen million in some sort of forced marriage—which is a little like being drafted to be a sex slave and an unpaid domestic worker at the same time. Consequently, 71 percent of enslaved people are female. (According to the numbers provided by the ILO report, 0.0004 percent of male slaves are sex slaves.) About one-fourth of all enslaved people are children. It's easy to think of modern slavery as something that afflicts a far-off, relatively undeveloped society, but remember, this is probably happening in your city.

While the ILO estimates that far more than forty million people have been roped into some form of slavery in the past five years (the number could be more than twice that), the situation may be on the verge of improvement. According to Kevin Bales, professor of contemporary slavery at the UK's University of Nottingham, "slavery is in a curious situation at this historical moment where it's closer to being eradicated or potentially eradicated than ever in history." In 2015, ending slavery was included in the UN's list of sustainable development goals, to be achieved by 2030, which is, arguably, more symbolic than effective, but at least people are talking about it. And while forty million is a lot of slaves—a popular and somewhat dubious factoid holds that there are "more slaves now than there ever have been"—Bales is quick to point out that what we have today is "by far the tiniest fraction of the global population to ever be in slavery."

The way this problem gets systematically rooted out, according to Trodd, also at the University of Nottingham, is by deputizing individuals, turning them into the tip of the anti-slavery spear. "Front-line people have to get trained," she said. "It's not always the obvious people. Sometimes it's all the taxi drivers have to know how to report something dodgy. Sometimes it's the meter inspectors who are going into homes and finding twelve Polish people locked in the cellar." And drafting people into the work of rooting out slavery involves, well, inconveniencing people. "I believe that now in Nottingham and in other cities, to be allowed to have a [taxi] license, or to do the mandatory annual license renewal, you do have to do the day's worth of training on this," she said.

Activists are forming what she called "local anti-slavery models for slavery free-cities." Nottingham in the UK and Austin, Texas, have announced citywide initiatives aimed at being slavery-free. Once we know which are the official slavery-free cities, Trodd said, "then we'll do that in an international sense."

That sounds easy enough in American and British cities, but the process is much more difficult in places like India, home to eight million enslaved people according to the most recent estimate from the Global Slavery Index. Trodd told me that in India, slavery affects "whole communities, whole villages, whole regions." Their entire lives consist of toiling in brick kilns and stone quarries—the most physically demanding jobs I can imagine—simply because their families "have been in debt bondage for generations."

These situations are justified—by the slave owners, of course—by a twisted internal logic. According to Bales, the slave owners explain that they're providing their slaves with what they need to survive because "they can't really be trusted to buy it with money," and that "if they get money they just buy alcohol and then they get in trouble." By this reasoning a slaveholder claims to be compassionate. And the real trouble is that the enslaved people lack the sort of frame of reference that would tell them that this argument is, well, a bunch of bullshit.

Disrupting these crimes resembles the actions that a union takes to disrupt the exploitative conditions in a factory that is abusing its paid workers. In Northern India, according to Bales, the process goes a little like this:

An NGO sends in a ringer—possibly a former slave—who speaks the local dialect. The ringer shows up around dinnertime with a nice batch of familiar local cuisine. "They just hang, and cook and chitchat," Bales said. As people get used to the ringer hanging around, that person will begin gently probing, bringing the problems to light organically. "So how long have you guys lived here? Oh, no one even knows? What are your different jobs? Oh, you all work for the same man? Interesting. Where's the school? Oh, there's no school." To people living in these conditions, these everyday facts of life probably never seem aberrant until someone comes along to ask the right questions.

If chipping away at this problem one village at a time sounds tedious and disheartening, you don't know the half of it. Finding slave labor involves some of the most arduous reconnaissance work you can imagine. But automation is taking over some of that work. The "Slavery from Space" project, spearheaded by the University of Nottingham, where Bales and Trodd work, is a fascinating, incredibly useful, and utterly time-consuming endeavor in which mountains of satellite imagery are handed over to a machine-learning system—what we call "artificial intelligence" or "AI"—which is then taught to identify the telltale shapes—literally shapes on the ground—that reveal a slaveholder's operation. But an AI can't do this work alone, so an eye-watering number of these images have to be analyzed by humans first. "That human observation . . . let us [identify] fifty-five thousand kilns across India, which human beings couldn't have done," Trodd said.

But while India's slave problem is immense, India is a relatively developed country, and to some degree its government willingly participates with anti-slavery NGOs. In the long-term fight against slavery, the stickiest wickets will be war-torn regions where no state actor has the ability, let alone the prerogative, to intervene against slaveholders. The last stand against slavery will happen in one of these places. It could be the DRC, Bales told me, or perhaps Northern Cambodia, or Myanmar—some place teetering on the edge of what he poetically referred to as "the falling apart place."

When that happens, activists, locals, and law enforcement officials will find these slavery situations one by one and convince the enslaved people they deserve better. After they walk away from captivity, can everyone dust off their hands and say "job well done"? Hardly. According to Austin Choi-Fitzpatrick in his book *What Slaveholders Think: How Contemporary Perpetrators Rationalize What They Do*: "To rescue someone in the afternoon and call it a day is not freedom. Sustainable emancipation requires transformations in the broader systems and structures connected to an individual's political, economic, and social life. This is no easy task."

Once they're all free, enslaved people emerge into a world that can be cruel and forbidding. Bales told me the story of a woman he met who'd recently been released from domestic slavery in France. "Isn't it nice to have choices now?" Bales recalled asking. He received only shrugs in response. "Look, everybody talks to me about these things called 'choices,' but no one will show me one of these things," the former slave said. "I know that I'm supposed to like them, but I don't know what they are, and I don't know if I eat it or I carry it around."

Slavery has effects on people's cognition that seem understudied. Bales told me about a concept he calls "aspaciality" in newly freed people. Since, in extreme cases, enslaved people are often forbidden to move in space at all without permission, any sort of freedom of movement can be fundamentally confusing. "You just take it out of your head that you can move any direction," he said. Someone with that kind of history, no matter how smart, can't be expected to walk out of captivity and choose a good laundry detergent, let alone what career to pursue or where to live.

In North Korea, the country with by far the highest prevalence of slavery, one in ten people is a slave. It's informative to look at what happens when North Koreans defect to the South and have to get by in that country's hyper-capitalist society. In 2017, the *Wall Street Journal* investigated the defector experience in South Korea, and the results were eye-opening: the system is inhospitable to North Koreans, and according to one defector, those who flee the North typically join the urban poor. The defectors have no idea how to use money—which seems to be the *Journal*'s primary interest—but moreover, the whole financial system in the South is confusing and riddled with unexpected cruelty, including scams for which the former North Koreans are totally unprepared.

There's yet another tough hurdle that will have to be tackled before we can finally close the slavery chapter in human history: we have to end prison labor—or at least the forms that qualify as slavery. According to Bales, as long as any state is "using its prison system as a way to enslave and profit," the job will never be complete.

In 2018, Kevin Rashid Johnson, an American prisoner and activist, wrote in the *Guardian* that prison labor as we know it is slavery. Inmates in some states, he noted, are "forced to work in the fields for free, entirely unremunerated," and he described them as being "cajoled into chain gangs and taken out to the fields where they are made to grow all the food that inmates eat," using "hand-held tools like wooden sticks and hoes." These situations sure sound like old-fashioned slavery to me.

This is tolerated in the United States because, well, it's in our Constitution. The Thirteenth Amendment abolished forced labor, "except as a punishment for crime whereof the party shall have been duly convicted."

As Bales notes, this would *arguably* be just, if the US justice system were flawless. But he points out that America has "systemic discrimination, the use of forced plea bargains to keep people from having a trial, privatized prisons that can't be investigated or inspected," and other factors that, to say the least, don't gel with the "duly convicted" wording in the Constitution.

We can only assume that a post-slavery world will be one in which the systemic injustice that forces innocent people—or people facing trumped-up charges—into unremunerated labor has ended. A very tall order in the US, admittedly. It would likely require a massive, focused effort aimed at proving that the system isn't just tantamount to slavery, but *is* slavery, and legally has to go. "I'm convinced it will take a superb investigative journalism team to crack it," Bales told me.

Fingers crossed on that.

Paradoxically, Bales noted, the patina of due process that the US successfully maintains makes this form of *potential* slavery thornier than slavery in countries where people travel down unambiguous pipelines into forced labor. "China is a perfect example," he said. "People are picked up on the street and may never be actually 'arrested' or charged or tried, or sentenced, and then end up in a prison factory for ten years." In China, you just have to be a member of the Falun Gong religious minority to be subjected to "arbitrary detention," according to Amnesty International.

So the last slave could walk free as part of a peace treaty in some conflict region, or the event just might happen when the last unjust penal system finally ends its worst policies. In either case, the end of slavery probably won't be what makes headlines that day. The hardest part of ending slavery is that it means creating societies in which former slaves can thrive. As Choi-Fitzpatrick writes, "Individuals do not live in isolation but are embedded in larger sets of norms, broader social dynamics, and longstanding communities."

It's up to those who have never known slavery to help build communities in which former slaves can discover the fullness of a free life. See? Told you I'd sound sanctimonious.

THE DAY THE LAST CEMETERY RUNS OUT OF SPACE

Likely in this century? > *Yes*

Plausibility Rating > *5/5*

Scary? > *Yes, but only because of all the spooky skeletons*

Worth changing habits? > *No*

(Sign posted at the entrance of St. Michael Cemetery, Boston, Massachusetts)

EXHUMATION OF GRAVES

Registration of claims closes on September 30.

Exhumation of graves will commence after registration of claims. Claimants will be notified of the exhumation by EPA at a later date.

- Exhumation, cremation, and storage/sea burial of cremated remains by EPA.
- Exhumation will be carried out by EPA's contractor.
- Each grave will be individually exhumed, under the close supervision of EPA.
- Next of kin and relatives who wish to witness the exhumation may do so.

- After the exhumation, the remains will be cremated at St. Michael Cemetery Crematorium.
- Next of kin may opt for the cremated remains to be stored in a government columbarium or sent for sea burial by EPA's appointed contractor. For the former, the cremated remains from each affected grave claimed by family members will be placed in an urn and installed in a standard niche allocated by EPA at a nearby government columbarium, subject to availability—as per the decision of the next of kin. Should the next of kin wish to choose the location of the niche, they may do so upon the payment of a fee of $250 per niche location.
- The costs of exhumation, cremation, and allocated standard niche with marble plaque at government crematorium and columbarium, or sea burial of cremated remains, will be borne by EPA.
- A marble plaque, inscribed with the deceased's name and date of death, will be mounted on the niche.
- Claimants who wish to add a photograph of the deceased onto the marble plaque may do so at their own expense.
- Next of kin who wish to make private arrangements to engage their own contractor to exhume the graves or store the cremated remains in a private columbarium or send the cremated remains themselves for sea burial may do so at their own expense.

Next of kin are encouraged to submit the Claim Registration Form early. Once the claim is registered, EPA will schedule the date of exhumation and claimant will be notified of the exhumation by NEA at a later date. (All unclaimed graves will be exhumed and the remains cremated and kept for three years before sea burial.)

◆

If the fictional sign you just read sounds in any way bizarre or outlandish, then you must not be from Singapore. In fact, that fake sign was transcribed almost verbatim from a very real sign I found posted at Choa Chu Kang Cemetery, the largest public cemetery in Singapore, and at the time, the only one considered active. I just transposed a few words to make the sign correspond to Boston instead of Singapore, but those policies of exhumation (side note: I would have expected there to be some soothing euphemism for "exhumation," like "interruption of final rest," but to their credit, they didn't bother), cremation, and scattering at sea, or placement in a "columbarium"—a sort of library for human ashes—are all completely real. One-third of the graves in Choa Chu Kang Cemetery were undergoing exhumation at the time of this writing, because the Singapore government has determined that cemeteries are a waste of space.

The Singaporean people I spoke to expect this to happen to all the cemeteries in Singapore in the coming years, even though the population of Singapore plateaued in 2017. Yet, almost without exception, the stated reason for the removal of cemeteries in Singapore is to make room for homes. In other words, projects like these persist not because the population demands it, but because, as of this writing, home prices in Singapore were skyrocketing thanks to buyers in China, Taiwan, and Korea, according to Bloomberg, and thus increasing revenues for the country's most powerful citizens: real estate barons.

Singapore is a wealthy and religiously diverse island nation, with an economy tightly controlled by the government, particularly where land use is concerned. And it's also the second most densely populated independent country in the world, with almost six million people crammed into about 720 square kilometers. This makes it a fascinating case study in death. Some religions, Islam, for instance, dictate that their adherents be buried. And they can be, because despite being full, some cemeteries in Singapore still do burials—very, very, expensive burials. But there's a catch: the government mandates that after fifteen years the dead be exhumed in the manner described on the sign.

My friend He Shuming, who goes by "Shu," is a filmmaker in Singapore. He told me what it was like having to move his grandfather's remains from what used to be a large, full-service memorial park called Mount Vernon to a public columbarium called Mandai—a sprawling, multistory facility in a much less central part of the city. There were upsides to the move, Shu told me. For instance, his other family members would all be placed there as well, so the living could just do one visit without having to travel to different places. Plus, Mandai has air-conditioning.

But Shu, who attended a school near Mount Vernon, misses the historic cemetery. "We used to go jogging around the cemetery. It's so nice. You see stones that date back to the early nineteen hundreds. There are people that were born in the early eighteen-somethings. It's pretty amazing; as a kid I didn't think anyone could be that old."

If you visit Mount Vernon's memorial park now, you'll find what's left of the cemetery wedged between noisy construction projects. Nearly all the graves in the cemetery, which is called Bidadari, have been exhumed and replaced with what will soon be eleven thousand new homes. There's also—this sounds like a joke, but isn't—a little *memorial to the cemetery that used to be there*. The memorial includes a few sample graves of the notable deceased, and signs telling some of their stories. One of the signs reads as follows: "Born in Singapore, Koona Vayloo Pillay was done out of his inheritance by a dishonest man but worked hard as a milk man to become wealthy again." Another sign informed me that there were once buried in the cemetery 58,200 Christians and 68,000 Muslims, along with many Hindus. Today, by my count, there are about 15 graves in total.

Bidadari was cleared out in a project that started in 2001. A riveting short documentary called *Moving House* was made that year by Tan Pin Pin showing how this process works: After receiving notice that their parents must be moved, the Chew family held a traditional Chinese ceremony requesting absolution for the disruption. Then they opted to stand by in the cemetery as a team of gravediggers painstakingly unearthed their parents' caskets with manual tools, sawed open the lids with a chain saw, fished out the bones, tattered clothes, and false teeth, and deposited them in grocery bags for the trip to the crematorium. "Personally, I don't agree with the exhumation exercise," says a member of the Chew family, "because when our ancestors die, they are buried in an auspicious location so their spirits can absorb the good feng shui elements from that location."

After people like the Chew family move their ancestors to the densely packed Mandai columbarium, Shu told me, the nature of mourning rituals fundamentally changes for people of traditional Chinese faith like the Chews and my friend Shu. "I don't know exactly how it works, but your soul is separate from your ashes," he told me. "At least that's how it was explained to me."

It's not just Singapore. With 0.8 percent of the planet's total population dying every year, and the population swell of the late 1940s through the late 1950s projected to generate an explosion of productivity for the death industry over the next two decades, there's little doubt that the economic realities of permanent subterranean interment of human remains are about to change radically, interrupting three centuries of burial customs in many societies. Other societies worked this all out a long time ago.

In Germany, for instance, grave sites are leased for approximately twenty years. If you're a dead German and the lease on your grave expires, your family can renew the lease if they still care about visiting you. If not, your bones get moved to, well, a mass grave. Austria has a similar policy, which created big news in 2012 when the remains of Hitler's parents were relocated to discourage neo-Nazis from showing up in the small village of Leonding and paying their respects. In Japan, meanwhile, the rate of cremation is effectively 100 percent.

The much greedier customs, the ones that are particularly common in—though not exclusive to—the English-speaking nations, involve a casket, which is a fully airtight wooden box a little over 2 meters long, 70 centimeters wide, and 60 centimeters tall, and containing about 70 kilograms of human remains, a kilogram of clothing, and 10 kilograms of embalming chemicals. Most of the time, that casket is enclosed inside a "vault"—a 1,500-kilogram cement box about 230 centimeters long, 90 centimeters deep, and 90 centimeters tall. All of that is interred in a hole 180 centimeters deep, and theoretically left there for all of eternity. At its inception, this process was—I suppose—intended to be repeated every time someone died, forever.

The coming glut of departures will overload many cemeteries— particularly in densely populated cities. London is expected to be out of cemetery space by 2045 at the latest, according to a piece in the *Guardian*. Hong Kong is out of grave and columbarium space, except at extremely high prices, and mainland China is on the verge of running out as well. In Cardiff, Wales, locals were fretting in 2018 that they might only have had two more years until no room is left, but the situation isn't always so urgent in Wales. The rural Welsh county of Rhondda Cynon Taf, for instance, says it can accommodate its dead until 2118.

So far, many panicked predictions around the world that space is about to run out haven't come true, because cemetery owners innovate.

"As the land becomes more scarce it becomes more expensive, so grave lots have become more expensive over the last half century—a lot more expensive," said David Charles Sloane, professor of urban planning at the University of Southern California and the author of *The Last Great Necessity: Cemeteries in American History*. Sloane said that in the 1970s, a cemetery proprietor told him, "We've got fifteen years max. We're done. We're full." But that cemetery, he said, "brought in a consultant, and two years later they found enough graves to last for fifty."

Because of what these land use consultants have accomplished, and are continuing to accomplish, when the last cemetery runs out of space, it's going to be a chaotic cemetery. Said Sloane of the changes wrought by the consultants: "They closed roads, and turned them into grave sites. They closed paths and turned them into the grave sites." Soon, you won't be able to find anyone in a crowded cemetery without following the GPS beacon on your phone. "There's going to have to be an app. But there *will* be an app," Sloane told me confidently.

He added that in places like Arlington National Cemetery, the best-known cemetery in the US, managers are experimenting with efforts to "dramatically increase the number of graves," by stacking the bodies of families in ever deeper graves. "If you have a kid—a single kid and two parents—they'll go down like twelve, thirteen, fourteen feet."

The site of several presidential graves, Arlington is a particularly stark example of the cost of losing cemeteries. Karen Durham-Aguilera, the former executive director of Army National Military Cemeteries, said in 2017 that barring some new (and unfair) set of eligibility requirements for burial, Arlington "will not be a burial option for those service members who served in the Gulf War and any conflict afterwards." Despite an expansion plan being implemented, the cemetery is projected to have zero remaining plots by the middle of the twenty-first century.

According to Sloane, there's no better place on Earth to see the Brave New World of American cemeteries than Los Angeles. The premier forward-thinking cemetery in California's marquee city is called—fittingly—Hollywood Forever Cemetery. It's a famous landmark and an offbeat cultural mecca. According to Sloane, "What they're trying to do is turn the cemetery back into a public space." I've spent a whole lot of time in Hollywood Forever, partly because my great-grandparents are interred in a mausoleum there, and partly because I've attended several of the cemetery's summertime outdoor film screenings, as well as a concert by the Swedish singer songwriter Jens Lekman.

Hollywood Forever is an absolute must-see if you're a tourist in LA. It's lavish and colorful, which makes sense considering it's the permanent home of legends like Judy Garland, Cecil B. DeMille, and Rudolph Valentino. But the sheer density of what's on display at Hollywood Forever gives some of the stranger cemeteries of New Orleans a run for their money. I'm singling out New Orleans here because its combination of Gothic and colonial artistic sensibilities, crowding, and the necessity to bury the dead in tombs rather than underground because of flooding have resulted in some of the most creepily charming, and often downright gorgeous, cemeteries in the world. For Hollywood Forever, which is right in the middle of Los Angeles, to come close to equaling such a high water mark for strangeness is no mean feat.

At Hollywood Forever, quite often there are no delineated "rows" or indeed any fixed aesthetic rules at all, allowing for a rich tapestry of cultural expressions and an integrated approach to the dispersal of different religions—assuming the dead didn't mind—which creates a sea of reddish-brown, black, and mottled gray headstones and sculptures with and without photos of the deceased, along with relatively modest aboveground tombs, next to enormous single-occupant tombs with their own moats and reflecting pools. Adding to the surreal ambiance is a flock of peacocks, which wanders freely between the stones. Currently, all the chaos is broken up by a network of asphalt roads, wide enough to accommodate parked cars on both sides. These make the cemetery easy to navigate, but given that plots there cost as much as $242,000 that's all bound to change.

"They've taken a huge amount of risks and made a lot of money," Sloane told me.

But space will run out, even at Hollywood Forever, and the coming end of the cemetery era will be marked by more and more exhumations—all of which will hopefully be intentional, unlike the time in 2001 when employees of the Menorah Gardens Cemetery just outside Fort Lauderdale, Florida, set about trying to cleverly rearrange their burial pattern à la Hollywood Forever and ended up exhuming dozens of bodies with a backhoe. When the dearly departed turned up in what employees thought were just piles of fill dirt, they sifted out the bones and tossed them into the wilderness before resuming their project.

After the scandal came to light, the cemetery's parent company (a holding corporation called SCI) got slapped with a class action lawsuit and state fines adding up to over $100 million. SCI also agreed to put everything right—which meant undoing some rearrangements that had split up family plots and left husbands and wives on opposite sides of the cemetery.

But Menorah Gardens Cemetery was just making the same impossible promise as *every* cemetery: eternal rest. In fact, cemeteries often put this promise right in their name. For example, there's a famous mortuary and cemetery in Houston called Chapel of Eternal Rest at Forest Park. And legendary lawman of the Wild West Wyatt Earp is buried in Little Hills of Eternity Memorial Park in Colma, California. Also, hello, Hollywood *Forever*?

This completely unsustainable concept is pretty new. For most of human history there was a widely practiced system of grave, um, recycling if you will, and it was perfectly rational. Granted, ostensibly permanent memorials were built at great expense throughout history for people like Egyptian pharaohs and the wives of India's Mughal emperors, but they were always the exception. The majority of history's average John and Jane Does didn't get so much as headstones.

As the practices of the German-speaking world suggest, Europeans have perfected a system of ceremonial burial followed by exhumation. If you create the right conditions for it, a body resting in a churchyard will decompose in about ten years—meaning these Europeans were even more efficient than the gravediggers of hyper-modern Singapore. In that short time, skin, organs, and hair all turn to dirt completely, leaving just a set of dry bones and, happily, no horrific odor. The anonymous bones are then exhumed. In the Middle Ages they were stacked up in ossuaries—bone houses—where many remain to this very day.

We should think, then, of the grim artistry of the famous "bone church" in Prague, or the macabre mazes of the dead in the Paris Catacombs, not as the handiwork of history's goth oddballs, but rather as the most pleasant answer anyone could come up with to the question "Hey, what do we do with all these bones?"

But lest you think that this chapter is strictly about innovations still to come, I should make clear that temporary burial has already started to make its comeback—and not just in Singapore and Hong Kong. The idea has now surfaced in the tenth most populous country in the world—i.e., Mexico. A shortage of graves in Mexico City became such a crisis in 2014 that a Singapore-style burial time limit law was proposed, meaning dead residents whose descendants can afford the extra cost remain buried, while those who can't pay will have to pick another option.

But Mexico is interesting for yet another reason. Whereas Americans are often accused of denying the existence of death altogether, death is quite literally part of the scenery for Mexicans, with the calavera, a stylized skull, being one of Mexican culture's most cherished symbols. Every year Mexicans celebrate the Day of the Dead on November 1—often with parties that take place in cemeteries.

It's because death is so central to the Mexican mindset that Jesus Guzman, an activist working for the Autonomous Union of Native Towns and Neighborhoods of the Federal District in Mexico City, takes the position that, by forcing native Mexicans not to bury their dead, Mexico City officials are erasing native culture. "Their worldview is not the same as ours," he told NBC News in 2014. "Can you imagine that with the stroke of a pen they can erase All Saints' Day and the Day of the Dead? They have no idea what they're doing." His group's widespread protests of the proposed cemetery law were ferocious, closing down a major avenue. For the time being, no exhumation policy has been implemented in Mexico City, so the shortage of graves has only grown worse.

Meanwhile, places like London have looked into other cemetery innovations. "Double-decker graves" were proposed in 2004, along with a proposal that old headstones have new names added to them. But according to a 2017 report from the House of Commons, this never happened. The practice, called "lift and deepen," has been kept "under review" by every successive government, meaning the problem just keeps getting kicked down the road.

Let's face it: Cemetery plots have been a crazy extravagance; the huge expanses of land cemeteries occupy in the middle of our cities consume a lot of space. So it's only natural that the living will eventually rebel against the practice. Look at New York City. The last two burial plots in all of Manhattan went up for sale in 2015 for $350,000 each, according to *New York* magazine. So that's one borough where you just can't be buried anymore. If you didn't get past the cemeteries' rope lines in the first four hundred years of Manhattan's existence, the doormen aren't going to let you in now.

With the rise of more Earth-friendly approaches to life in general, there has been a parallel trend in green-friendly eco-graves for those who feel guilty about taking up all that space. For instance, Hillside Memorial Park and Mortuary in Culver City, California—the final resting place of such luminaries as Leonard Nimoy—includes an environmentally conscious option called "Gan Eden," which USC professor Sloane called a "quite well-designed tiny little sliver of a section." There are no cement vaults there, and the dead can simply be buried in a shroud rather than a heavy-duty casket.

I visited Gan Eden, and, as Sloane said, it's tiny. It's big enough for maybe fifty burials in its current form, and thanks to the lush green grass and other obsessively pruned landscaping elements, it doesn't quite exude a "natural" vibe. For a purist like me, Sloane recommends Ramsey Creek Preserve, an impressively rustic wooded space in Westminster, South Carolina, where bodies truly are returned to nature. Ramsey Creek really is just a patch of wilderness, and the gravestones there are simply natural stones. Walking among the graves is no different from taking an idyllic hike. A visitor to the Preserve would find crinkling leaves, prancing deer, and singing birds—but few obvious signs of bodies buried beneath the topsoil.

Maybe the availability of options like these will smooth the transition from the land-wasting way that people have been buried for so long. As someone who has often said "just toss me in the woods when I die," I'm the target market for businesses like Ramsey Creek, or at least I was for most of my life.

I've always seen burial as a vain extravagance, because here in Southern California cemeteries are vast, green lawns, forever in need of water—a resource that is in short supply. Unlike places with similar climates, like Spain and Israel, where most of the burial grounds are dirt lots or are full of low-impact local flora, nearly all the cemeteries here are bright green advertisements for eternal, drought-exacerbating environmental frivolity.

My feelings about burial shifted, however, while I was in Singapore, particularly when I toured Bukit Brown Cemetery, which closed in 1973. Once considered the biggest Chinese graveyard outside of China, it's now slated for one of Singapore's exhumation and construction projects—this time to make way for a new highway, which after repeated financial and logistical setbacks was slated to be put in place in 2019. After the highway is finished, there are additional plans, I was told, to replace the rest of the cemetery with housing.

For now, Bukit Brown is both a nature preserve and a living history museum. On one hand it's full of hidden grandeur. Turn-of-the-century Singaporean businessman Ong Sam Leong's gravesite covers an expanse of ground larger than my house at around six hundred square meters. Yes, Ong's grave is absolutely a waste of space, but just for a second forgive him for that. His seemingly forgotten tomb at the top of a grassy hill with an incredible view of the city is a sculptor's magnum opus, featuring a moat, Chinese-style gargoyles for diverting rainwater, and other carved figures that espouse the virtues of Confucianism and depict various Chinese fables.

On the other hand, Bukit Brown is a public cemetery, filled to the brim with workaday Singaporeans. Each gravesite is a sort of shrine built into a tuft of ground, with a rounded stone surface and an area that allows several people to stand or kneel at a time, thus inviting mourners to visit often. The graves aren't laid out according to a space-maximizing grid, but—as the Chew family noted in *Moving House*—according to feng shui. Granting that there's enormous effort involved in constructing such elaborate grave sites, Bukit Brown is the furthest thing from a California lawn cemetery. Instead of enforcing an artificial order, Bukit Brown is in conversation with the natural beauty surrounding it. The effect isn't cemetery-like in the way I understand "cemetery"—as something austere and serene. It's more like being buried in the spot in my parents' backyard where I used to take my toys—a place where I felt truly happy and safe rather than *merely* peaceful.

My tour guide at Bukit Brown was Claire Leow, a former journalist who cofounded a loose coalition of volunteers under the banner

"All Things Bukit Brown" and leads a small corps of volunteer tapho-
philes (no, the word for someone who takes interest in cemeteries is not
"necrophiliacs," thank you very much), spreading awareness that, well,
this cemetery is really cool, and the government is planning to destroy it.
And if you talk to Claire for long, it's easy to see why cemeteries mean
so much to her.

Like Shu's, her family members' remains were moved from Bidadari
to public columbaria, but she's unimpressed by the convenience. She
visited her brother's urn in a columbarium two years ago, she told me.
His plaque is high on a wall. "If I step back far enough, I can just see the
edge of this urn." Instead of a dedicated space for mourning, she said,
"there's a tiny little pen-sized hole for me to stick in a plastic flower, and
I think, *This is rubbish! This is absolute rubbish! If anything this destroys
all my memories of him.*"

Interestingly, Leow's memories of her brother were facilitated by the
cemetery itself, since he died before she was born. She and her mother
visited every other week, even though her mother could never bear to
explain how he'd died. "We were poor. He didn't really have a proper
tomb, and then it collapsed, no one had the money to fix it, but we
still went to visit him. There were cracks in the marble and we tried to
put it together every time, and cut some grass. I really felt very close to
him, you know?" Leow told me.

One day, Leow's mother spoke directly to her brother's grave. "I
shouldn't have gone off that morning," Claire recalled overhearing her
saying. "You were always such a good student and you ran for the school
bus." It's only through that expression of regret spoken to her brother's
grave that Leow deduced that he'd been hit by a car while running to
catch a bus.

According to Leow, this is what we'll lose when we stop burying our
loved ones: "having the cemetery as a space," as she puts it. She compares
the creation of memories in a cemetery to having a conversation in
person, as opposed to on the phone. "You can see my face. You can see
my expressions, my hand gestures. They just add a bit more, obviously,
to the conversation. And I think that's what cemeteries are for."

EPILOGUE

It's entirely possible that many of my scenarios have filled you with fear—that reading about them has been a grueling endurance test. But if you've made it to the end, I hope at least some of your fears about the future have been put to bed. Yes, catastrophes and mass extinctions are horrible, and some seemingly positive changes in the future have dark downsides, but hopefully the process of making them tangible has taken away some of their evil magic.

With that in mind, before I let you go I'm going to take you on a journey through what is, without question, the darkest future day of them all: the day everything ends.

In anticipation of writing about this last scenario, I asked Mr. Optimism himself, Steven Pinker, the bestselling author I mentioned in the introduction, how he copes with the concept of existence ending for everyone and everything, and he told me in an email that he *doesn't*. "I tend to act as if 'a billion years from now' is equivalent to 'never'—I just refuse to care about timescales of that order of magnitude," he wrote. "Too many other unfathomable things will happen between now and then."

Well, I can't help myself, Dr. Pinker. So as a parting thought, let's stop and look at the days when some of those "unfathomable things" have actually happened and everything turns to nothing. I have to know: What exactly is doomsday and is it really inevitable?

If you're an egghead who reads science books, you probably take it as a given that it is. If you're a scientist, on the other hand, there's a good chance you take issue with things being called "inevitable." Daniel Whiteson, a physicist at the University of California, Irvine, and the author of *We Have No Idea: A Guide to the Unknown Universe*, told me, "It's impossible to say anything confidently about what's going to happen in a thousand years or billion years, because we're just learning every year how clueless we are."

But a certain breed of science nerd seems to take actual comfort in an ultimate and inevitable apocalypse—or if not comfort, per se, then a certain gleeful, misanthropic relish. This perverse apocalyptic zeal is best exemplified by the ultra-viral YouTube animations made by the German design studio known as "Kurzgesagt—In a Nutshell." Kurzgesagt videos explain natural phenomena in fun, easy-to-digest terms, pausing every so often to cheerfully note the inevitability of your death, dear viewer, not to mention the extinction of your entire species. In one of their videos, they elaborate on this perspective, calling it "optimistic nihilism"—a term they coined themselves. Their explanation of what optimistic nihilism is sounds like a speech delivered by Ayn Rand, just before she murders you:

> *Every humiliation you suffer in your life will be forgotten. Every mistake you made will not matter in the end. Every bad thing you did will be voided. If our life is all we get to experience, then it's the only thing that matters. If the universe has no principles, the only principles relevant are the ones we decide on. If the universe has no purpose, then we get to dictate what its purpose is.*

I get that the Kurzgesagt people are attempting a selfless, facts-only worldview that eschews "anthropocentrism," or pro-human bias. That's to be admired, sort of. I also appreciate many of the ethical and philosophical takeaways of "optimistic nihilism," and I realize that my desire for my species to keep existing forever—or at least, not die horribly—is, by definition, anthropocentric.

But that bias is rooted in feelings of existential horror that I can't shake, so admittedly, I'll always approach life with that slant. What's more, I believe anthropocentrism has its virtues. I feel a very strong sense of revulsion when I imagine my entire species literally going extinct. Don't you? If you don't, I'm not sure we can hang, because you sound like a movie villain, apt to do God-knows-what when I turn my back.

Going on the assumption that you *are* a supporter of humanity continuing to exist, here is:

Attempt to put your mind at ease #1: *Humanity as we know it isn't going to be the same forever, but we wouldn't want it to be anyway.*

Bad news first: it looks like nearly every species that currently exists will go extinct eventually, no matter what. As pioneering evolutionary biologist Leigh Van Valen hypothesized in 1976 about groups of organisms, "All groups for which data exist go extinct at a rate that is constant for a given group," which is somewhat irksome. Refusing to soften the blow, he went on, "no definite exceptions exist although a few are possible."

But here's why I wouldn't read too much into that: it doesn't happen all at once. New species, in a way, "replace" older ones. Sparrows are relatives of dinosaurs that showed up toward the middle of dinosaur times, and they're still around today.

Meanwhile, even as species come and go, in about a million years the effects of solar radiation on the Earth's surface will have decreased the concentration of atmospheric carbon dioxide, making most kinds of photosynthesis impossible. As a 1982 paper in the journal *Nature* concluded, this pretty much spells the end of life on Earth as we know it. But don't get too bummed, because according to a 1992 response paper from scientists Ken Caldeira and James F. Kasting, the end of life on Earth *as we know it* doesn't spell the end of life *period*. They postulate a shift to reliance on a different kind of photosynthesis known as C4 photosynthesis—something maize is already capable of—which can potentially keep life going on Earth for hundreds of millions of years.

So within that time frame, picture animals—humans included—continuing to evolve alongside all those corn-based plants. We're the dinosaurs in this analogy, and the sparrows are the similar, but better-adapted life forms that will carry on after we're gone. It might also help to imagine dogs producing offspring more suited to this future, and that process could give way to an equally future-resistant new doglike species. Present-day humans and our associated species may all die off, technically, but that just leaves more room for our descendants.

What's more: maybe the organisms we give way to will transcend such primitive notions as the longing for immortality, and will instead embrace oblivion like a species made up entirely of enlightened Zen Buddhists. After all, our planet itself is a finite resource. And its finitude could one day leave our descendants with nowhere to live. So even if we keep struggling to survive, *they'd* better make peace with death, right? Because the planet ain't forever, either.

Attempt to put your mind at ease #2: *Maybe we won't need Earth.*

This is the part where things are going to get very unsettling, but it gets better so stick with me:

Statistically speaking, sometime in the next six hundred thousand years, the Earth will most likely collide with an asteroid that has a diameter of one kilometer or more. According to the calculator on another of my favorite websites, the Earth Impact Effects Program, that would be the equivalent of about 47,000 megatons of TNT, enough to wreak the same environmental havoc as an entire regional nuclear war. But humans, or whatever earthling species exists at that point, may well have some sort of photon torpedo that can easily prevent that from happening. Then again, we've already established in the chapter on volcanoes that earthlings will probably have to deal with a catastrophic super-volcanic event in the next million years or so. That could potentially be worse than an asteroid.

But it's *possible* that humanity could keep chugging along, not just by getting better and better at fighting disasters on Earth but by escaping the confines of our homeworld altogether. We're in the data-free realm of pure theory now, but in 1964 Soviet astrophysicist Nikolai Kardashev posited that humanity might one day be able to ascend to a status he called "type III civilization," meaning we're so advanced that we're able to make use of all the energy in the entire galaxy. One hopes that by then humans will have moved on to lifestyles that require less energy per individual, but I don't think that's Kardashev's point.

Kardashev wasn't just a starry-eyed sci-fi daydreamer. In his 1985 paper "On the Inevitability and the Possible Structures of Supercivilizations," he explains in detail how a sufficiently advanced civilization—human or otherwise—will find itself building such huge, complex instruments to facilitate technological progress that it will have to derive energy from sources like supermassive black holes, such as the one at the center of the Milky Way galaxy. The futurist Michio Kaku, who is also a trained physicist, thinks it will take somewhere between 100,000 and 1,000,000 of our Earth years for us to get there.

The day we make it to this point, we'll be a "galactic civilization," traveling to and from the center of our galaxy to collect energy, on multi-generational voyages lasting thousands of years. After all, the black hole in our galaxy is twenty-six thousand light years away, and we'll probably never be able to build spaceships that can exceed the speed of light. So to build our energy infrastructure, we'll have to create entire societies that float through space, populated by people who'll never set foot on Earth. And that might be just as well, because we might not need Earth anymore by that point.

We might instead live in something along the lines of O'Neill cylinders, which are theoretical rotating, cylindrical spacecraft with full, life-sustaining ecosystems featuring all the comforts of home. (And by "home" I mean "home planet.") These cylinders are meant to have not just gravity, but simulated dynamic weather, topography, and ecology, meaning dew-speckled meadows in the morning and hooting owls at night. There'll be cities, suburbs, camping trips, lakes, miniature salty oceans, and amber waves of grain. And we'll experience it all while floating in our tin cans like proverbial Major Toms, except thanks to artificial gravity the only actual floating we'll do is in our astro swimming pools.

It's hard to know whether it'll happen before or after those cozy cylinders are open for business, but the sun is set to swallow the Earth in about 7.6 billion years. Fortunately, at that point it's likely that the Earth will no longer be the planet we've all come to know but, instead, a lifeless, deserted husk that humans (or human-esque creatures) abandoned eons before. The day the great swallowing finally arrives, we humans could very well be watching the fireworks from the plush confines of our O'Neill cylinders, or from mining colonies aboard terraformed asteroids, or maybe even from fully functioning civilizations on habitable planets orbiting suns with trillion-year life spans, in contrast to our rather short-lived sun.

Whichever it is, on that day, here's what our descendants may observe—again *from a safe distance*. (I say "may," crossing my fingers that we *will* have figured out by that point some non-Earth option for getting by.) The sun will have been undergoing a slow (from a human perspective) expansion into a red giant, and the now very scorched, dry, lifeless Earth will be going about its business, trying to orbit the sun one last time, but will instead tweak its orbit, circling closer and closer toward the sun like—there's no kind way to say this—a turd in a toilet circling the drain. This will go on for perhaps two months according to a 2015 article by David Rothstein, an astronomy postdoctoral fellow at Cornell University. That will make for strange times on Earth as the world heats up and the sun takes up more and more of the daytime sky, until the sky is nothing but sun. Then one day, Earth will be devoured. It'll happen all at once, like in 2012, when the star BD+48 740 was thought to have swallowed one of its unnamed planets. One day that year, scientists observed that the star had too much lithium, and then deduced from the presence of a lithium-rich planet nearby that the star had suddenly eaten that planet's neighbor, meaning all that lithium was like the chocolate on a baby's chin. So on that day of the Earth's demise, the sun will have taken a little bit of extra iron, oxygen, and silicon into its solar tummy. But with any luck, not too much extra carbon, because our carbon-based descendants will have fled millennia earlier.

But wait a minute, don't we still have to worry about the death of the universe?

Attempt to put your mind at ease #3: *We know less about the far future than we sometimes like to think.*

Whiteson, the physicist at UC Irvine, told me that the "heat death" of the universe isn't actually inevitable. You can instead think of it as the best answer physicists can currently give to the question of where all the trend lines in our understanding of physics lead when you take them as far as they go. Without getting bogged down in math equations, let's just say the universe is expanding, and entropy is increasing, and if that doesn't change, there's a theoretical endpoint where everything is basically devoid of energy, including atoms and subatomic particles, which fall apart. And that means in effect there's no matter or energy left anywhere.

"It looks like we're going that direction," Whiteson said. But, he told me, "that's basically making a linear extrapolation. *If these things continue the way they're going now, what would happen?* Yes, the universe would be very spread out and cold."

Once again I'm going to give you some bad news first, and then some good news: heat death might not have a chance to happen in this way because it all might end the day the Big Bang's asshole brother, the Big Crunch, shows up.

You'll need a quick history lesson from Whiteson about the universe here: In the very first micro-moment—"the first ten-to-the-minus-thirty-five seconds," to be precise—the universe banged itself into existence. But then that stopped, and the universe shifted into "gradual, very slow expansion," for about ten billion years.

Now here's the disconcerting part: about five billion years ago, for reasons we don't yet understand, a mysterious force called dark energy "started pushing the universe apart, and has continued for about five billion years. We have no theory to describe it, and no mechanism that we can use to explain it." The reason this is so scary is that based on what we *do* know about this accelerating expansion, it's entirely possible, Whiteson told me, that dark energy "turns around and starts decelerating the universe, and then accelerating it inward into a super Big Crunch." That would compress the universe into a tiny, dense globule, where—I'm just guessing here—it's a bit too crowded to live.

This could happen, Whiteson said, but here's the more important takeaway: physicists "really just have no idea what's causing this, and we can't make confident extrapolations at all."

This isn't because scientists are just guessing and you shouldn't listen to them—you should *definitely* listen to scientists—it's just that this scientific frontier is exceptionally wild. Whiteson pointed out to me that dark energy was discovered in 1998, which is after the creation of Pokémon. And this end-of-the-universe concept only got an academic name in 2002, when astronomy researcher Milan Ćirković at the Astronomical Observatory of Belgrade wrote a resource letter naming this burgeoning field "physical eschatology"—"eschatology" being the study of the end-times, a term that's usually only used in conjunction with theology. In his letter, Ćirković casts a wide enough net that it includes not just the end of the universe, but "the future evolution of astrophysical objects."

Much of our thinking about something that won't happen for perhaps *trillions of years* has been pieced together from things we learned in the past couple of decades. "Scientists ten gazillion years from now could look back and treat this whole period [the way scientists today treat] the Big Bang. This could just be the first few bits of the universe warming up," Whiteson told me.

More to the point, in light of everything we don't know, he said, "the universe could continue on forever."

I'm sure there are people who will find it naïve of me to spend all this time trying to convince my readers that life can go on forever, but I have a secret motive: I want to convince you that *the future is worth it.* Some of the horrors I've outlined won't be avoided, and some will. Some of the wonderful things I've predicted won't happen, and others will. I can't predict which way the future will lean. But if we fundamentally don't believe in a future at all, I'm pretty sure of one thing: it'll be more horror than wonder.

Weirdly, "doom" is a much cooler concept than "hope" (among some groups at least), and I suspect that's why these days I so often see people with eyes aglow, talking about how climate change is an unstoppable force that will one day kill us all. That's wrong on three counts. Climate change, being caused by humans, is very stoppable, and most assuredly won't kill all of us. More important, as I type these words, the deadliest California wildfires in history, which were exacerbated by climate change, have killed at least one hundred people. Climate change isn't a day in the future; it's a process happening in the present, and we brought it on ourselves because we didn't believe the future was real.

As long as we believe we're utterly doomed, there's no way for us to build a livable future for ourselves. The trouble is, as we've just learned, the future isn't a final outcome, an ellipsis, or a dreamy fade to black with soaring music; it's a collection of days. And the only way those days will be any damn good at all is if we imagine the ones we want, believe we really *can* have them, and try to make them happen.

ACKNOWLEDGMENTS

Before I wrote a book, I always assumed acknowledgments sections were polite tips of the hat to people who encouraged the author. I know better now. The following people didn't just believe in me—they worked their asses off to help me put *The Day It Finally Happens* together, and it's kind of laughable that my name is the only one on the front cover just because I sat down and wrote the words.

First of all, Paige Pearl (née Devitt) pushed me to start this project, helped me write the proposal, ensured that I would actually accomplish things on my reporting trips, arranged some of my interviews, and weeded out my worst ideas, including a mountain of material that—thankfully—no longer exists, except in the layer of hell where the worst deleted book passages go. She also "put up with me"—to use an Oscars speech cliché—which means she saw me through many, many, very literal panic attacks. "I'm sorry you have so many ideas for things that will never exist," she tells me sometimes. It's entirely thanks to Paige that this book is not one of them.

The illustrations and graphics in this book, along with the research behind them, are the work of Bryan Bischof and Leo Rosenberg of Quasicoherent Labs, Inc. I can't mention them without thanking Will Chernoff for telling me they exist. The Quasicoherent Labs guys were a godsend, because they offered a service I didn't think existed, but which I nonetheless needed: a one-stop shop that could (as their name suggests) translate my insane, blue-sky ideas into something that makes sense, crunch the relevant numbers, and formulate a visual presentation for the data they found. In my opinion, the illustration that opens the immortality chapter is worth the price of this book alone, because it's so deeply researched and cleverly presented that you can spend a whole morning (as I did) turning it around in your hands, peering at it from different angles, and gaining more and more insight.

John Orlow endured the nightmare of interview transcriptions for me and I would be in a mental hospital right now if he hadn't. Sam Roudman was that rare fact-checker who manages to make a piece of writing more fun to read rather than more boring. Mark Balane did stealth graphic design work, along with Ian Gordon and Shawn Scott. Nate Miller took my author photo. Peter Miller helped out with research and fact-checking. Justin Caffier allowed me to text him ideas and thoughts that were not otherwise fit for human consumption, a necessary disposal service when you're trying to write a book people can actually read.

Jamie Taete, Grace Wyler, Dave Schilling, Harry Cheadle, Arielle Pardes, and Matt Taylor are all colleagues who, in various ways, nurtured the ideas that later became *The Day It Finally Happens*, long before I'd ever given any thought to writing a book. Brian Merchant was indispensable in approximately a million ways: unwittingly showing me the path to being an author, liking the idea, and passing it along to his agent—now also my agent—Eric Lupfer, who is a visionary (yes, there are visionary literary agents). Claire Leow, He Shuming, Fadi Abou Akleh, Yusuf Khurram, Paul O'Dowd, and Donna Lu were helpful guides during my travels. In some ineffable way, music by Cliff Martinez, Four Tet, HEALTH, Snail Mail, and Porches unlocked my ability to write at times when I otherwise couldn't have.

Rick Horgan and Emily Greenwald gave this book a home at Scribner, which was more than enough to earn my gratitude, but they also proved to be generous editors who shepherded the project through every stage of the writing process. Huw Armstrong gave this book a home at Hodder & Stoughton, and his enthusiasm gave me a much-needed jolt of confidence.

I owe a huge debt of gratitude to the gifts that fell into my lap at birth, including my race (white), upbringing (easy), and class (middle). I also wish to thank my Mom and Dad, my sister Maritte, and my dog Lilo.

Last but most of all, the highly influential presence of my Uncle Sam in my life, from my birth until his death right around the time I started work on this book, was something I always took for granted until he was gone. Sam exposed me to books by Kurt Vonnegut, which would have been enough, but he also lived by a unique set of values that I try to emulate. He was big on compassion, kindness, and humor, but he also had a lifelong habit of gently pushing people past what they perceived as the boundaries of their abilities, so he could derive vicarious joy from watching them succeed. I hope he would have liked this book. I wasn't sure I could write it, but then I did.

NOTES

INTRODUCTION

xi   "aren't dangerous enough": Mike Pearl, "How Scared Should I Be of Pit Bulls?," *Vice*, November 19, 2015, https://www.vice.com/en_us/article/qbxxxd/how -scared-should-i-be-of-pit-bulls-107.

xi   "fatalities from falling tree limbs": Thomas W. Schmidlin, "Human Fatalities from Wind-Related Tree Failures in the United States 1995–2007," *Journal of the International Society for the Prevention and Mitigation of Natural Hazards*, November 18, 2008, 13.

xi   "4.5 million annual dog bites": Centers for Disease Control "Dogs," and Prevention, updated July 14, 2016, https://www.cdc.gov/healthypets/pets /dogs.html.

xiii   "0.8 degrees Celsius": Rajendra Pachauri et al., "Climate Change 2014: Synthesis Report," *Fifth Assessment Report of the Intergovernmental Panel on Climate Change* 2015, 2.

xiii   "increasing our emissions once again": Rhodium Group Energy & Climate Staff, "Preliminary US Emissions Estimates for 2018," January 8, 2019, https:// rhg.com/research/preliminary-us-emissions-estimates-for-2018.

xiii   "4 degrees Celsius by 2084": Xiaoxin Wang et al., "Climate Change of 4°C Global Warming Above Pre-industrial Levels," *Advances in Atmospheric Sciences*, July 2018, 757.

xiv   "watery future for major coastal cities": Josh Holder et al., "The Three-Degree World: The Cities That Will Be Drowned by Global Warming," *Guardian*, November 3, 2017, https://www.theguardian.com/cities/ng-interactive/2017 /nov/03/three-degree-world-cities-drowned-global-warming.

xiv   "Americans get their news from Facebook": John Gramlich, "10 Facts About Americans and Facebook," Pew Research Center Fact Tank, April 10, 2018, http://www.pewresearch.org/fact-tank/2019/02/01/facts-about-americans -and-facebook.

xiv   "72 percent are worried": Aaron Smith and Monica Anderson, "Automation in Everyday Life," Pew Research Center Internet & Technology, October 4, 2017, http://www.pewinternet.org/2017/10/04/automation-in-everyday-life.

xv "cooked up a crazy hypothetical": George C. Mitchell, *Matthew B. Ridgway: Soldier, Statesman, Scholar, Citizen* (Pittsburgh: Cathedral Publishing, 1999), 72.

THE DAY THE UK FINALLY ABOLISHES ITS MONARCHY

4 "monarchy-related tourism": "Monarchy 2017," *Brand Finance*, 2017, 5.

5 "no rigorous, transparent, academic research": Claire Haven-Tang, "Fact Check: Do Tourists Visit Britain Because of the Royal Family?," *Conversation*, December 1, 2017, https://theconversation.com/fact-check-do-tourists-visit-britain-because-of-the-royal-family-88335.

6 "70 percent of Chinese shoppers": "Monarchy 2017," *Brand Finance*, 2017, 4.

6 "As of this writing": Scott Mendelson, "Box Office: *Avengers: Endgame* Probably Won't Top *Avatar*, And That's Good For Disney," *Forbes*, June 3, 2019, https://www.forbes.com/sites/scottmendelson/2019/06/03/avengers-endgame-avatar-star-wars-force-awakens-james-cameron-disney-box-office/#70b79a77879a2019.

6 "£513 million in profit": Anthony D'Alessandro, "*Avengers: Endgame* To Near Rare Breakeven Point With $1.1B Global Opening," *Deadline*, April 27, 2019, https://deadline.com/2019/04/avengers-endgame-breakeven-profit-after-opening-weekend-box-office-marvel-1202603237/.

6 "Britain's Loyalest Royalist": YouTube user *Wall Street Journal*, "Is This Britain's Loyalest Royalist?" YouTube, September 8, 2015, https://www.youtube.com/watch?v=SnxM3DkqCfI.

9 "election was suspect": Yoan Kolev, "1946: Third Bulgarian Kingdom Ends with a Referendum," Radio Bulgaria, August 23, 2014, http://bnr.bg/en/post/100450616/1946-third-bulgarian-kingdom-ends-with-a-referendum.

10 "six realms": "New rules on royal succession come into force," BBC News, March 26, 2015, https://www.bbc.com/news/uk-32073399.

11 "pays for the royal family": "Crown Estate Makes Record £304m Treasury Payout," BBC News, June 28, 2016, https://www.bbc.com/news/uk-36643314.

12 "royal brand's share": "Monarchy 2017," *Brand Finance*, 2017, 4.

13 "Guest said of his stint": Richard Grant, "Nowt So Queer as Folk," *Guardian*, January 9, 2004, https://www.theguardian.com/film/2004/jan/10/features.weekend.

THE DAY A TECH BILLIONAIRE TAKES OVER THE WORLD

20 "a wonder it hasn't happened": Hans Joachim Morgenthau, *Politics Among Nations: The Struggle for Power and Peace*, 6th ed. (New York: McGraw-Hill, 1995), 202.

21 "global value chain": Gary Gereffi et al., *Global Value Chain Analysis: A Primer*, Duke University Center on Globalization, Governance & Competitiveness, July 2016, 7.

21 "beyond being mere companies": Balaji Srinivasan, "Silicon Valley's Ultimate Exit," Speech to Y Combinator Conference, October 25, 2013, https://www .youtube.com/watch?v=cOubCHLXT6A.

22 "met with the US president": Peter Kafka, "Balaji Srinivasan, Who May Run the FDA for Trump, Hates the FDA. But Silicon Valley Likes Srinivasan," *Recode*, January 14, 2017, https://www.recode.net/2017/1/14/14276530/balaji -srinivasan-trump-fda-twitter-andreessen-horowitz.

22 "allegedly thinks shouldn't exist": Elizabeth Spiers (@espiers), "He's an ex of mine. (I am living in the strangest computer sim.) Super smart but can't imagine him wanting to run FDA except to dismantle it," Twitter, January 14, 2017, 5:05 p.m., https://twitter.com/espiers/status/820391496008470529.

22 "recommended Srinivasan to the president": Elizabeth Dwoskin, "The Secretive Brain Trust of Silicon Valley Insiders Who Are Helping Trump," *Washington Post*, November 21, 2016.

22 "well-publicized libertarian leanings": Sean Sullivan, "The Politics of Jeff Bezos," *Washington Post*, August 7, 2013.

23 "investigating 'the singularity' for *Vice*": Mike Pearl, "How Scared Should I Be of the Singularity?," *Vice*, October 4, 2016, https://www.vice.com/en_us /article/qbnk77/how-scared-should-i-be-of-the-singularity.

23 "anything to win the contest": Shannon Liao, "The Eight Most Outrageous Things Cities Did to Lure Amazon for HQ2," *Verge*, October 19, 2017, https:// www.theverge.com/2017/10/19/16504042/amazon-hq2-second-headquarters -most-funny-crazy-pitches-proposals-stonecrest-new-york.

23 "giant saguaro cactus": Yvonne Sanchez, "Amazon Rejects Tucson's Gift of a 21-Foot Saguaro Cactus," *Arizona Republic*, September 9, 2017.

23 "stadium full of hockey fans": @jyrki21, "We are currently cheering for Amazon to set up shop in Ottawa during a TV timeout. I'm not making this up. #Canucks #Sens," Twitter, October 17, 2017, 8:47 p.m., https://twitter.com /Jyrki21/status/920451152621244417.

24 "Erin Biba was hounded": Erin Biba, "What It's Like When Elon Musk's Twitter Mob Comes After You," *Daily Beast*, May 28, 2018, https://www.thedailybeast .com/what-its-like-when-elon-musks-twitter-mob-comes-after-you.

24 "Colombian death squads": Associated Press, "Chiquita Brands faces new death squad charges in Colombia," August 31, 2018.

THE DAY DOPING IS ALLOWED AT THE OLYMPICS

27 "debating each other in 2016": Regan Penaluna, "Head to Head: Should We Allow a Doping Free-for-All," *Nautilus,* August 18, 2016.

29 "missed the email": Simon Hattenstone, "Maria Sharapova on failing that drug test: 'I felt trapped, tricked,'" *Guardian*, September 9, 2017.

29 "2 percent performance improvement": Alexis Mauger et al., "Influence of Acetaminophen on Performance During Time Trial Cycling," *Journal of Applied Physiology*, January 2010, 98–104.

30 "notorious wave of records broken": Jamie Strashin, "Should track and field erase its record book?," CBC News, July 31, 2017, https://www.cbc.ca/sports /olympics/trackandfield/track-and-field-erase-record-book-1.4221985.

30 "his steroids or mine": Pat Putnam, "Good Things Come in Large Packages," *Sports Illustrated*, August 23, 1971.

31 "were considered cheaters": Duncan Stone, "When Doping Wasn't Considered Cheating," *Conversation*, February 9, 2018, https://theconversation.com /when-doping-wasnt-considered-cheating-63442.

31 "bioethicist Thomas Murray once wrote": Thomas Murray, "Sports Enhancement," *Hastings Center Bioethics Briefings*, undated, https://www.thehast ingscenter.org/briefingbook/sports-enhancement/.

31 "unusually high prevalence": Karim Khan, "Meldonium Use by Athletes at the Baku 2015 European Games. Adding Data to Ms Maria Sharapova's Failed Drug Test Case," *British Journal of Sports Medicine Blog*, March 8, 2016, http://blogs.bmj.com/bjsm/2016/03/08/meldonium-use-by-athletes-at-the -baku-2015-european-games-adding-data-to-ms-maria-sharapovas-failed-drug -test-case/.

32 "actual effects of meldonium": Andrew Pollack, "Effects of Meldonium on Athletes Are Hazy," *New York Times*, March 10, 2016, https://www.nytimes .com/2016/03/11/sports/tennis/effects-of-meldonium-on-athletes-are-hazy .html.

32 "testing female athletes": Ruth Padawer, "The Humiliating Practice of Sex-Testing Female Athletes," *New York Times Magazine*, June 28, 2016.

33 "everyone knew at the time": Kate Galbraith, "Is Mark McGwire on Steroids?," *Slate*, August 25, 1998, https://slate.com/news-and-politics/1998/08 /is-mark-mcgwire-on-steroids.html.

33 "admitted as much": "McGwire Apologizes to La Russa, Selig," ESPN.com, January 12, 2010, http://www.espn.com/mlb/news/story?id=4816607.

33 "announces what he eats": Matthew Evans, "Diet in a Day: Olympic Gold Medal Swimmer Adam Peaty," *Men's Health*, July 24, 2017.

33 "released Oxycontin": Purdue Pharma, "About Purdue Pharma," undated, http://www.purduepharma.com/about/#&panel1-16.

33 "revenues of about $2.8 billion": Barry Meier, "In Guilty Plea, OxyContin Maker to Pay $600 Million," *New York Times*, May 10, 2007.

33 "big fat lawsuit": Tina Bellon, "U.S. State Lawsuits Against Purdue Pharma over Opioid Epidemic Mount," Reuters, May 15, 2018.

35 "2014 lab test on rats": Dmitry Zaretsky et al., "The Ergogenic Effect of Amphetamine," *Temperature*, 2014, 242–47.

35 "as the Earth gets hotter": Kirk Smith et al., "The last Summer Olympics? Climate change, health, and work outdoors," *Lancet*, August 13, 2016, 642–44.

36 "2004 review": Fred Hartgens et al., "Effects of Androgenic-Anabolic Steroids in Athletes," *Sports Medicine*, July 2004, 514–46.

37 "life spans of former Olympic medalists": R. Zwiers et al., "Mortality in Former Olympic Athletes: Retrospective Cohort Analysis," *BMJ*, December 2012.

THE DAY HUMANS BECOME IMMORTAL

41 "2013 op-ed": Roger Cohen, "When I'm Sixty-Four," *New York Times*, December 24, 2013, https://www.nytimes.com/2013/12/25/opinion/cohen-when -im-sixty-four.html.

42 "anti-aging activist": Aubrey de Grey, "How We Can Finally Win the Fight Against Aging?," filmed November 2016 at TEDxMünchen, Munich, https:// www.youtube.com/watch?v=AvWtSUdOWVI.

42 "three leading causes of death": CDC, "Achievements in Public Health, 1900–1999: Control of Infectious Diseases," *Morbidity and Mortality Weekly Report*, July 30, 1999, https://www.cdc.gov/mmwr/preview/mmwrhtml /mm4829a1.htm.

42 "kills 90 percent of people": Aubrey de Grey, "Life Span Extension Research and Public Debate: Societal Considerations," *Studies in Ethics, Law, and Technology*, January 2007, 6.

42 "aging is the damage": C. López-Otín et al., "The Hallmarks of Aging," *Cell*, June 6, 2013, 1195.

THE DAY ANYONE CAN IMITATE ANYONE ELSE PERFECTLY

52 "Face2Face: Real-Time Face Capture": Justus Thies et al., "Face2Face: Real-Time Face Capture and Reenactment of RGB Videos," *2016 IEEE Conference on Computer Vision and Pattern Recognition,* 2387–95.

53 "deepfakes": Samantha Cole, "AI-Assisted Fake Porn Is Here and We're All Fucked," *VICE Motherboard,* December 11, 2017, https://motherboard.vice.com/en_us/article/gydydm/gal-gadot-fake-ai-porn.

53 "Jordan Peele": David Mack, "This PSA About Fake News from Barack Obama Is Not What It Appears," BuzzFeed News, April 17, 2018, https://www.buzzfeednews.com/article/davidmack/obama-fake-news-jordan-peele-psa-video-buzzfeed.

55 "catfishing scams": Nicholas Searle, "My Geriatric 'Catfishing' Cautionary Tale," *Salon,* March 5, 2016, https://www.salon.com/2016/03/05/my_geriatric_catfishing_cautionary_tale/.

THE DAY THE LAST HUMAN-DRIVEN CAR ROLLS OFF THE LOT

62 "reimagining roads as harmonious places": Shin Kato et al., "Cooperative Driving of Autonomous Vehicles Based on Localization, Inter-Vehicle Communications and Vision Systems," *JSAE Review,* October 2001, 503–9.

62 "one in China": Neal E. Boudette, "Autopilot Cited in Death of Chinese Tesla Driver," *New York Times,* September 14, 2016.

62 "and three": Jackie Wattles, "Tesla Model X Was in Autopilot Before Fatal Crash," *CNN Business,* March 31, 2018, https://money.cnn.com/2018/03/31/technology/tesla-model-x-crash-autopilot/.

62 "in the US": Charles Fleming, "Tesla Car Mangled in Fatal Crash Was on Autopilot and Speeding, NTSB Says," *Los Angeles Times,* July 26, 2016.

62 "Gill Pratt of the Toyota Research": Tom Vanderbilt, "Autonomous Cars: How Safe Is Safe Enough?," *Car and Driver,* October 3, 2017.

62 "seven million miles": Timothy B. Lee, "Waymo Announces 7 Million Miles of Testing, Putting It Far Ahead of Rivals," *Ars Technica,* June 6, 2018, https://arstechnica.com/cars/2018/06/waymo-announces-7-million-miles-of-testing-putting-it-far-ahead-of-rivals/.

62 "another driver's fault": Jaclyn Cosgrove et al., "Waymo Self-Driving Car Involved in Arizona Crash—But Wasn't at Fault, Police Say," *Los Angeles Times,* May 5, 2018.

63 "2018 study published in *Nature*": Edmond Awad et al., "The Moral Machine Experiment," *Nature,* October 24, 2018, 59–64.

63 "having sex in them": Scott A. Cohen et al., "Autonomous Vehicles and the Future of Urban Tourism," *Annals of Tourism Research*, January 2019, 33–42.

63 "Full Tilt": Clive Thompson et al., "Full Tilt: When 100% of Cars Are Autonomous," *New York Times Magazine*, November 8, 2017.

63 "population leader": Tom Phillips et al., "India Is World's Most Populous Nation with 1.32bn People, Academic Claims," *Guardian*, May 24, 2017.

64 "started in the mid-2000s": Amy Waldman, "In Today's India, Status Comes with Four Wheels," *New York Times*, December 5, 2005.

64 "multi-decade public works project": Amy Waldman, "Mile by Mile, India Paves a Smoother Road to Its Future," *New York Times*, December 4, 2005.

64 "injury data": "Global Status Report on Road Safety," World Health Organization, 2009.

65 "downfall of social media": Vivek Wadhwa, "Five Tech Predictions for 2012," *Washington Post*, December 30, 2011.

65 "crisis-level air pollution": Michael Safi, "Delhi's Air Pollution Is Now So Bad It Is Literally Off the Chart," *Guardian*, June 15, 2018.

66 "hardware will only cost $5,000": Paul Lienert, "Self-Driving Costs Could Drop 90 Percent by 2025, Delphi CEO Says," Reuters, December 4, 2017.

66 "self-driving car software free": Ryan Felton, "Baidu Open-Sources Its Software to Speed Up the Development of Autonomous Car Tech," *Jalopnik*, April 24, 2017.

THE DAY SAUDI ARABIA PUMPS ITS LAST BARREL OF OIL

72 "seventeenth highest GDP": "Projected GDP Ranking (2019–2023)," *Statistics Times*, April 2, 2018, http://statisticstimes.com/economy/projected-world-gdp-ranking.php.

72 "super bullish": John Kemp, "Hedge Fund Oil Bulls on the Rampage as Bears Vanish: Kemp," Reuters, April 23, 2018.

73 "45 percent": "Summary for Policymakers of IPCC Special Report on Global Warming of 1.5°C Approved by Governments," Intergovernmental Panel on Climate Change Newsroom, October 8, 2018.

73 "fantastical commercial": YouTube user Arch Daily, "Saudi Arabia Plans Futuristic City, 'Neom,'" YouTube, October 16, 2017, https://www.youtube.com/watch?v=N53DzL3_BHA.

74 "project website for Neom": Neom, "Neom Fact Sheet," (Full Promotional Video) undated, https://www.neom.com/content/pdfs/NEOM-Fact-Sheet-en.pdf.

74 "prospect of Neom working out": "Report: Political Instability May Slow Prog-

ress of Saudi Mega-City," *Middle East Monitor*, February 7, 2018, https://www
.middleeastmonitor.com/20180207-report-political-instability-may-slow-prog
ress-of-saudi-mega-city/.

74　"18 percent of all proven petroleum": "Saudi Arabia Facts and Figures," OPEC,
undated, https://www.opec.org/opec_web/en/about_us/169.htm.

74　"82.3 percent of Saudi Arabia's exports": "Saudi Arabia," The Observatory
of Economic Complexity, undated, https://atlas.media.mit.edu/en/profile
/country/sau/.

74　"non-oil exports will rise": *Saudi Gazette*, "Full Text of Saudi Arabia's Vision
2030," *Al Arabiya*, April 26, 2016, https://english.alarabiya.net/en/perspective
/features/2016/04/26/Full-text-of-Saudi-Arabia-s-Vision-2030.html.

74　"13 percent": "Best Countries for Business," *Forbes*, December 19, 2018,
https://www.forbes.com/places/saudi-arabia.

76　"publicly flogged": Ian Black, "Pressure Grows on Saudi Arabia over Blogger
Facing Second Flogging," *Guardian*, January 15, 2015, https://www.theguard
ian.com/world/2015/jan/15/pressure-saudi-arabia-over-blogger-raif-bada
wi-flogging.

76　"the crown prince had him murdered": Shane Harris et al., "CIA Concludes
Saudi Crown Prince Ordered Jamal Khashoggi's Assassination," *Washington
Post*, November 16, 2018.

76　"women began to receive driver's licenses": Ben Hubbard, "Making History,
Saudi Arabia Issues Driver's Licenses to 10 Women," *New York Times*, June
4, 2018, https://www.nytimes.com/2018/06/04/world/middleeast/saudi-ara
bia-drivers-licenses-women.html.

77　"youth unemployment rate in 2030": "Saudi Youth Unemployment Forecast
to Exceed 42% by 2030," *Arabian Business*, November 26, 2016, https://
www.arabianbusiness.com/saudi-youth-unemployment-forecast-exceed-42
-by-2030-653770.html.

77　"private sector jobs in the kingdom": Ahmed Al Omran, "Saudi Arabia Raises
the Alarm over Rising Unemployment," *Financial Times*, April 24, 2018.

77　"one-trick pony": Carla Power, "Saudi Arabia Bulldozes Over Its Heritage,"
Time, November 14, 2014.

78　"birthplace of the Prophet Muhammad": David Usborne, "Redevelopment
of Mecca: Bulldozers Bear Down on Site of Mohamed's Birth," *Independent*,
February 20, 2014.

78　"reputability": Karsten Strauss, "The World's Most Reputable Countries
2016: U.S. Ranks 28th," *Forbes*, June 24, 2016, https://www.forbes.com/sites
/karstenstrauss/2016/06/24/the-worlds-most-reputable-countries-2016-u-s-a
-ranks-28th/#141a32847a9f.

78　"Americans have an unfavorable view": "Country Ratings," Gallup Historical

Trends, August 22, 2018, https://news.gallup.com/poll/1624/perceptions-foreign
-countries.aspx.

THE DAY A REAL JURASSIC PARK OPENS

80 "convicted of fraud": Doha Madani, "Fyre Festival Organizer Billy McFarland Sentenced to 6 Years on Fraud Charges," NBC News, October 11,
2018, https://www.nbcnews.com/news/us-news/fyre-festival-organizer-billy
-mcfarland-sentenced-6-years-fraud-charges-n919086.

81 "no closer to the science fiction fantasy": Robert Lee Hotz, "Scientists Recover
DNA from Time of Dinosaurs," *Los Angeles Times*, June 10, 1993.

81 "most of it is from the Cretaceous period": Susan Ward, "Welcome to the
World of Amber," Emporia State University website, January 1996, http://
www.euroamber.ca/brief_history_and_facts_on_amber.pdf.

81 "mosquitoes preserved": Susan Ward, "Myths and Truths About Amber,"
Emporia State University website, January 1996, http://academic.emporia
.edu/abersusa/myths.htm.

81 "thought to be a bit of a stretch": "Here Come the DNAsaurs," *Newsweek*,
June 13, 1993, https://www.newsweek.com/here-come-dnasaurs-194026.

82 "Cohen/Boyer patents": Stanley N. Cohen and Herbert W. Boyer, "Process
for Producing Biologically Functional Molecular Chimeras," United States
Patent Office, December 2, 1980.

82 "521 years": Matt Kaplan, "DNA Has a 521-Year Half-Life," *Nature*, October
10, 2012, https://www.nature.com/news/dna-has-a-521-year-half-life-1.11555.

82 "cloned ibex": Charles Q. Choi, "First Extinct-Animal Clone Created,"
National Geographic, February 10, 2009.

84 "expected count of 238 animals": Michael Crichton, *Jurassic Park* (New York:
Alfred A. Knopf, 1990), 161.

THE DAY ANTIBIOTICS DON'T WORK ANYMORE

90 "report commissioned in 2014": Jim O'Neill et al., "Tackling Drug-Resistant
Infections Globally: Final Report and Recommendations," *Review on Anti-
microbial Resistance*, May 2016.

91 "the end of modern medicine": Press Association, "Antibiotic Resistance Could
Spell End Of Modern Medicine, Says Chief Medic," *Guardian*, October 13,
2017.

91 "Nobel Prize acceptance speech": Alexander Fleming, "Penicillin," Nobel
Lecture, December 11, 1945, https://www.nobelprize.org/uploads/2018/06
/fleming-lecture.pdf.

91 "accidentally ingested antibiotics": Ernest E. Faville et al., "Successful Farming," Meredith Corporation, 1950.

91 "2010 article by Ralph Loglisci": Ralph Loglisci, "New FDA Numbers Reveal Food Animals Consume Lion's Share of Antibiotics," Center for a Liveable Future, December 23, 2010, http://livablefutureblog.com/2010/12/new-fda-num bers-reveal-food-animals-consume-lion%E2%80%99s-share-of-antibiotics.

91 "some controls in place": Alison Moodie, "Will New FDA Rules Curb the Rise of Antibiotic-Resistant Superbugs?" *Guardian*, January 8, 2017.

91 "slowly rolling out similar controls": Charlotte Middlehurst, "Can China Kick Its Animal Antibiotic Habit?" *Guardian*, June 19, 2018.

91 "a third of prescriptions": "CDC: 1 in 3 Antibiotic Prescriptions Unnecessary," Centers for Disease Control and Prevention, May 3, 2016, https://www.cdc .gov/media/releases/2016/p0503-unnecessary-prescriptions.html.

92 "lost some of its efficacy": G. Ziv et al., "Intramuscular Treatment of Subclinical Staphylococcal Mastitis in Lactating Cows with Penicillin G, Methicillin and Their Esters," *Journal of Veterinary Pharmacology and Therapeutics*, September 1985, 276–83.

92 "flesh-eating bacteria": Silvia Paz Maya et al., "Necrotizing Fasciitis: An Urgent Diagnosis," *Skeletal Radiology*, January 2014, 577–89.

92 "famous in the US and UK": Dennis L. Stevens, "The Flesh-Eating Bacterium: What's Next?," *Journal of Infectious Diseases*, March 1999, 366–74.

92 "places like convalescent homes": S. F. Bradley et al., "Methicillin-Resistant Staphylococcus Aureus: Colonization and Infection in a Long-Term Care Facility," *Annals of Internal Medicine*, September 15, 1991, 417–22.

92 "fully recovering six months later": "Meet Grant Hill," Stop MRSA Now, undated, http://www.stopmrsanow.org/meet-grant-hill.html.

92 "career-ending MRSA infection": A. J. Perez, "Giants TE Daniel Fells to Have 10th Surgery to Treat MRSA," *USA Today*, December 7, 2015.

93 "Bad Bugs, No Drugs": "Bad Bugs, No Drugs," Infectious Diseases Society of America, 2004 (note: removed from the website), https://www.idsociety.org /Template.cfm?Section=Antimicrobials&Template=/ContentManagement /ContentDisplay.cfm&ContentID=9718.

93 "five times the risk of infection": Jon Van, "'85 Salmonella Outbreak Largest Ever, Study Says," *Chicago Tribune*, December 11, 1987.

93 "nonfatally poisoned": Thomas J. Török, M.D., et al., "A Large Community Outbreak of Salmonellosis Caused by Intentional Contamination of Restaurant Salad Bars," *Journal of the American Medical Association*, August 6, 1997, 389–95.

94 "Africa and Asia": Monica H. Green, "Taking 'Pandemic' Seriously: Making the Black Death Global," *Medieval Globe*, 2016, 1.

NOTES261

94 "eighty-eight million rats": Andrew Buncombe, "The Verminators: On the Frontline of Mumbai's Battle with 88 Million Rats," *Independent*, August 20, 2012.

94 "two million rats": Polly Mosendz, "New York Doesn't Have More Rats Than People After All," *Newsweek*, November 6, 2014.

95 "clothes of the dead": Carlo M. Cipolla, *Before the Industrial Revolution: European Society and Economy 1000–1700* (New York: W. W. Norton & Company, 1974), 20.

96 "ubiquitous availability of antibiotics": Dr. Philip Mathew, "India's War Against Over-the-Counter Antibiotic Abuse," *The Week*, June 6, 2017.

96 "reemerging disease": Marc Galimand, "Resistance of *Yersinia Pestis* to Anti-microbial Agents," *Antimicrobial Agents and Chemotherapy*, October 2006, 3233–36.

97 "Canadian health-care workers": Kevin J. Mitchell et al., "Sickness Presentee-ism: The Prevalence of Coming to Work While Ill Among Paediatric Resident Physicians in Canada," *Paediatrics & Child Health*, May 2017, 84–88.

97 "at risk for streptococcal infections": Miwako Kobayashi et al., "A Cluster of Group A Streptococcal Infections in a Skilled Nursing Facility—the Potential Role of Healthcare Worker Presenteeism," *Journal of the American Geriatrics Society*, November 7, 2016, 279–84.

97 "condoms are much more effective": Gabriela Paz-Bailey et al., "The Effect of Correct and Consistent Condom Use on Chlamydial and Gonococcal Infection Among Urban Adolescents," *Archives of Pediatrics and Adolescent Medicine*, June 2005, 536–42.

97 "2017 US study": Casey E. Copen, "Condom Use During Sexual Inter-course Among Women and Men Aged 15–44 in the United States: 2011–2015 National Survey of Family Growth," *National Health Statistics Reports*, August 10, 2017, 1–17.

98 "banned in the US since 1972": Richard D. Lyons, "F.D.A. Curbs Use of Germicide Tied to Infant Deaths," *New York Times*, September 23, 1972.

98 "mortality rate from MRSA bacteremia": M. Pastagia et al., "Predicting Risk for Death from MRSA Bacteremia," *Emerging Infectious Diseases*, July 2012, 1072–80.

98 "vancomycin-resistant Staphylococcus aureus": W. A. McGuinness et al., "Vancomycin Resistance in *Staphylococcus Aureus*," *Yale Journal of Biology and Medicine*, June 23, 2017, 269–81.

98 "daptomycin-resistant Staphylococcus aureus": A. S. Bayer et al., "Mecha-nisms of Daptomycin Resistance in Staphylococcus Aureus: Role of the Cell Membrane and Cell Wall," *Annals of the New York Academy of Sciences*, January 2013, 139–58.

100   "global data on sepsis": Issrah Jawad et al., "Assessing Available Information on the Burden of Sepsis: Global Estimates of Incidence, Prevalence and Mortality," *Journal of Global Health*, June 2012, 1–9.

100   "not widely available": Argyris S. Michalopoulos, "The Revival of Fosfomycin," *International Journal of Infectious Diseases*, November 2011, e732–39.

100   "Greek report on problem-child drugs": Matthew E. Falagas et al., "Potential of Old-Generation Antibiotics to Address Current Need for New Antibiotics," *Expert Review of Anti-infective Therapy*, 593–600.

THE DAY THE LAST FISH IN THE OCEAN DIES

105   "extremely bad stuff happened": Hillel J. Hoffman, "The Permian Extinction— When Life Nearly Came to an End," *National Geographic*, undated, https://www.nationalgeographic.com/science/prehistoric-world/permian-extinction/.

106   "temperature-dependent hypoxia": Justin Leonard Penn et al. (including Jonathan Payne), "Temperature-Dependent Hypoxia Explains End-Permian Mass Extinction in the Oceans," GSA Annual Meeting in Seattle, Washington, USA—2017, https://gsa.confex.com/gsa/2017AM/webprogram/Paper304319.html.

106   "over sixty thousand years": Seth D. Burgess et al., "High-Precision Timeline for Earth's Most Severe Extinction," *Proceedings of the National Academy of Sciences of the United States of America*, March 4, 2014, 3316–21.

106   "several million metric tons of plastic garbage": Jenna R. Jambeck et al., "Plastic Waste Inputs from Land into the Ocean," *Science*, February 13, 2015, 768–71.

106   "highly degraded seascapes": Antonio Pusceddu et al., "Chronic and Intensive Bottom Trawling Impairs Deep-Sea Biodiversity and Ecosystem Functioning," *Proceedings of the National Academy of Sciences of the United States of America*, June 17, 2014, 8861–66.

106   "a few more centuries": Fred Pearce, "Less Gloopy Oceans Will Slow Climate Change," *New Scientist*, March 21, 2014, https://www.newscientist.com/article/dn25272-less-gloopy-oceans-will-slow-climate-change/.

106   "dead zones": Damian Carrington, "Oceans Suffocating as Huge Dead Zones Quadruple Since 1950, Scientists Warn," *Guardian*, January 4, 2018.

107   "90 percent of fish stocks": United Nations Food and Agriculture Organization, "General situation of world fish stocks," 2018, http://www.fao.org/newsroom/common/ecg/1000505/en/stocks.pdf.

108   "96 percent of marine species": David Raup, "Size of the Permo-Triassic Bottleneck and Its Evolutionary Implications," *Science*, October 12, 1979, 217–18.

108 "chytrid fungus infections": Cherie Briggs Lab, "Frog-Killing Chytrid Fungus in California," Ecology, Evolution, and Marine Biology, UC Santa Barbara, https://labs.eemb.ucsb.edu/briggs/cherie/research/frog-killing-chytrid-fungus -california.

108 "Southern California kit fox": Peter Maas, "Globally Extinct Mammals," The Sixth Extinction, undated, https://petermaas.nl/extinct/lists/globally-ex tinct-mammals/.

109 "49 percent of all vertebrates": J. Tanzer et al., "Living Blue Planet Report," World Wildlife Fund, 2015, http://ocean.panda.org.s3.amazonaws.com/media /Living_Blue_Planet_Report_2015_08_31.pdf.

109 "so many turtles": Jon Mooallem, *Wild Ones: A Sometimes Dismaying, Weirdly Reassuring Story About Looking at People Looking at Animals in America*, (New York: Penguin Press, 2013), 135.

109 "number of sea turtles in the Caribbean": Carol Ruckdeschel et al., *Sea Turtles of the Atlantic and Gulf Coasts of the United States* (Athens, GA: University of Georgia Press, 2006), 95.

110 "30 percent of the coral died": Ben Smee, "Great Barrier Reef: 30% of Coral Died in 'Catastrophic' 2016 Heatwave," *Guardian*, April 18, 2018.

110 "estimates of the total loss": Terry P. Hughes et al., "Global warming transforms coral reef assemblages," *Nature*, April 18, 2018, 492–96.

111 "coelacanth shares DNA with a salamander": Chris T. Amemiya et al., "The African Coelacanth Genome Provides Insights into Tetrapod Evolution," *Nature*, April 18, 2013, 311–16.

111 "doesn't share with a shark": ReefQuest Centre for Shark Research, "The Coelacanth—a Morphological Mixed Bag," Biology of Sharks and Rays, undated, http://www.elasmo-research.org/education/classification/coelacanth .htm.

111 "animal habitats": "Shipping Threat to Endangered Whale," BBC News, August 28, 2001, http://news.bbc.co.uk/2/hi/science/nature/1513434.stm.

111 "inconvenient routes": "Reducing Ship Strikes to North Atlantic Right Whales," NOAA Endangered Species Conservation, undated, https://www .fisheries.noaa.gov/national/endangered-species-conservation/reducing-ship -strikes-north-atlantic-right-whales.

111 "too loud, or that fall below 100 hertz": Brandon L. Southall et al., "Reducing Noise from Large Commercial Ships," U.S. Department of Transportation-Maritime Administration, Spring 2018, https://nmssanctuaries.blob.core .windows.net/sanctuaries-prod/media/docs/20180411-reducing-noise-uscg.pdf.

112 "$123.13 billion": "Environmental Remediation Market—Global Forecast to 2022," Markets and Markets, October 28, 2016, https://www.marketsand markets.com/PressReleases/environmental-remediation.asp.

112 "Yoni Zohar's marine technology lab": Megan Hanks, "Yoni Zohar Explains How His Lab Became the First to Farm Bluefin Tuna in Land-Based Aquaculture," *UMBC News*, February 22, 2016, https://news.umbc.edu /yoni-zohar-explains-how-his-lab-became-the-first-to-farm-bluefin-tuna-in -land-based-aquaculture.

113 "op-ed in *Nature*": Christopher D. Golden et al., "Nutrition: Fall in Fish Catch Threatens Human Health," *Nature*, June 15, 2016, 317–20.

113 "pumping in cold water": Christopher Knaus, "Plan to Pump Cold Water on to Barrier Reef to Stop Bleaching Labelled 'Band-Aid,'" *Guardian*, April 6, 2017.

THE DAY THE US COMPLETELY BANS GUNS

119 "41 percent increase": Paloma Esquivel, "In a Violent Year in San Bernardino, Unsolved Homicides Leave Families Grasping for Answers," *Los Angeles Times*, January 7, 2017, https://www.latimes.com/local/lanow/la-me-ln-san -bernardino-unsolved-20161226-htmlstory.html.

119 "44 percent of homicides in San Bernardino": "The Most Dangerous Cities in America, Ranked," CBS News, https://www.cbsnews.com/pictures/the -most-dangerous-cities-in-america/25/.

119 "3 percent of American adults": Lois Beckett, "The Gun Numbers: Just 3% of American Adults Own a Collective 133m Firearms," *Guardian*, November 15, 2017, https://www.theguardian.com/us-news/2017/nov/15/the-gun-numbers -just-3-of-american-adults-own-a-collective-133m-firearms.

119 "74 percent of gun owners": Kim Parker et al., "America's Complex Relationship with Guns," Pew Research Center Social & Demographic Trends, June 22, 2017, http://www.pewsocialtrends.org/2017/06/22/americas-complex-rela tionship-with-guns/.

120 "said owning a gun makes you safer": Mark Murray, "Poll: 58 Percent Say Gun Ownership Increases Safety," NBC News, March 23, 2018, https:// www.nbcnews.com/politics/first-read/poll-58-percent-say-gun-ownership -increases-safety-n859231.

121 "5 percent of Americans are hunters": "2016 National Survey of Fishing, Hunting, and Wildlife-Associated Recreation," U.S. Fish and Wildlife Service, October 2018, https://wsfrprograms.fws.gov/subpages/nationalsurvey /nat_survey2016.pdf.

121 "more permissive over the past few decades": Ali Rowhani-Rahbar et al., "Loaded Handgun Carrying Among US Adults, 2015," *American Journal of Public Health*, November 8, 2017.

121 "drop in the firearm suicide rates": Andrew Leigh et al., "Do Gun Buybacks

Save Lives? Evidence from Panel Data," *American Law and Economics Review*, October 1, 2010.

122–23 "gun rights backstop": Eugene Volokh, "State Constitutional Rights to Keep and Bear Arms," *Texas Review of Law & Politics*, December 22, 2006.

124 "Merck Pharmaceuticals distributes cocaine hydrochloride": Enno Freye et al., *Pharmacology and Abuse of Cocaine, Amphetamines, Ecstasy and Related Designer Drugs: A Comprehensive Review on Their Mode of Action, Treatment of Abuse and Intoxication* (Berlin: Springer Science + Business Media, 2009), 33.

124 "legal methamphetamine": "Desoxyn," U.S. Food and Drug Administration, revised February 2015, https://www.accessdata.fda.gov/drugsatfda_docs /label/2017/005378s034lbl.pdf.

124 "prescription pads specifically for alcohol": Megan Gambino, "During Prohibition, Your Doctor Could Write You a Prescription for Booze," *Smithsonian*, October 7, 2013, https://www.smithsonianmag.com/history/during-prohi bition-your-doctor-could-write-you-prescription-booze-180947940/.

126 "works only 70 percent of the time": Brian Freskos, "How a Gun Trace Works," *The Trace*, July 8, 2016, https://www.thetrace.org/2016/07/how-a-gun-trace -works-atf-ffl/.

126 "thoroughly racialized": Michelle Alexander, *The New Jim Crow: Mass Incarceration in the Age of Colorblindness* (New York: The New Press, 2012), 118.

127 "Gingrich": Newt Gingrich, "Remarks at the National Rifle Association Meeting," C-SPAN, April 13, 2012, https://www.c-span.org/video/?305367-8 /newt-gingrich-remarks-national-rifle-association-meeting&start=23.

127 "ideological underpinnings of his work": YouTube user: VICE, "3D Printed Guns," March 25, 2013, https://www.youtube.com/watch?v=DconsfGsXyA.

127 " 'Y'all Qaeda,' 'Vanilla ISIS,' and 'Yee Hawdists' ": Brian Ries, " 'Y'all Qaeda': People Aren't Taking the Armed Militia in Oregon Too Seriously," *Mashable*, January 4, 2016, https://mashable.com/2016/01/04/oregon-militia -yall-qaeda/#FoHb00JiSGqG.

127 "LaVoy Finicum, was shot dead": Julie Turkewitz et al., "Police Shooting of Oregon Occupier Declared Justified, but F.B.I. Faces Inquiry," *New York Times*, March 8, 2016, https://www.nytimes.com/2016/03/09/us/oregon-lavoy -finicum-shooting.html.

128 "Timothy McVeigh": Mike Harvkey, "Why I Read the Most Controversial Books in Print Today," *Publishers Weekly*, May 8, 2015, https://www.publish ersweekly.com/pw/by-topic/industry-news/tip-sheet/article/66570-why-i -read-the-four-most-controversial-books-in-print-today.html.

128 "number of groups": "The Year in Hate: Trump Buoyed White Supremacists in 2017, Sparking Backlash Among Black Nationalist Groups," Southern Poverty Law Center, February 21, 2018, https://www.splcenter.org/news/2018/02/21

/year-hate-trump-buoyed-white-supremacists-2017-sparking-backlash-among -black-nationalist.

129 "Eric Frein": Kyle Swenson, "He Grew Up Listening to His Father's Anti-Police Rants. A Lawsuit Claims It Drove Him to Murder," *Washington Post*, September 27, 2017, https://www.washingtonpost.com/news/morning-mix/wp/2017 /09/27/was-a-pennsylvania-cop-killer-driven-to-murder-by-his-fathers-anti -government-rants/.

129 "one thousand law enforcement officers": Rheana Murray, "Accused Cop Killer Eric Frein Repeatedly Appears, Then Eludes Manhunt," ABC News, September 24, 2014, https://abcnews.go.com/US/accused-cop-killer-eric-frein -repeatedly-appears-eludes/story?id=25734478.

129 "finally arrested": "US Marshal Describes Moment Eric Frein Was Captured," 6 ABC Action News, October 31, 2014, http://6abc.com/news/us-marshal -describes-moment-eric-frein-was-captured/373904/.

129 "Americans opposed drone strikes": Alyssa Brown et al., "In U.S., 65% Support Drone Attacks on Terrorists Abroad," Gallup, March 25, 2013, https:// news.gallup.com/poll/161474/support-drone-attacks-terrorists-abroad.aspx.

THE DAY NUCLEAR BOMBS KILL US ALL

134 "The FCC's investigation": "Preliminary Report: Hawaii Emergency Management Agency's January 13, 2018 False Ballistic Missile Alert," Federal Communications Commission Public Safety and Homeland Security Bureau, January 30, 2018.

136 "Atomic Bomb Casualty Commission": Roman Mars et al., "Atomic Tattoos," 99% Invisible, January 15, 2019, https://99percentinvisible.org/episode /atomic-tattoos/.

136 "*Atom Central*": YouTube user: atomcentral, "Unedited Atomic Bomb Explosion W Sound," YouTube, January 5, 2017, https://www.youtube.com /watch?v=YKwkTYeukE4.

138 "280-kiloton": Mac William Bishop, "North Korea's Vow to Shut Punggye-ri Nuclear Site Appears Mostly Symbolic," NBC News, April 30, 2018, https:// www.nbcnews.com/news/north-korea/north-korea-s-vow-shut-punggye-ri -nuclear-site-appears-n869991.

139 "what the chances were of a nuclear war": Milo Beckman, "We're Edging Closer to Nuclear War," *FiveThirtyEight*, May 15, 2017, https://fivethirtyeight .com/features/were-edging-closer-to-nuclear-war/.

140 "total number of nuclear warheads": "Nuclear Arsenals," International Campaign to Abolish Nuclear Weapons, undated, http://www.icanw.org/the-facts /nuclear-arsenals/.

140 "firestorms after the bombs the US dropped": Lillian Goldman Law Library, "The Atomic Bombings of Hiroshima and Nagasaki: Chapter 9—General Description of Damage Caused by the Atomic Explosions," The Avalon Project, undated, http://avalon.law.yale.edu/20th_century/mp09.asp.

140 "firestorm in Hiroshima": A. B. Pittock et al., "Environmental Consequences of Nuclear War Volume I: Physical and Atmospheric Effects," *Physics Today*, 1987, 97–98.

140 "relic of a 1950s mindset": Michael Krepon, "Massive Retaliation," *Arms Control Wonk*, August 20, 2009, https://www.armscontrolwonk.com/archive/402436/massive-retaliation/.

140 "brashness": Bernard Brodie, *Strategy in the Missile Age* (Princeton: Princeton University Press, 1959), 257.

141 "probably a precise plan": J. Scott Applewhite, "Military Aides Still Carry the President's Nuclear 'Football,'" *USA Today*, May 5, 2005.

141 "a ton of these lying around": "US Nuclear Arsenal (as of January 2017)," Union of Concerned Scientists, https://www.ucsusa.org/sites/default/static/arsenal/assets/US-Nuclear-Forces_Jan-2017.pdf.

142 "account of Akiko Takakura": Hiroshima Peace Cultural Center, "Testimony of Akiko Takakura," Atomicarchive, http://www.atomicarchive.com/Docs/Hibakusha/Akiko.shtml.

142 "Yoshitaka Kawamoto, who was thirteen": Hiroshima Peace Cultural Center, "Testimony of Yoshitaka Kawamoto," Atomicarchive, http://www.atomicarchive.com/Docs/Hibakusha/Yoshitaka.shtml.

143 "four hundred times more radioactive material": Proceedings of the IAEA/WHO/EC International Conference, "Ten Years After Chernobyl: What Do We Really Know?," April 1996, https://inis.iaea.org/collection/NCLCollectionStore/_Public/28/058/28058918.pdf.

143 "Chernobyl-related cancer deaths": World Health Organization, "1986–2016: CHERNOBYL at 30," April 25, 2016, http://www.who.int/mediacentre/news/releases/2005/pr38/en/.

144 "1.25 degrees celsius": Andrew Freedman, "The (Nuclear) Winter of Our Discontent," Climate Central, March 6, 2012, https://www.climatecentral.org/news/the-nuclear-winter-of-our-discontent.

144 "dire picture of the winter": Michael J. Mills et al., "Multidecadal Global Cooling and Unprecedented Ozone Loss Following a Regional Nuclear Conflict," *Earth's Future*, 2014, 161–76.

144 "1.4 billion metric tons": YouTube user: CSER Cambridge, "Feeding Everyone No Matter What," Centre for the Study of Existential Risk, September 2, 2016, https://www.youtube.com/watch?v=SiiKC8Osxw8.

145 "two billion people would die": Ira Helfand, "Nuclear Famine: Two Billion

People at Risk?," *International Physicians for the Prevention of Nuclear War*, November 2013, http://www.ippnw.org/nuclear-famine.html.

145 *"Feeding Everyone No Matter What"*: David Denkenberger et al., *Feeding Everyone No Matter What* (Cambridge, MA: Academic Press, 2015).

145–46 "sixteen thousand copies of the biggest nukes in history": Sam Biddle, "How Many Nukes Would It Take to Blow Up the Entire Planet?" *Gizmodo*, April 5, 2012, https://gizmodo.com/5899569/how-many-nukes-would-it -take-to-blow-up-the-entire-planet.

146 "B61": Zachary Keck, "Why the B-61-12 Bomb Is the Most Dangerous Nuclear Weapon in America's Arsenal," *National Interest*, October 9, 2018.

146 "retired and slated for dismantlement": Kelsey Davenport, "Nuclear Weapons: Who Has What at a Glance," Arms Control Association, June 2018, https:// www.armscontrol.org/factsheets/Nuclearweaponswhohaswhat.

146 "promised an expanded nuclear arsenal": Donald Trump, "Remarks by President Trump in Meeting with State and Local Officials on Infrastructure Initiative," White House, February 12, 2018, https://www.whitehouse.gov /briefings-statements/remarks-president-trump-meeting-state-local-officials -infrastructure-initiative/.

146 "New START": Henry Meyer et al., "Nuclear Fears Haunt Leaders with U.S.-Russian Arms Pact's Demise," *Bloomberg*, February 16, 2019, https:// www.bloomberg.com/news/articles/2019-02-16/nuclear-doom-haunts-leaders -with-u-s-russian-arms-pact-s-demise.

146 "tiny nuclear warheads": Ankit Panda, "Why Pakistan's Newly Flight-Tested Multiple Nuclear Warhead–Capable Missile Really Matters," *Diplomat*, January 25, 2017, https://thediplomat.com/2017/01/why-pakistans-newly-flight-tested -multiple-nuclear-warhead-capable-missile-really-matters/.

146 "force Pakistan to nuke itself": Rajat Pandit, "Will Call Pakistan's Nuke Bluff If Tasked to Cross Border: Army Chief," *Times of India*, January 12, 2018.

147 "54 percent of humanity": United Nations, Department of Economic and Social Affairs, Population Division, "The World's Cities in 2018," data booklet, 2018.

148 "doomsday machine": Herman Kahn, *On Thermonuclear War* (Princeton: Princeton University Press, 1960), 144–55.

149 "doomsday clock": John Mecklin et al., "It Is 2 Minutes to Midnight," 2018 Doomsday Clock Statement, January 25, 2018, https://thebulletin.org/sites /default/files/2018%20Doomsday%20Clock%20Statement.pdf.

THE DAY A BABY IS BORN ON THE MOON

153 "Elon Musk's SpaceX": Jackie Wattles, "SpaceX Promised to Fly Tourists to the Moon. How's That Going?," CNN, June 7, 2018, https://money.cnn .com/2018/06/07/technology/future/spacex-falcon-heavy-moon-tourists /index.html.

153 "Robert Bigelow's Bigelow Aerospace": Howard Bloom, "How to Get Back to the Moon in 4 Years—This Time to Stay," *Scientific American*, February 22, 2017, https://blogs.scientificamerican.com/guest-blog/how-to-get-back -to-the-moon-in-4-years-this-time-to-stay/.

153 "His 1991 paper": Jim Dunstan, "From Flag Burnings to Bearing Arms to States Rights: Will the Bill of Rights Survive a Trip to the Moon?," 1991, 95, 98.

154 "very well-grounded fear": Haym Benaroya, *Building Habitats on the Moon: Engineering Approaches to Lunar Settlements* (New York: Springer Praxis Books, 2018), 165.

155 "animals that begin their lives": Dorothy B. Spangenberg, "LifeSat: The General Biology Module," *SAE Transactions*, 1990, 1326–29.

155 "Spangenberg also experimented": D. B. Spangenberg et al., "Development Studies of *Aurelia* (Jellyfish) Ephyrae Which Developed During the SLS-1 Mission," *Advances in Space Research*, August 1994, 239–47.

THE DAY THE ENTIRE INTERNET GOES DOWN

162 "the Oracle system Starbucks uses": Art Zeile, "Starbucks Has a Venti-Sized Computer Problem," *TheStreet*, April 28, 2015, https://www.thestreet.com /story/13128128/1/starbucks-has-a-venti-computer-problem.html.

164 "PanAmSat Corporation's Galaxy IV satellite": Laurence Zuckerman, "Satellite Failure Is Rare, and Therefore Unsettling," *New York Times*, May 21, 1998.

165 "picture of bliss": Shawn Hubler, "The Loudness of Pager-Free Silence," *Los Angeles Times*, May 21, 1998.

165 "all the power in Quebec": Sten Odenwald, "The Day the Sun Brought Darkness," NASA, March 13, 2009, http://www.nasa.gov/topics/earth/features /sun_darkness.html.

166 "oiled butt": Paul Ford, "How *PAPER* Magazine's web engineers scaled their back-end for Kim Kardashian (SFW)," *The Message*, January 21, 2015, https:// medium.com/message/how-paper-magazines-web-engineers-scaled-kim-kar dashians-back-end-sfw-6367f8d37688.

166 "Mirai botnet": Lorenzo Franceschi-Bicchierai, "Twitter, Reddit, Spotify Were Collateral Damage in Major Internet Attack," *Vice Motherboard*, October

21, 2016, https://motherboard.vice.com/en_us/article/d7ywak/twitter-reddit-spotify-were-collateral-damage-in-major-internet-attack.

167 "four hundred of these cables": "Submarine Cable Frequently Asked Questions," Telegeography, 2019, https://www2.telegeography.com/submarine-cable-faqs-frequently-asked-questions.

167 "failures *were* caused by shark bites": Keith Schofield, "Sharks Are Not the Nemesis of the Internet—ICPC Findings," International Cable Protection Committee, July 1, 2015, https://cdn.arstechnica.net/wp-content/uploads/2015/07/ICPC-sharks.pdf.

168 "Hayastan Shakarian": "Woman Who Cut Internet to Georgia and Armenia 'Had Never Heard of Web,'" *Telegraph*, April 11, 2011.

168 "leave them exposed": YouTube user TomoNews US, "Deep Sea Cables: Facebook, Microsoft Lay Massive Underwater Data Cable Across Atlantic—TomoNews," YouTube, September 25, 2017, https://www.youtube.com/watch?v=_drQT3eMli4.

168 "don't bother to hide": YouTube user Techno Exploit, "The Manufacturing and Beach Landing of Marea—Most Technologically Advanced SUBSEA Cable [2017]," YouTube, September 24, 2017, https://www.youtube.com/watch?v=AO1C260H2mE.

168 "about three seconds": YouTube user Brighton Tools, "M18™ FORCE LOGIC™ HYDRAULIC CABLE CUTTER," YouTube, April 27, 2017, https://www.youtube.com/watch?v=nBaQvr5-xWQ.

169 "eliminating any single point of failure": "Compliance," Google Cloud Help, undated, https://support.google.com/googlecloud/answer/6056694?hl=en.

169 "sixteen such servers spread internationally": "Data Center Locations," Google Data Centers, undated, https://www.google.com/about/datacenters/inside/locations/index.html.

169 "eleven such crucial cable landings": Sam Biddle, "How to Destroy the Internet," *Gizmodo*, May 23, 2012, https://gizmodo.com/5912383/how-to-destroy-the-internet.

169–70 "Fourteen people in different countries": James Ball, "Meet the Seven People Who Hold the Keys to Worldwide Internet Security," *Guardian*, February 28, 2014.

170 "'instances' of the thirteen name servers": http://www.root-servers.org/.

171 "twenty-year-old vulnerability": Cade Metz et al., "Researchers Discover Two Major Flaws in the World's Computers," *New York Times*, January 3, 2018.

172 "flip a switch": Dana Liebelson, "The Government's Secret Plan to Shut Off Cellphones and the Internet, Explained," *Mother Jones*, November 26, 2013, https://www.motherjones.com/politics/2013/11/internet-phone-kill-switch-explained/.

172 "eighteen-page report": "Risk Management Strategy—Internet Routing, Access and Connection Services," Department of Homeland Security, July 2011, https://www.dhs.gov/xlibrary/assets/itsrm-for-internet-routing-report.pdf.

172 "representatives from hardware manufacturers": "Information Technology Sector: Charters and Membership," DHS, undated, https://www.dhs.gov /information-technology-sector-council-charters-and-membership.

172 "repairing undersea cables": Matt Burgess, "Ever Wondered How Underwater Cables Are Laid? We Take a Trip on the Ship That Keeps Us Online," *Wired*, November 30, 2016, https://www.wired.co.uk/article/subsea-internet-cable -ship-boat.

172 "sixteen hours": Lindsay Goldwert, "How Do You Fix an Undersea Cable?," *Slate*, January 8, 2007, http://www.slate.com/articles/news_and_politics /explainer/2007/01/how_do_you_fix_an_undersea_cable.html.

173 "auditing firm Deloitte": George Arnett, "One in Four UK Smartphone Owners Does Not Make Phone Calls Weekly," *Guardian*, September 8, 2015.

174 "smart grids": "Smart Grid for a Smart Chicago," City of Chicago, undated, https://www.chicago.gov/city/en/progs/env/smart-grid-for-a-smart-chicago .html.

174 "urging utilities to automate": "Grid Modernization and the Smart Grid," US Department of Energy, undated, https://www.energy.gov/oe/activities /technology-development/grid-modernization-and-the-smart-grid.

174 "traffic lights": Jack Karsten, "Smart Transportation Technology Promises to Lower the Costs of Traffic," *Brookings Techtank*, December 14, 2017, https://www .brookings.edu/blog/techtank/2017/12/14/smart-transportation-technology -promises-to-lower-the-costs-of-traffic/.

174 "multiple outages": Tad Vezner, "CenturyLink Vendor Again Blamed for 911 Outage in Multi-State Outage," *Grand Forks Herald*, August 2, 2018, http:// www.grandforksherald.com/news/government-and-politics/4480850-century link-vendor-again-blamed-911-outage-multi-state-outage.

174 "fire monitoring": Alberto De San Bernabe Clemente et al., "A WSN-Based Tool for Urban and Industrial Fire-Fighting," *Sensors*, November 6, 2012, 15009–35.

174 "triage at mass casualty events": Leslie A. Lenert et al., "An Intelligent 802.11 Triage Tag for Medical Response to Disasters," AMIA 2016 Annual Symposium Archive, 2005, https://www.ncbi.nlm.nih.gov/pmc/articles/PMC1560742/.

174 "Egypt's lower class": Mark Milian, "Reports Say Egypt Web Shutdown Is Coordinated, Extensive," CNN, January 28, 2011, http://www.cnn.com/2011 /TECH/web/01/28/egypt.internet.shutdown/index.html.

174–75 "blackout cost the local economy": Parmy Olson, "Egypt's Internet Black-out Cost More Than OECD Estimates," *Forbes*, February 3, 2011, https://

www.forbes.com/sites/parmyolson/2011/02/03/how-much-did-five-days-of
-no-internet-cost-egypt/#2cafb2bd4d49.

175   "50 percent of Egyptians online": "Focus on Egypt," Media Use in the Middle East, 2017, http://www.mideastmedia.org/survey/2017/chapter/focus-on
-egypt/.

175   "fourteen thousand internet users": "North Korea Internet usage, broadband,
and telecommunications reports," Internet World Stats, undated, https://
www.internetworldstats.com/asia/kp.htm.

175   "hacking sector": Timothy W. Martin, "How North Korea's Hackers Became
Dangerously Good," *Wall Street Journal*, April 19, 2018, https://www.wsj
.com/articles/how-north-koreas-hackers-became-dangerously-good-15241
50416.

THE DAY THE LAST SLAUGHTERHOUSE CLOSES

180   "the Dutch philosopher": Cor van der Weele, "Meat and the Benefits of
Ambivalence," *The Ethics of Consumption*, 2013, 290–95.

180   "animal-loving vegetarians": Kathryn Asher et al., "Study of Current and
Former Vegetarians and Vegans," Humane Research Council, December
2014, 4.

180   "A series of psychological studies": Jonas R. Kunst et al., "Meat Eaters by
Dissociation: How We Present, Prepare and Talk About Meat Increases Willingness to Eat Meat by Reducing Empathy and Disgust," *Appetite*, October
1, 2016, 758–74.

180   "puzzling 2018 US consumer survey": "Food Demand Survey," Oklahoma
State University Department of Agricultural Economics, January 18, 2018, 4.

182   "finally condemned them": Vidhi Doshi, "Modi Finally Speaks Out Against
Lynchings of 'Beef Eaters,'" *Washington Post*, June 29, 2017, https://www
.washingtonpost.com/world/modi-finally-speaks-out-against-lynchings-of
-beef-eaters/2017/06/29/f171e042-5ccf-11e7-aa69-3964a7d55207.

183   "rate at which animals die": Hannah Ritchie et al., "Meat and Seafood Production & Consumption," OurWorldInData.org, https://ourworldindata
.org/meat-and-seafood-production-consumption.

184   "this magic-wand scenario": Rachel Nuwer, "What Would Happen If the
World Suddenly Went Vegetarian?" *BBC Future*, September 27, 2016, http://
www.bbc.com/future/story/20160926-what-would-happen-if-the-world
-suddenly-went-vegetarian.

184   "Nomadic pastoralist cultures": Ousman Tall, "Herders vs Farmers: Resolving
Deadly Conflict in the Sahel and West Africa," *OECD Insights*, April 16, 2018,

http://oecdinsights.org/2018/04/16/herders-vs-farmers-resolving-deadly-con
flict-in-the-sahel-and-west-africa/.

185 "building more comfortable restraints": Temple Grandin, "Proper Cattle
Restraint for Stunning," updated September 2018, http://www.grandin.com
/humane/restrain.slaughter.html.

185 "cows moo prodigiously": Mac McClelland, "This Is What Humane Slaughter
Looks Like. Is It Good Enough?," *Modern Farmer*, April 17, 2013, https://
modernfarmer.com/2013/04/this-is-what-humane-slaughter-looks-like-is-it
-good-enough/.

185 "banned kosher and halal slaughter": Samuel Osborne, "Belgium Votes to
Ban Kosher and Halal Slaughter In Its Biggest Territory," *Independent*, May
8, 2017, https://www.independent.co.uk/news/world/europe/belgian-region
-walloon-bans-kosher-halal-meat-islam-jewish-a7723451.html.

185 "Swiss activist group": Pour l'Égalité Animale, "Enquête en Abattoir Suisse,"
2018, https://abattoirs-suisses.ch/moudon/.

186 "more greenhouse gases than driving": "Rearing Cattle Produces More Greenhouse Gases Than Driving Cars, UN Report Warns," United Nations News,
November 29, 2006, https://news.un.org/en/story/2006/11/201222-rearing
-cattle-produces-more-greenhouse-gases-driving-cars-un-report-warns.

186 "37 percent": "Livestock a Major Threat to Environment," FAO Newsroom,
November 29, 2006, http://www.fao.org/newsroom/en/news/2006/1000448
/index.html.

186 "twenty-five times": "Overview of Greenhouse Gases," United States Environmental Protection Agency, undated, https://www.epa.gov/ghgemissions
/overview-greenhouse-gases.

187 "number one driver of deforestation": "What's Driving Deforestation?," Union
of Concerned Scientists, undated, https://www.ucsusa.org/global-warming
/stop-deforestation/whats-driving-deforestation#.XG4a6C3Myu4.

187 "according to a 2011 study": "Climate and Environmental Impacts,"
Environmental Working Group, 2011, https://www.ewg.org/meateaters
guide/a-meat-eaters-guide-to-climate-change-health-what-you-eat-matters
/climate-and-environmental-impacts/.

187 "PETA not only approves": "PETA's 'In Vitro' Chicken Contest," PETA,
undated, https://www.peta.org/features/vitro-meat-contest/.

188 "try the stuff": Matti Wilks et al., "Attitudes to *In Vitro* Meat: A Survey
of Potential Consumers in the United States," *PLOS ONE*, February 16,
2017.

188 "declared war on cultured meat": Caitlin Dewey, "Why Cattle Ranchers and
Tech Start-Ups Are Beefing Over the Meaning of 'Meat,'" *Washington Post*,

https://www.washingtonpost.com/news/wonk/wp/2018/03/02/why-cattle-ranchers-and-tech-start-ups-are-beefing-over-the-meaning-of-meat/.

189   "Tyson Foods invested": "Tyson Ventures Announces Investment in Future Meat Technologies," Tyson Foods, May 2, 2018, https://www.tysonfoods.com/news/news-releases/2018/5/tyson-ventures-announces-investment-future-meat-technologies.

190   "McDonald's announced": Geoffrey Mohan, "McDonald's Will Shift to More Humane Chicken Slaughter Policy," *Los Angeles Times*, October 27, 2017, https://www.latimes.com/business/la-fi-mcdonalds-chicken-20171027-story.html.

190   "costs a facility": William Neuman, "New Way to Help Chickens Cross to Other Side," *New York Times*, October 21, 2010, https://www.nytimes.com/2010/10/22/business/22chicken.html.

190   "Israel's cultured meat technology": Sue Surkes, "China Makes Massive Investment in Israeli Lab Meat Technology," *Times of Israel*, September 17, 2017, https://www.timesofisrael.com/china-makes-massive-investment-in-israeli-lab-meat-technology/.

191   "family-owned beef farming operations": "Industry Statistics," National Cattlemen's Beef Association, 2017, http://www.beefusa.org/beefindustry statistics.aspx.

191   "pasture and rangeland": Dave Merrill et al., "Here's How America Uses Its Land," *Bloomberg*, July 31, 2018, https://www.bloomberg.com/graphics/2018-us-land-use/.

191   "two billion subsistence farmers": George Rapsomanikis, "The Economic Lives of Smallholder Farmers," Food and Agriculture Organization of the United Nations, 2015, http://www.fao.org/3/a-i5251e.pdf.

191   "downsides for vegetable-lovers": Michael Pollan, *The Omnivore's Dilemma: A Natural History of Four Meals* (New York: Penguin Press, 2006).

192   "ecological and safety risks": Peter Hess, "Turns Out That Using Human Poop to Fertilize Crops Isn't Such a Great Idea," *Vice Motherboard*, April 22, 2016, https://motherboard.vice.com/en_us/article/8q8xnk/turns-out-that-using-human-poop-to-fertilize-crops-might-not-be-such-a-great-ide.

192   "spare animal parts": "Environmental Impact," National Renderers Association, undated, http://www.nationalrenderers.org/environmental/.

193   "company called Modern Meadow": "Modern Meadow Launches Zoa, the First Ever Biofabricated Leather Material Brand," Modern Meadow, September 26, 2017, http://www.modernmeadow.com/press/modern-meadow-launches-zoa-the-first-ever-biofabricated-leather-material-brand/.

193   "Zoa website claims": Modern Meadow, "Grown of Zoa," https://web.archive.org/web/20181119223356/http://zoa.is/. Archived on November 19, 2019.

194 "his own amputated leg": Beckett Mufson, "This Guy Served His Friends Tacos Made from His Own Amputated Leg," *Vice*, June 12, 2018, https://www .vice.com/en_us/article/gykmn7/legal-ethical-cannibalism-human-meat-tacos -reddit-wtf.

194 "Bistro In Vitro": "Celebrity Cubes," Bistro In Vitro, undated, https://bistro -invitro.com/en/dishes/celebrity-cubes/.

THE DAY HUMANS GET A CONFIRMED SIGNAL FROM INTELLIGENT EXTRATERRESTRIALS

200 "One in six stars": "At Least One in Six Stars Has an Earth-sized Planet," NASA, January 10, 2013, https://www.nasa.gov/mission_pages/kepler /news/17-percent-of-stars-have-earth-size-planets.html.

200 "2016 Princeton study": Timothy D. Morton et al., "False Positive Probabilities for All *Kepler* Objects of Interest: 1284 Newly Validated Planets and 428 Likely False Positives," *Astrophysical Journal*, May 10, 2016, 1–15.

200 "tens of billions of habitable planets": Eric Berger, "Number of Potentially Habitable Planets in Our Galaxy: Tens of Billions," *Ars Technica*, May 10, 2016, https://arstechnica.com/science/2016/05/number-of-potentially-hab itable-planets-in-our-galaxy-tens-of-billions/.

200 "two trillion": Christopher J. Conselice et al., "The Evolution of Galaxy Number Density at Z < 8 and Its Implications," *Astrophysical Journal*, October 2016, 1–17.

200 "Proxima Centauri": Pat Brennan, "ESO Discovers Earth-Size Planet in Habitable Zone of Nearest Star," NASA, August 24, 2016.

200 "Tau Ceti": Fabo Feng, et al., "Color Difference Makes a Difference: Four Planet Candidates around τ Ceti," *The Astronomical Journal*, September 5, 2017, 135.

201 "seven potentially habitable planets": Kenneth Chang, "7 Earth-Size Planets Orbit Dwarf Star, NASA and European Astronomers Say," *New York Times*, February 22, 2017.

202 "no fewer than eighteen scientists,": "BSRC People," Berkeley SETI Research Center, undated, https://seti.berkeley.edu/people.html.

202 "volunteers numbering in the millions": Sarah Scoles, "A Brief History of SETI@Home," *Atlantic*, May 23, 2017, https://www.theatlantic.com/science /archive/2017/05/aliens-on-your-packard-bell/527445/.

202 "set of nine protocols": "Protocols for an ETI Signal Detection," SETI Institute, undated, https://www.seti.org/protocols-eti-signal-detection.

203 "predict their reaction": Jung Yul Kwon et al., "How Will We React to the Discovery of Extraterrestrial Life?," *Frontiers in Psychology*, January 10, 2018, 1–12.

204 "sent imaginations soaring in 2015": Ross Andersen, "The Most Mysterious Star in Our Galaxy," *Atlantic*, October 13, 2015.

204 "sci-fi fans": Liam Shaughnessy, "Our Favorite Hypothetical Alien Megastructures," *Vice Motherboard*, October 21, 2015, https://motherboard.vice.com /en_us/article/jpgqxg/our-favorite-hypothetical-alien-megastructures.

THE DAY THE NEXT SUPERVOLCANO ERUPTS

210 "Mary Shelley": Erin Zaleski, "The Summer Storm That Inspired *Frankenstein* and *Dracula*," *Daily Beast*, September 3, 2016, https://www.thedailybeast .com/the-summer-storm-that-inspired-frankenstein-and-dracula.

211 "two enormous masses": "How Large Is the Magma Chamber That Is Currently Under Yellowstone?," USGS, https://www.usgs.gov/faqs /how-large-magma-chamber-currently-under-yellowstone?qt-news_science _products=0#qt-news_science_products.

213 "potential for other types of disasters": "Five Things Most People Get Wrong About the Yellowstone Volcano," USGS, May 8, 2015, https://volcanoes.usgs .gov/volcanoes/yellowstone/faqs_misconceptions.html.

214 "centuries to thousands of years": Haley E. Cabaniss et al., "The Role of Tectonic Stress in Triggering Large Silicic Caldera Eruptions," *Geophysical Research Letters*, May 16, 2018, 3889–95.

214 "six days in 2010": Katharine Sanderson, "Questions Fly over Ash-Cloud Models," *Nature*, April 27, 2010.

215 "glassy juvenile components": A. Vogel et al., "Reference Data set of Volcanic Ash Physicochemical and Optical Properties," *Journal of Geophysical Research: Atmospheres*, 9485–514.

216 "speculation and fanciful depictions": "Modeling the Ash Distribution of a Yellowstone Supereruption," USGS Volcano Hazards Program, August 27, 2014, https://volcanoes.usgs.gov/volcanoes/yellowstone/yellowstone_sub_page_91 .html.

216 "non–life threatening layer of ash": "Ash Eruption and Fallout," USGS, undated, https://pubs.usgs.gov/gip/msh/ash.html.

217 "2,500 times that much ash": "Questions About Yellowstone Volcanic History," USGS Volcano Hazards Program, undated, https://volcanoes.usgs.gov /volcanoes/yellowstone/yellowstone_sub_page_54.html.

217 "volcanic winter": M. R. Rampino et al., "Volcanic Winter and Accelerated Glaciation Following the Toba Super-Eruption," *Nature*, 1992, 50–52.

217 "early humans in east Africa": Chad L. Yost, "Subdecadal Phytolith and Charcoal Records from Lake Malawi, East Africa, Imply Minimal Effects on Human

Evolution from the ~74 Ka Toba Supereruption," *Journal of Human Evolution*, March 2018, 75–94.

217 "humans were having a lovely time": E. I. Smith et al., "Humans Thrived in South Africa Through the Toba Eruption About 74,000 Years Ago," *Nature*, March 22, 2018, 511–15.

THE DAY THE LAST SLAVE GOES FREE

221 "essentially divided into": "Global Estimates of Modern Slavery: Forced Labour and Forced Marriage," International Labour Organization, September 19, 2017, https://www.ilo.org/wcmsp5/groups/public/@dgreports/@dcomm /documents/publication/wcms_575479.pdf.

221 "sustainable development goals": "Resolution adopted by the General Assembly on 25 September 2015," United Nations, September 25, 2015, http://www .un.org/ga/search/view_doc.asp?symbol=A/RES/70/1&Lang=E.

222 "eight million enslaved people": "India," Global Slavery Index, 2018, https:// www.globalslaveryindex.org/2018/findings/country-studies/india/.

223 "Slavery from Space": Doreen S. Boyd et al., "Slavery from Space: Demonstrating the Role for Satellite Remote Sensing to Inform Evidence-Based Action Related to UN SDG Number 8," *Journal of Photogrammetry and Remote Sensing*, August 2018, 380–88.

224 "Sustainable emancipation requires transformations": Austin Choi-Fitzpatrick, *What Slaveholders Think: How Contemporary Perpetrators Rationalize What They Do* (New York: Columbia University Press, 2017).

224 "one in ten people is a slave": "Executive Summary," Global Slavery Index, 2018, https://www.globalslaveryindex.org/2018/findings/executive-summary/.

224 "defector experience in South Korea": "North Korean Defectors Struggle to Master Money," *Wall Street Journal*, March 28, 2017, https://www.wsj.com /video/north-korean-defectors-struggle-to-master-money/009D1B6C-804D -4F1F-A3C6-F498E8E5E98E.html.

225 "prison labor as we know it is slavery": Kevin Rashid Johnson, "Prison Labor Is Modern Slavery. I've Been Sent to Solitary for Speaking Out," *Guardian*, August 23, 2018.

225 "arbitrary detention": "CHINA 2017/2018," Amnesty International, undated, https://www.amnesty.org/en/countries/asia-and-the-pacific/china/report -china/.

THE DAY THE LAST CEMETERY RUNS OUT OF SPACE

229 "population of Singapore plateaued": Abhishek Vishnoi, "Singapore Population Growth Stalls as Non-Residents Decrease," *Bloomberg*, September 27, 2017, https://www.bloomberg.com/news/articles/2017-09-28/singapore-population -growth-stalls-as-non-residents-decrease.

229 "buyers in China, Taiwan, and Korea": Andrea Tan, "Singapore Home Prices Jump the Most in Almost Eight Years," *Bloomberg*, April 1, 2018, https:// www.bloomberg.com/news/articles/2018-04-02/singapore-home-prices-post -biggest-jump-in-almost-eight-years.

230 "eleven thousand new homes": Rachel Tan, "Singaporeans Unfazed by Bidada-ri's Cemetery Past for Planned HDB Estate," *Straits Times*, September 1, 2013, https://www.straitstimes.com/singapore/singaporeans-unfazed-by-bidadaris -cemetery-past-for-planned-hdb-estate.

230 "riveting short documentary": *Moving House*, directed by Tan Pin Pin, Sin-gapore, 2001, https://vimeo.com/43520630.

231 "leased for approximately twenty years": Frank Thadeusz, "Germany's Tired Graveyards: A Rotten Way to Go?," *Spiegel Online*, January 7, 2008, http:// www.spiegel.de/international/germany/germany-s-tired-graveyards-a-rotten -way-to-go-a-527134.html.

231 "Hitler's parents": "Hitler's Parents' Gravesite Available as Lease Ends," CBS News, March 30, 2012, https://www.cbsnews.com/news/hitlers-parents -gravesite-available-as-lease-ends/.

231 "effectively 100 percent": "Ashes to Ashes," *Economist*, October 31, 2012, https://www.economist.com/graphic-detail/2012/10/31/ashes-to-ashes.

231 "2045 at the latest": Ana Naomi de Sousa, "Death in the City: What Happens When All Our Cemeteries Are Full?," *Guardian*, January 21, 2015, https:// www.theguardian.com/cities/2015/jan/21/death-in-the-city-what-happens -cemeteries-full-cost-dying.

231 "Hong Kong Is out of grave and columbarium space": Justin Heifetz, "Hong Kong Has No Space Left for the Dead," *Vice Motherboard*, October 23, 2017, https://motherboard.vice.com/en_us/article/xwaqm7/hong-kong-has-no-space -left-for-dead-people-china.

231 "China is on the verge of running out": Rachel Nuwer, "China's 3,000 Cemeteries Will Run Out of Space in Just Six Years," *Smithsonian*, October 10, 2013, https://www.smithsonianmag.com/smart-news/chinas-3000-cem eteries-will-run-out-of-space-in-just-six-years-1339090/.

231 "Cardiff, Wales": Matt Discombe, "A New Cemetery Is Being Planned for Cardiff as the City Is Running Out of Space to Bury People," *WalesOnline*,

March 6, 2018, https://www.walesonline.co.uk/news/wales-news/new-cem etery-being-planned-cardiff-14370448.

231 "Rhondda Cynon Taf": Rachel Flint, "Wales' Burial Space Running Out, Warns Church," BBC News, March 15, 2018, https://www.bbc.com/news /uk-wales-politics-43336061.

232 "Army National Military Cemeteries": Claire Barrett, "No More Burials at Arlington in 25 Years? Famed Cemetery Is Running Out of Space," *Military Times*, March 31, 2017, https://www.militarytimes.com/news/pentagon-con gress/2017/03/31/no-more-burials-at-arlington-in-25-years-famed-cemetery -is-running-out-of-space/.

233 "plots there cost as much as $242,000": Janet Lever, "I Got My Dream Plot in Hollywood Forever Cemetery—Almost," *Los Angeles*, February 2, 2018, https://www.lamag.com/culturefiles/got-dream-plot-hollywood-forever-cem etery-almost/.

233 "exhuming dozens of bodies with a backhoe": "Rabbis Re-Consecrate Menorah Gardens," CBS4 Miami, January 27, 2011, https://miami.cbslocal .com/2011/01/27/menorah-gardens-to-be-re-consecrated/.

234 "agreed to put everything right": Daniel Chang, "Menorah Gardens Broward County Cemetery to Be Reconsecrated," *Palm Beach Post*, January 27, 2011, https://www.palmbeachpost.com/article/20110127/news/812039292.

234 "ten years": Michael Leidig, "Dust to Dust (But Not If Your Dearly Departed Is Buried in Germany)," *Telegraph*, November 16, 2003, https://www.telegraph .co.uk/news/worldnews/europe/germany/1446872/Dust-to-dust-but-not-if -your-dearly-departed-is-buried-in-Germany.html.

235 "shortage of graves in Mexico City": "Running Out of Cemeteries, Mexico City Digging Up the Dead," CBS News, October 28, 2014, https://www.cbsnews .com/news/running-out-of-cemeteries-mexico-city-digging-up-the-dead/.

235 "Their worldview is not the same as ours": "Mexico City Is Running Out of Burial Space, But Many Resist Cremation," NBC News, October 28, 2014, https://www.nbcnews.com/news/latino/mexico-city-running-out-burial -space-many-resist-cremation-n235896.

235 "Double-decker graves": Nigel Morris et al., " 'Double-Decker' Graves Planned for Packed Cemeteries," *Independent*, January 16, 2004, https://www.indepen dent.co.uk/news/uk/this-britain/double-decker-graves-planned-for-packed -cemeteries-73953.html.

235 "lift and deepen": Catherine Fairbairn, "Reuse of Graves," House of Commons Library, June 6, 2017, http://researchbriefings.files.parliament.uk/documents /SN04060/SN04060.pdf.

235 "$350,000 each": Mara Altman, "How Do You Sell the Last Two Burial Plots

in Manhattan?," *Intelligencer*, October 21, 2015, http://nymag.com/daily /intelligencer/2015/10/last-two-manhattan-burial-plots-for-sale.html.

237 "to make way for a new highway": Christopher Tan, "LTA Confirms Third Delay in Bukit Brown Road Project; New Completion Deadline by Early 2019," *Straits Times*, November 15, 2017, https://www.straitstimes.com /singapore/transport/lta-confirms-third-delay-in-bukit-brown-road-project -new-completion-deadline-by.

EPILOGUE

241 "extinct at a rate that is constant": Leigh Van Valen, "A New Evolutionary Law," *Evolutionary Theory*, January 1973, 1–30.

241 "Sparrows": Stephen L. Brusatte et al., "The Origin and Diversification of Birds," *Current Biology*, October 5, 2015.

241 "end of life on Earth": J. E. Lovelock et al., "Life Span of the Biosphere," *Nature*, April 8, 1982, 561–63.

241 "different kind of photosynthesis": Ken Caldeira, "The Life Span of the Biosphere Revisited," *Nature*, December 1992, 721–23.

242 "collide with an asteroid": "Asteroid of One-Kilometer or Larger Strikes Earth Every 600,000 Years," *MIT Tech Talk*, September 10, 2003, http://news.mit .edu/2003/asteroid-0910.

242 "47,000 megatons of TNT": Robert Marcus et al., "Earth Impact Effects Program," undated, https://impact.ese.ic.ac.uk/ImpactEarth/Impact Effects/.

242 "type III civilization": Nikolai Kardashev, "Transmission of Information by Extraterrestrial Civilizations," *Soviet Astronomy*, 1964, 217.

242 "huge, complex instruments": Nikolai Kardashev, "On the Inevitability and the Possible Structures of Supercivilizations," *The Search for Extraterrestrial Life: Recent Developments*, 1985, 497–504.

243 "between 100,000 and 1,000,000 of our Earth years": Michio Kaku, "The Physics of Interstellar Travel," undated, http://mkaku.org/home/articles /the-physics-of-interstellar-travel/.

243 "O'Neill cylinders": Gerard K. O'Neill, *The High Frontier: Human Colonies in Space* (New York: William Morrow and Company, 1977).

244 "circling closer and closer": Dave Rothstein, "How Long Would It Take the Earth to Fall into the Sun? (Intermediate)," Ask an Astronomer, Astronomy Department at Cornell University, updated June 27, 2015, http://curious.astro .cornell.edu/about-us/39-our-solar-system/the-earth/other-catastrophes/57 -how-long-would-it-take-the-earth-to-fall-into-the-sun-intermediate.

244 "Earth will be devoured": Klaus-Peter Schroder et al., "Distant Future of the

Sun and Earth Revisited," *Monthly Notices of the Royal Astronomical Society*, May 2008, 155–63.

244 "star BD+48 740": Colin Schultz, "Earth Will Die a Hot Horrible Death When the Sun Expands and Swallows Us, and Now We Know What That Looks Like," *Smithsonian*, August 21, 2012, https://www.smithsonianmag.com/smart-news/earth-will-die-a-hot-horrible-death-when-the-sun-expands-and-swallows-us-and-now-we-know-what-that-looks-like-28965223/.

245 "physical eschatology": Milan M. Ćirković, "Resource Letter: PEs-1: Physical Eschatology," *American Journal of Physics*, 2003, 122–33.